D1189620

Landscapes of Learning

✳➻✿➻✳➻✿➻✳➻✿➻✳➻✿

LANDSCAPES
OF
LEARNING

✳➻✿➻✳➻✿➻✳➻✿➻✳➻✿

Maxine Greene

WILLIAM F. RUSSELL PROFESSOR
IN THE FOUNDATIONS OF EDUCATION
TEACHERS COLLEGE, COLUMBIA UNIVERSITY

TEACHERS COLLEGE PRESS
TEACHERS COLLEGE, COLUMBIA UNIVERSITY
NEW YORK AND LONDON

For reprint permission, grateful acknowledgment is made to:

Alfred A. Knöpf, Inc. for "The Motive for Metaphor" and "Six Significant Landscapes" by Wallace Stevens from *The Collected Poems of Wallace Stevens,* © 1959, 1964 by Wallace Stevens.

University of California Press for poem from *Sonnets to Orpheus* by Rainer Maria Rilke. Copyright © 1960 by C.F. MacIntyre.

The Bobbs-Merrill Co., Inc. for a poem by Anne Finch from *by a Woman writt,* edited by Joan Goulianos, © 1973.

David Laing for a poem by Dilys Laing, first published in *The Collected Poems of Dilys Laing,* Case Western Reserve Press, 1965.

Library of Congress Cataloging in Publication Data

Greene, Maxine.
    Landscapes of learning.

    1. Educational anthropology. 2. Education—philosophy. 3. Educational sociology. 4. Education of women. I. Title.
LB45.G68   370.19'3   78-6571

ISBN   0-8077-2534-X

Manufactured in the U.S.A.

87   86   85   84   83   82   2   3   4   5   6

For Carol

Acknowledgements

Lawrence A. Cremin and Frank Jennings suggested that I do this book, and I thank them for their support and encouragement.

Mary L. Allison provided expert and sensitive editorial assistance, and she has my gratitude as well.

MG

Contents

Preface

THE essays in this book are based on lectures written between 1974 and 1977 and originally read before various professional audiences. Most of them have been reconceived and rewritten for this publication, largely because of changes that have recently taken place in the culture—changes too pervasive and significant for a teacher educator to ignore. The rise of what many are calling a "new irrationalism" cannot but pose new problems for the educational practitioner, especially when that phenomenon is so paradoxically linked to a demand for a "return to basics" and for more and more traditional emphases in the schools.

The increase in cynicism about progress cannot but affect what happens in education. There has been an erosion of belief in the efficacy of human interventions when economic difficulties mount, when inequities multiply, when the environment is polluted. People who once had faith in social activism and commitment have withdrawn from the social arena into their own problematic privacy. Meanwhile, there is a growing tendency to distance the poor and the excluded once again, to resist compensatory measures, and to blame the disadvantaged for their most visible disabilities. Talk of participation in policy-making by those affected is heard less and less often. Technological expertise has taken over; things are done *to* people or *for* them; apathy and passivity increase. Uncritical, frequently bored, individuals become ever more susceptible to mystification. All this must have an influence on what is communicated by means of education, whether that education is carried on in schools, by television programs, in offices, in community centers, or on the streets.

The essays that follow are addressed to men and women involved in educating, not in schooling alone. My primary interest has been to draw attention to the multiple realities of our culture in such a way as

1

to arouse readers to pose critical questions of their own. Throughout, there is talk of emancipation and "wide-awakeness," of the need to transcend passivity. Transcendence has to be chosen; it can be neither given nor imposed. It is my view that persons are more likely to ask their own questions and seek their own transcendence when they feel themselves to be grounded in their personal histories, their lived lives. That is what I mean by "landscapes."

I take from the philosopher Maurice Merleau-Ponty the idea that the life of reason develops against a background of perceived realities, that to remain in touch with one's original perceptions is to be present to oneself. A human being lives, as it were, in two orders—one created by his or her relations with the perceptual fields that are given in experience, the other created by his or her relations with a human and social environment. It is important to hold in mind, therefore, that each of us achieved contact with the world from a particular vantage point, in terms of a particular biography. All of this underlies our present perspectives and affects the way we look at things and talk about things and structure our realities. To be in touch with our landscapes is to be conscious of our evolving experiences, to be aware of the ways in which we encounter our world.

In many of the pieces that compose this book, I have referred to or used examples from works of imaginative literature. The reason is that, as many have pointed out, encounters with literary works of art make it possible for us to come in contact with ourselves, to recover a lost spontaneity. This is because, in order to enter into the illusioned world of the novel (or the short story or the poem), we must break with the mundane and the taken-for-granted. We must, as it were, bracket out the ordinary world. By allowing ourselves to enter the imaginary mode of awareness, we submit ourselves to the guidance of an author as we lend a book some of our life.

Under Kafka's guidance, let us say, we form the materials of our experience in such a way as to correspond to the Land Surveyor's terrible search through the Castle for the Count, or whoever is the authority. No longer in the domain of the conventional and the routine, we discover the ways in which structures or hierarchies or even bureaucracies are actually given to our consciousness. The meaning of authority—authority, in itself, as we apprehend it—becomes visible to us, even palpable. We are, as phenomenologists say, returning to "things themselves." It is true that literary experiences are not the only ones that make this possible, but, in certain respects, they are the most accessible experiences for educators remote from themselves. In any event, the evocations of literary works throughout these pages are intended to summon up possibilities, whether they can be fully realized here or not.

The questions that are posed against the background consciousness I have been describing are likely to be the ones that are truly relevant, truly worthwhile. They are likely to be directed towards the actualities of experience and, therefore, to provoke significant reflection. If they do this, the questioner may well be moved to be a learner, since learning is, in one dimension, a conscious search for some kind of coherence, some kind of sense. Learning also is a process of effecting new connections in experience, of thematizing, problematizing, and imposing diverse patterns on the inchoateness of things. The objective of educators is to enable others to learn *how* to learn. If they are personally involved in what can be a most demanding human enterprise, those others—students, or co-investigators—may be caught up much more readily than if the teachers' sense-making efforts have all taken place in the past. And, clearly, there is nothing to stop teacher-learners from deliberately communicating the rules and norms they have incarnated and acted upon while engaging with different subject matters and mastering various skills. Learners must be conscious of what they are doing in such engagements, aware of their own efforts to order and to know. Teacher-learners, equally conscious of their pursuits of meaning and clarity, cannot help but suggest something of what it signifies to pursue or to understand.

But there is more. In the pages that follow there are many discussions of conflicts in our culture, crises and deficiencies of various kinds. We all learn to become human, as is well known, within a community of some kind or by means of a social medium. The more fully engaged we are, the more we can look through others' eyes, the more richly individual we become. The activities that compose learning not only engage us in our own quests for answers and for meanings; they also serve to initiate us into the communities of scholarship and (if our perspectives widen sufficiently) into the human community, in its largest and richest sense. Teachers who are alienated, passive, and unquestioning cannot make such initiations possible for those around. Nor can teachers who take the social reality surrounding them for granted and simply accede to them. Again, I am interested in trying to awaken educators to a realization that transformations are conceivable, that learning is stimulated by a sense of future possibility and by a sense of what might be. So there is talk in this book about the need for social *praxis,* about critical consciousness, about equality and equity, as well as about personal liberation.

The essays are, more or less arbitrarily, divided in four parts. The first deals with emancipatory education and the connection between critical reflection and self-awareness as well as the connection between "wide-awakeness" and morality. The second part deals with various social issues and their implications for an approach to pedagogy. The third has to do with the artistic-aesthetic; the fourth, with the predicaments of women. The themes—critical awareness, self-understanding, and social commitment—recur in all the essays; on occasion, they overlap. This is because one person wrote them, a teacher with her own passion for coherence, her own sense of incompleteness, her own desire to ask questions of the world.

December 1977

Maxine Greene

EMANCIPATORY
EDUCATION

I

The Predicaments of American Selfhood: A Response to the New Irrationalism

"WHAT a piece of work is a man! How noble in reason! How infinite in faculties!... And yet to me what is this quintessence of dust?"[1] Shakespeare's Hamlet was speaking at the beginning of the modern age, but the feeling of loss and contradiction communicated by his poetry is oddly relevant to our own time. The image of self we have inherited was defined in the 18th century, at a moment of high optimism and faith in human rationality. The American ("that New Man," as de Crèvecoeur called him[2]) was described as indeed "noble in reason," much like the Renaissance man. Moreover, he was thought to be distinctively self-determining and almost infinitely perfectible. Even today that delineation possesses a concreteness, as if it referred to something objectively real, an actual personality. There is a sense in which Americans are loath to question its validity, in spite of all their present experiences of personal diminution and their doubts about their effectuality.

The predicament is multivalent. Few would sacrifice what they take to be their inalienable human rights, including the right to liberty. Few would seriously deny that freedom depends on the opportunity to think for oneself, to make one's own sense of the world. Some, looking back, might still agree with Thomas Jefferson's view that reasoning and scientific thinking are necessary if the chains of moral and political superstition are ever to be broken. Despite all this, many persons today are deliberately choosing against the rational way. They prefer the way of mysticism or sensuality. They prefer magic, ancient myths, orphic wisdom, or astrology. It is not that these modes of thinking and being provide answers to the nagging questions, but rather because

7

they make discursive thinking seem unnecessary; they make the questions recede. Chanting distracts from the urge to ask; mantras fix and narrow attention; relaxation techniques overcome tension and uncertainty. People move in limbo, in an ongoing present. Do they despair? Are they free? They smile.

What does this mean for democracy, for education? Throughout our history there has been an insistence on the relationship between rationality (or intelligence or understanding) and the freedom of dignity of men and women. The roots of the democratic ethic, and certainly of the philosophy of democratic education, are to be found in the conviction that human beings can achieve autonomy and efficacy once they learn how to inquire, to communicate, to use their cognitive capacities. This conviction was reinforced by each advance made by the sciences in the 19th century. Even those troubled by the excesses of industry and commerce, by the trauma of "the locomotive in the garden,"[3] celebrated the possibilities of mastery. Experimental thinking seemed appropriate in an open world. It was a way of breaking with restrictiveness and fixity. By the end of the century, there was talk of the scientific method being the method of human intelligence at its creative best.[4]

Not only did scientific discovery appear to advance the cause of progress, it contributed, most believed, to the physical welfare of individuals and freed them to live safer and more wholesome lives. Scientists themselves were conceived to be members of honorable communities, where truth was valued above all things, where knowledge could be funded openly, in the full light of day. "Science is made by men," writes Werner Heisenberg; at the beginning of this century, it was clear to most observers that science derived from experiments conducted by living human beings. The results of science, Heisenberg also says, "are attained through talks among those who work in it and who consult one another about their interpretation of. . .experiments."[5] With such a conception in mind, educators like John Dewey could not but consider the laboratory normative for classroom life. What would more readily provoke intelligent inquiry, cooperative endeavor, the free exchange of ideas? What better way was there to give a young person a sense of his or her potentiality?

It is not surprising that when Dewey wrote about "the lost individual"[6] in 1929, he put so much emphasis on the connection between a "stable and efficacious individuality"[7] and the joy to be found in the "free working of mind." He said:

It is a property of science to find its opportunities in problems, in questions. Since knowing is inquiring, perplexities and difficulties are the meat on which it thrives. The disparities and conflicts that give rise to problems are not something to be dreaded, something to be endured with whatever hardihood one can command; they are things to be grappled with."[8]

He went on to talk about difficulties in personal relations and about such frictions as "one of the chief causes of suffering." He said that suffering increases if we cannot treat such frictions as problems "to be dealt with intellectually." Instead, we withdraw into ourselves when we have personal difficulties and experience a distress that might "in part be converted into the enjoyment that attends the free working of mind, if we took them as occasions for the exercise of thought. . . ." There is something Browningesque—vigorous and expansive—about the image of the person presented here. Thinking and the scientific attitude are viewed as antithetical to stasis, self-indulgence, and constraint.

Contemporary challenges to the rational and scientific are clearly not attacks on the "free working of mind." If anything, the rejection of the cognitive today is (paradoxically enough) justified by talk of liberation, heightened consciousness, and the right to refuse alien controls. The most obvious reason for this, of course, is that scientific endeavor now appears to be subsumed under technical activity, engineering, and manipulative controls. More seriously, the outcomes of all this seem abruptly to have taken on a life of their own. The developments with the most dramatic (and the most understandable) impact are the ones that have worked to overwhelm or mutilate the individual human being, or—as in the case of space exploration—have excluded ordinary persons, entertained them but set them aside. Once the favored child of scientific discovery, the presumed beneficiary of what was achieved in laboratories, the lay individual now finds those very achievements obliterating his or her dignity and fundamental worth. Incapable of comprehending the symbol systems of modern science, unable to distinguish between what is "pure" and what is "applied," the ordinary person thinks mainly of brainwashing techniques, nuclear holocausts, extermination mechanisms, or devastations of land, sea, and air.

Also, even for the relatively uninformed, there is a lived experience of what Jacques Ellul calls "encirclement" by impersonal technique.

No technician anywhere would say that he is submitting men, collec-
tively or individually, to technique. The biogeneticist who experiments
on the human embryo, or the film director who tries to affect his audience to the greatest degree, makes no claim that he is working on
man. The individual is broken into a number of independent fragments, and no two techniques have the same dimensions or depth, nor
does any combination of techniques (for example, propaganda plus
vocational guidance) correspond to any part of the human being. The
result is that every technique can assert its innocence. Where, then, or
by whom, is the human individual being attacked? Nowhere and by no
one. Such is the reply of technique and technicians.[9]

The point is that people are experiencing themselves being worked on
by forces as invisible as they are impersonal—red dyes in food,
asbestos in the workplace, listening devices on the telephone, behavior
modification in the school; phenomena of this sort are constantly
being *(ex post facto)* disclosed. People struggle to cope with official
agencies, with the telephone company, or with the justice system. They
confront bureaucracy wherever they turn, "a form of dominion,"
Hannah Arendt said, characterized by "rule by Nobody."[10] No one
takes responsibility; yet individuals feel that their rights and liberties
are being eroded by people more adept, efficient, and powerful than
they can ever be. And, in a mysterious way, all this seems linked to
science as much as to ubiquitous technique.

There is more. The sciences, in addition to being increasingly
mathematicized, have become positivistic. This means that scientists
(unlike the practitioners Dewey seems to have had in mind) are likely
to lose perspective on what they, as human beings, are doing when
they apply their empirical and analytic methods in a domain of inquiry. Devoid of perspective on their own grounding in experience, in
a particular location in the world, they are likely to treat their own
investigations as in some sense godlike. They may overlook the fact
that what they discover (and what they define as objectively and un-
arguably "real") is a function of certain protocols and procedures developed at a particular moment in the history of thought. They may
equate all knowledge with what follows from scientific practice and
neglect what Dewey once called the "realm of meanings to which truth
and falsity as such are irrelevant."[11] Dewey had in mind poetic meanings and moral meanings, as available as truth-meanings to human
experience and as testimony to the continuity between experiencing
and what we take, at any moment, to be our world.

The positivistic separation between the knower and the known, along with the stress on what is finished, objective, and *given*, increases the possibility of individual submergence. This is because ordinary persons are no longer able to hold in mind that all knowledge (including scientific knowledge) is interpretive, that subject cannot be separated from object where understanding the world is concerned. Presented with expert, "official" descriptions of everything from the physical world to the economic situation, from the energy crisis to crime in the streets, they begin to react to all explanations as if they had the status of absolute or natural laws. Everything that is presumably knowable appears to be part of the self-enclosed universe of scientific understanding; ordinary persons, lacking expertise, can only accomodate. The alternatives, for many people, are submission or withdrawal. What then happens to their images of themselves?

Perhaps inevitably, a dualism has developed, what Dewey called "a split between the inner and the outer."[12] The self is sought in some inward domain, popularly called "consciousness." If the self—or identity, or personhood—is conceived to be primarily inner and spiritual, it can be thought of as inviolable. As in the Hindu formulation, Brahman (the individual soul) is akin to Atman (the World Soul) and therefore impervious to physical manipulations and behavioral controls. At once, it escapes empirical formulation and sometimes language itself. When someone like B. F. Skinner denies the existence of inner states on the ground that such existence can never be empirically demonstrated, the one committed to interiority might say that this actually supports the claim that there exists a realm apart from the empirical. The deliberate neglect of that realm by Western experimenters, it is often said, has testified to the partial, truncated character of their science, even when it is celebrated as the "free working of mind." This may partially account for current upsurges of interest in scientific or pseudo-scientific studies of the effects of various hallucinogens, biofeedback techniques, yoga discipline, psychic surgery, and the like.

The crucial issue, where the individual is concerned, is the new dualism, the fascination with interiority. Theodore Roszak has been one of the spokesmen for this phenomenon, which he talks about as a defiance of "objective consciousness" and a determination to grasp reality through the exercise of "non-intellective powers,"[13] visionary experiences, and shamanism. Nor surprisingly, Roszak has often referred back to William Blake and his rebellion against constraints, his exposure of the "mind-forg'd manacles"[14] we wear.

And, indeed, there are many evocations of the Romantic tradition in Western literature in what is thought of as a new irrationalism today. Wordsworth, Emerson, Melville, Dostoyevsky, and others certainly did rebel against authoritarianism, calculativeness, abstraction, and constraint. Whether spontaneity concerned them, or authenticity, or free will, they were clearly taking issue with the predetermined, with legitimations presented as objectively real, with rational structures external to and at odds with what they felt and perceived. We need only recall Herman Melville's Ishmael warning against the "unseasonable meditativeness" that makes a man lose touch with his experienced world, or saying (with regard to the "whiteness of the whale") "to analyse it seems impossible."[15] Some things elude rational explanation, he is saying; yet they mean profoundly more, oftentimes, than what is measurable.

Or we might recall Dostoyevsky's Ivan Karamazov, desperately longing for order and justice in the universe, knowing there can be no universal harmony. "I have a longing for life," he says, "and I go on living in spite of logic. Though I might not believe in the order of the universe, yet I love the sticky leaves as they open in the spring. I love the blue sky. I love some people, whom one loves you know sometimes without knowing why."[16] Such rebellions against logic and abstraction are not rebellions against the cognitive mode, nor do they signify rejections of science *per se*. Even William Blake called for a "fourfold" rather than a one-dimensional vision; he never proposed living forever in the domain of innocence. In the contexts of their own lived worlds, the Romantic writers seemed, above all, to be struggling for coherence and to become present to themselves.

It is my belief that those who have made a "consciousness revolution"[17] today (often in the idioms of Romantic writing) are expressing their own longings to come in touch with themselves and with their original intuitions of reality. I believe that they are trying to recapture the themes of their lived lives and of the worlds they have constituted as they have grown. Because they feel imposed upon by too many official schemata, by others' namings and demarcations of things around, they feel both mystified and restive. They grope for ways of emancipating themselves. It is not the scientific method itself that strikes them as oppressive, nor is it scientism alone. Without being clearly aware of it, they are afflicted by some of the consequences of scientism or positivism, most particularly the subject-object split and the links to technological controls.

What is most serious and most troubling is the sense that the self as participant, as inquirer, as creator of meanings, has been obliterated. And this, in turn, leads to the preoccupation with what John

Lilly calls "self-metaprogramming"[18] and what Robert Hunter describes as "seismic activity in the intuitive deeps."[19] Hunter, in fact, talks about how "unhampered" the intuitive regions are when compared with the cognitive. "Below the level of cognition," he writes, "...the processes of our minds are not hitched to so cumbersome a vehicle as language. They move that much faster."[20] This kind of argument, like many of the arguments for "expanded consciousness," appeals to many people, perhaps especially to those who spend hours looking at television, or those "turned on" to acid rock, or those who simply want to be free to be.

It is not hard to understand such an appeal. Nor is it hard to understand the need, somehow or other, to come in touch with whatever the "true self" is conceived to be, to become more conscious of consciousness. But then a suspicion arises that persons who choose to exist "beyond the wasteland"[21] actually do find non-cognitive (or subcognitive) processes more enticing than reflective thought. Many talk as if self-awareness is an achievement, self-justifying, or curative in its own right. Those who participate in sensitivity training or other new kinds of "therapy" are likely to become inattentive to social realities —about which, they feel, they can do nothing anyway. Nothing seems more remote from their attention than the kind of knowing called *praxis,* a type of radical and participant knowing oriented to transforming the world.

More than half a century ago, Dewey talked about the tendency to build castles in the air when energies are "checked by uncongenial surroundings." When people construct imaginary worlds, they often allow them to "substitute for an actual achievement which involves the pains of thought." He went on to discuss the split between mind and conduct and the ways in which this can characterize an entire social situation. There are times, he said, when the social situation throws those normally given to reflection back "into their own thoughts and desires without providing the means by which these ideas and aspirations can be used to reorganize the environment." And then:

> Under such conditions, men take revenge, as it were, upon the alien and hostile environment by cultivating contempt for it, by giving it a bad name. They seek refuge and consolation within their own states of mind, their own imaginings and wishes, which they compliment by calling both more real and more ideal than the despised outer world.[22]

It would appear that this sort of life, excluding "the pains of thought," lays an individual open to new kinds of oppression. After all, the most

effectual way of coping with manipulation or conditioning is to become cognizant of what is happening (and, if possible, to find out who
is responsible). To take refuge within one's inwardness may well be to
disarm oneself as a social being, to render oneself doubly vulnerable to
the mystifications that legitimate manipulation and conditioning. Under such circumstances, can the self remain inviolable? Or does a kind
of inviolability have to be achieved—through critical reflection, in the
pain of thought?

Much depends upon how consciousness is conceived. Is it indeed to
be understood as pure interiority, as awareness? Or is it, as some
philosophers say, a mode of grasping, moving outwards, coming in
touch with the world? William James, Jean-Paul Sartre, Maurice
Merleau-Ponty, Alfred Schutz, and many others have made the point
that consciousness is not to be understood simply as a kind of inwardness, a sense of being aroused and alive. Nor is it to be described as an
entity, a breath, something akin to what Gilbert Ryle once called a
"ghost in a machine."[23] Consciousness thrusts toward the world, not
away from it; it thrusts towards the situations in which the individual
lives her or his life. It is through acts of consciousness that aspects of
the world present themselves to living beings. These acts include imagining, intuiting, remembering, believing, judging, conceiving, and
(focally) perceiving. Alone or in collaboration, they bring individuals
in touch with objects, events, and other human beings; they make it
possible for individuals to orient themselves to, to interpret, to constitute a world.

According to this view, consciousness is translucent.[24] Each act of
consciousness has an object: consciousness is always *of* something; it
is characterized by intentionality. To say that I am conscious of someone approaching me is to say that I am perceiving a figure down the
street as a man coming closer and closer to my space. As he comes
nearer to me, I may intuit a threatening quality in his stance, or I may
judge him to be intoxicated, or I may suddenly remember that he was
once a co-worker of mine. Who he turns out to be, for me, depends
upon the way I finally become conscious of him. At best, I can only
come in touch with certain aspects of the man, because my understanding of him depends upon my vantage point and previous experiences. I know that there are sides to him that are hidden from me;
there are profiles of his personality, of his character, that are out of my
reach. To have anything approximating a complete knowledge, I
would have to be able to see him from all conceivable angles, in all the
dimensions of his life. I would have to consult him about himself, talk

to his friends and relatives, and interpret his behavior from many points of view. But this is just an accidental encounter on the street; I see him from a particular perspective—as someone vaguely remembered, say, someone on the fringes of my life. His reality, from my vantage point, is the object of my vague remembering. I would grasp his presence differently if he were my student, my employer, or my dear friend.

Consciousness as perspectival grasping is our way of encountering the natural and human world. Not surprisingly, examples of what this signify abound in literature. Consider Ivan Karamazov and the sticky leaves or Ishmael and the whiteness of the whale. Wordsworth's autobiographical poem, *The Prelude,*[25] provides a range of examples, because it deals explicitly with the multiple acts of consciousness that create a personal history. Subtitled "The Growth of a Poet's Mind," it suggests the connection between an awareness of those acts of consciousness and the emergence of identity. In some respects, it is a poem about one human being's self-formation, recaptured through a return (in inner time) to his original landscape, the place where it all began.

The poem begins with the poet's decision to leave the constraints of the city where he has been a "discontented sojourner" and go back to the Lake Country where he grew up. When he arrives there, he first becomes conscious of the hills and cottages in the mode of memory. He remembers his "unconscious intercourse with beauty" when he was a child, and he sees images of silver mist and water colored by clouds. He remembers the "fits of vulgar joy" that gave way in time to something deeper and more coherent, an imaginatively achieved unity with nature, an understanding that "we half create what we perceive." He can grasp that vision now because he is *there,* in his home place, as a physical being; his body, after all, was the original source of his perspective. He tries to come in touch with his first perceptions, with the moment when he began orienting himself to the landscape. Only as he learned to name, to thematize, he realizes, could he see the wind "shouldering the naked crag," imagine "huge and mighty forms that do not live like living men." He recalls himself beginning to ponder, to constitute a world and make it meaningful. Because he has regained touch with the primordial landscape, he feels present to himself, in touch with himself as never before.

Clearly, he would have been unable to interpret his experiences if he had not gradually become acquainted with his culture's modes of sense-making, what has been called "the stock of knowledge at hand."[26] His learning took place, however, against the background of a rich perceptual life, against awareness that rooted him in a landscape and provided an enduring ground. This would not have happened if he were disembodied, if his consciousness had contracted within itself instead of transcending towards the things he saw around him. It did transcend, from his earliest days, and he, the living poet, could now integrate what he remembers, intuits, feels, imagines, believes, and knows. Taking a range of perspectives as a grown man, he could fashion an entire network of relationships in his experience. He could *become* a network of relationships,[27] as the activities of consciousness intersected with one another, as he achieved a whole.

What is real for the poet is his experience interpreted over time. There was no separation, in Wordsworth's case, between subject (the poet's mind) and object (the English world around). So it actually is for the ordinary person; so is it, as well, for natural and social scientists. The problem is that we do not remain aware of our reality as existing beings when we look out upon (or inquire into) what too often strikes us as an independently existing, "alien and hostile" place. We close our eyes to our situatedness, our location in an intersubjective world. We become unable to think about the ways in which our perspectives are affected by our involvements, by our projects, by the work we do. We forget that, even when we do the purest kind of scientific study, we are grounded in experience, in an ineluctably human reality. We forget, similarly, that there can be no such phenomenon as an objectless consciousness, that there is no refuge within.

Nor is there a hidden personal reality to be uncovered intuitively or mystically. Schutz wrote that, "The meaning of our experiences . . . constitutes reality."[28] To talk of meaning is to talk of interpretation, not immediate awareness. It is to allow for the fact that there are multiple realities available to human consciousness, and a network of relationships to effect that have much to do with the living self. There are, as Schutz put it, diverse "provinces of meaning." Each one—be it the province of science, art, play, or dream—is composed of a sect of more or less compatible experiences. Each set of experiences is interpreted in accord with a characteristic cognitive style. The experiences involved in scientific investigations, for instance, are interpreted empirically and analytically, with a minimum of personal engagement. Those associated with the various arts are interpreted imaginatively, expressively, or non-discursively, with a great deal of personal involvement.

There is, as well, what is sometimes called "the paramount reality" —the reality of everyday life. This is the domain in which we do our work, interact with others, and try to bring about the kinds of changes that will sustain our purposes. Although we are likely to take it as "given," normal, fundamentally unalterable, the world of everyday life is what it is because we have learned to interpret the experiences we have together on the basis of our own previous experiences and those handed down to us by our elders, which "in the form of 'knowledge at hand' function as a scheme of reference."[29] Each of us, because our biographies, our projects, and our locations differ, encounters the social reality of everyday from a somewhat distinctive perspective, a perspective of which we are far too often unaware.

The crucial point is that we, as conscious beings, constitute the world we inhabit through the interpretations we adopt or make for ourselves. To take that world for granted as predefined or objectively *there* is to be uncritical, submissive, and submerged. Obviously, this does not mean that the world is an illusion or that it does not exist independently. It simply means, as Merleau-Ponty expressed it, that all our knowledge of the world, even our scientific knowledge, is gained from our human points of view, "or from some experience of the world without which the symbols of science would be meaningless."[30] Each of us, he said, is a subject "destined to be in the world"; our concern is with a disclosure of the world, a clarification of what it means to be.

This view is at the furthest remove from the view associated with contemporary irrationalism. This is because it affirms the existential importance of cognition, or rationality, while providing a grounding in the lived world. The lived world must be seen as the structuring context for sense-making of any sort, even for scientific inquiry. To acknowledge this is to acknowledge the necessity to ground scientific discoveries in experience, or in what Michael Polanyi called "personal knowledge."[31] Positivism, then, must be challenged, if we are to reaffirm our potency; the objectivism that supports mystification must be exposed. It must become clear again that reflection is not only rooted in experience, its entire purpose is to inform and clarify experience—or the lived world. If we add to this a conceived possibility of remaining in touch with our perceptual backgrounds and thus remaining present to ourselves, we may be better able to ward off the depredations of technique.

Clearly, it takes critical reflection upon our own realities to capture such awareness. It requires a degree of wide-awakeness too many people avoid. Much depends on our ability to be cognizant of our standpoints and to be open to the world. "Nothing determines me from the outside," wrote Merleau-Ponty, "not because nothing acts upon me, but, on the contrary, because I am from the start outside myself and open to the world. We are *true* through and through, and have with us, by the mere fact of belonging to the world, and not merely being in the world in the way that things are, all that we need to transcend ourselves."[32]

It may be a submission to debasement that makes it seem so hard today to transcend in this fashion. For all the talk of heightened consciousness, boredom and passivity are all around. For all the free play of sexuality, there is a kind of passionlessness wherever we look. More and more people seek out modes of detachment, of inner flight. There is a fascination with the therapeutic, but there is a fascination with madness as well. We need only recall *One Flew Over the Cuckoo's Nest* or the works of R. D. Laing.[33] There are numbers of people who believe that madness is in some sense liberating, that the insane individual is healthier than the sane (if sanity means adjustment to the inhumane). We might think of the play, *Equus,* and of the psychiatrist in that play lamenting the need to deliver the boy from madness. Dr. Dysart describes himself as someone standing in the dark with a pick in his hand, "striking at heads" so as to destroy passion.[34] He sees himself forcing a plastic normality on those he treats, while feeling a chain biting into his own mouth.

Many of us can respond to this. In the United States today, we know what it is to feel dominated and constrained. We have to struggle for our emancipation; some of us are familiar with the feeling of a chain in the mouth. But the problems will not be solved by the invention of new either/ors, by forced choosing between the outer and the inner. No one's self is ready-made; each of us has to create a self by choice of action, action in the world. Such action, if it is to be meaningful, must be informed by critical reflection, because the one who is submerged, who cannot see, is likely to be caught in *stasis,* unable to move. But the kinds of choices that are necessary can only be made when there are openings, when appropriate social conditions exist. So the matter of the diminution of self is two-pronged: it demands reflective thinking on the part of individuals, and it demands social change. Even as we think about dignity and transcendence, therefore, we need to think of human *praxis,* or the kind of knowing that surpasses and transforms, that makes a difference in reality.[35]

What does all this mean for education? One implication has to do with subject matter, with curriculum. Students must be enabled, at whatever stages they find themselves to be, to encounter curriculum as possibility. By that I mean curriculum ought to provide a series of occasions for individuals to articulate the themes of their existence and to reflect on those themes until they know themselves to be in the world and can name what has been up to then obscure. If this is to happen, disciplinary opportunities of many kinds must be provided, the subject matters embodying the schemata used in our tradition to make sense of things. As students are enabled consciously (and critically) to order their experiences by means of such schemata, they ought to be left free to look out upon their own landscapes, or what may be thought of as their own perceptual ground.

Journeys to some Lake Country enable certain students to recover their landscapes; music and dancing work for others, as do encounters with varied works of art. Paulo Freire used video-taped renderings of natural settings and daily life. Asking his fellow investigators (his co-learners, who were peasants) to decode them, he enabled them to overcome their traditional silences and, in so doing, to articulate the themes of their shared lives.[36] The point is that learning must be a process of discovery and recovery in response to worthwhile questions rising out of conscious life in concrete situations. And learning must be in some manner emancipatory, in the sense that it equips individuals to understand the history of the knowledge structures they are encountering, the paradigms in use in the sciences, and the relation of all of these to human interests and particular moments of human time. It should be possible as well for people to learn the significance of technique and to understand the dangers of instrumental controls through confrontations with some centers of technology, even with bureaucracies. The idea is to enable them to pose searching and significant questions with respect to what works upon them and conditions them—to learn how to recognize mystification, whatever the source.

If learning focuses upon lived life, it should enable persons to recognize lacks in the situations through which they move. Recognizing lack or deficiency (infringements on personality, exclusion, or neglect), they may learn how to repair and transcend. Much depends on how their life situations are understood, on the degree to which they can avoid taking what *is* for granted, on what they are willing to risk. Given the complexity of our technetronic society, given its hierarchies and its distinctions, we cannot invest all our hopes in education, certainly not in what happens in the schools.

But we can try—in whatever educational roles we find ourselves. We can affirm the joys of living mindfully, or pursuing meanings as we live. The narrator, in the novel *Invisible Man,* asks at the end: "Why do I write, torturing myself to put it down? Because in spite of myself

I've learned some things. . . ." He talks about how certain ideas keep filing away at his lethargy and about how important it is to tell other people about them. He talks of denouncing and defending, hating and loving, and about how he must stop hibernating and move upwards into the air, visible at last, refusing invisibility.

> In going underground, I whipped it all except the mind, the *mind*. And the mind that has conceived a plan of living must never lose sight of the chaos against which that pattern was conceived. That goes for societies as well as for individuals. Thus, having tried to give pattern to the chaos which lives within the pattern of your certainties, I must come out, I must emerge.[37]

Emergence like that, transcendence like that, are necessary if persons are to achieve a sense of effectuality again. If they can remain in touch with their perceptual landscapes, if they can be critical and aware, they may be able to overcome passivity and the temptation to withdraw. We must all choose ourselves as learners open to the profiles of a world we can never fully know, willing to live (as Virginia Woolf once wrote) "in the presence of reality." We may be, objectively, nothing more than a "quintessence of dust." But we can choose, and we can sometimes transform.

References

1. William Shakespeare, *Hamlet* (New Haven: Yale University Press, 1947), Act II, Scene 2, p. 65.
2. Hector St. John de Crevecoeur, *Letters from an American Farmer* (London, 1882), Everyman, p. 43.
3. See Leo Marx, *The Machine in the Garden* (New York: Oxford University Press, 1967), pp. 13-14.
4. See John Dewey, *The Quest for Certainty* (London: George Allen and Unwin, 1930), pp. 43-49.
5. Werner Heisenberg, *Physics and Beyond* (New York: Harper & Row, 1971), Preface.
6. John Dewey, *Individualism Old and New* (New York: Capricorn Books, 1962), p. 52.
7. Ibid., p. 73.
8. Ibid., p. 162.
9. Jacques Ellul, *The Technological Society* (New York: Vintage Books, 1967), p. 389.

10. Hannah Arendt, "On Violence," *Crises of the Republic* (New York: Harvest Books, 1972), p. 137.
11. Dewey, *Experience and Nature* (New York: Dover Publications, 1958), p. 411.
12. Dewey, *Democracy and Education* (New York: Macmillan Company, 1916), p. 402.
13. Theodore Roszak, *The Making of a Counter Culture* (New York: Anchor Books, 1969), p. 236.
14. William Blake, "London," in *William Blake,* ed. J. Bronowski (Baltimore: Penguin Books, 1958), p. 52.
15. Herman Melville, *Moby Dick* (New York: Random House, 1930), p. 277.
16. Fyodor Dostoyevsky, *The Brothers Karamasov* (New York: Modern Library, 1945), p. 312.
17. See Charles Reich, *The Greening of America* (New York: Random House, 1970).
18. John C. Lilly, *The Center of the Cyclone: An Autobiography of Inner Space* (New York: Bantam Books, 1973), pp. 177-183.
19. Robert Hunter, *The Storming of the Mind: Inside the Consciousness Revolution* (Garden City, NY: Doubleday Anchor, 1972), p. 103.
20. Ibid.
21. See Theodore Roszak, *Where the Wasteland Ends* (Garden City, NY: Doubleday and Company, 1972).
22. Dewey, *Democracy and Education, op. cit.,* p. 405.
23. Gilbert Ryle, *The Concept of Mind* (New York: Barnes and Noble, 1949), pp. 15-16.
24. Jean-Paul Sartre, *Being and Nothingness* (New York: Philosophical Library, 1956), pp. li-liii.
25. William Wordsworth, *The Prelude: Selected Poems and Sonnets,* ed. Carlos Baker (New York: Holt, Rinehart and Winston, 1962).
26. Albert Schutz, "Teiresias," in *Studies in Social Theory,* Collected Papers II, ed. Arvid Brodersen (The Hague: Martinus Nijhoff, 1964), pp. 283f.
27. Maurice Merleau-Ponty, *Phenomenology of Perception* (New York: Humanities Press, 1967), p. xx.
28. Schutz, "On Multiple Realities," in *The Problem of Social Reality,* Collected Papers I, ed. Maurice Natanson (The Hague: Martinus Nijhoff, 1967), pp. 209-212.
29. Ibid., p. 208.
30. Merleau-Ponty, *op. cit.,* p. viii.
31. Michael Polanyi, *Personal Knowledge: Towards a Post-Critical Philosophy* (New York: Harper Torchbooks, 1962).
32. Merleau-Ponty, *op. cit.,* p. 456.
33. See R. D. Laing, *The Divided Self* (Baltimore: Penguin Books, 1965).
34. Peter Shaffer, *Equus* (New York: Atheneum, 1974), p. 106.
35. Sartre, *Search for a Method* (New York: Alfred A. Knopf, 1963), pp. 91-100; also see Paulo Freire, *Pedagogy of the Oppressed* (New York: Herder and Herder, 1970), pp. 27-40.
36. Freire, *op. cit.,* pp. 75-90.
37. Ralph Ellison, *Invisible Man* (New York: Signet Books, 1950), p. 50.

2

The Rational and the Emancipatory: Towards a Role for Imaginative Literature

C RITICAL philosophy today tries to grasp "the self-formative process of the active subject."[1] The very term "critical" refers to the human capacity for self-reflection as it does to reflective rationality. But it is extremely difficult to feel ourselves active subjects in today's world; emancipatory activity seems continually thwarted in our everyday lives. The technocratic consciousness bears down upon us, along with what is called "functional rationality."[2] We are caught up in product orientations, credentialling practices, and preoccupations with utility. Not only do we find ourselves objectified by external controls; we internalize the legitimations given for those controls. We accede to explanations we scarcely understand and, without thinking very much about it, submit to what the powerful and faceless say. We are afflicted, even without our realizing it, with "false consciousness." This means, according to Herbert Marcuse, a "confinement of experience, a restriction of meaning."[3] Our sense of the rootedness of knowledge in experience diminishes, as does our comprehension of the ways in which persons bring meaning into being and constitute their shared realities.

The pedagogical problem is, in part, to remind people of these things, to arouse them to some degree of committed rationality. In one guise or another, this has been a root concern of educators, psychologists, and philosophers since the Enlightenment. The responses to it have been multiple: experiential education, logical or linguistic

22

analysis, psychoanalysis, and various pedagogies of the oppressed.[4] A complement to any one of these for teachers or teachers-to-be might well be the study of certain signal works of imaginative literature, particularly some of those written in the 19th and early 20th centuries. Because they were created at a time when the idea of progress was becoming problematic, when taken-for-granted values of ordinary life were being questioned, the works I have in mind have a peculiar capacity to disclose to modern readers aspects of our own lived worlds. In addition to that, however, an engagement with materials created in the past can become an initiation into the history to which we all belong. The past may take on for us "the outline," as Maurice Merleau-Ponty once wrote, "of a preparation of premeditation of a present that exceeds it in meaning although it recognizes itself in it."[5] If this happens, the effort to grasp the self-formative process may become grounded in an ongoing interrogation of the social world we and our fellow beings have constructed over time.

In the writings that questioned bourgeois society in years past, there was a "conscious transcendence of the alienated existence," as Marcuse says.[6] In fact, the incompatibility between the images of life to be found in that prose and poetry and the normal "order of business" may be evidence of their truth. Readers, over the years, have been able to perceive that truth when they have opened themselves to those works. In so doing, they have taken new standpoints on their normal life situations; they have gone beyond their own taken-for-grantedness. Marcuse also points out, however, that modern society has so much absorptive and assimilative power that the critical elements in this kind of literature have been obscured.

The insoluble problems in a work like Flaubert's *Madame Bovary,* for instance, have never been resolved; they have been suppressed. This means that the novel's power of "artistic alienation" has been undermined. Instead of seeing Emma Bovary's plight as an indictment of Yonville society with its pecuniary ideals and its falsifications of life (I would say), we read the story as an account of a spoiled, deluded "romantic" whose own illusions caused her death. We are, in consequence, incapable of recognizing her predicament as that of countless middle-class housewives (if not their fellow inhabitants of materialistic society)—pathetically uninformed, assuaged by objects, treated by others and treating themselves as commodities. We feel no more alienated from our normal "order of business" than when we watch commercials on a television screen.

When we consider how effectively modern society has absorbed the most startling products of the *avant garde,* and even the revolutionary imagination, it is easy to understand Marcuse's view. From denim pants to cocaine and free sex, from Robert Rauschenberg's paintings to Joseph Heller's satires, inventions once conceived to be shocking or subversive have been appropriated by the comfortable. The most terrible indictments of the carnage in Vietnam, the most depressing renditions of contemporary *ennui,* have become coffee table ornaments; even protest has been objectified and made into a possession set out for display. Nevertheless, it seems to me that an adequate pedagogy might still enable modern learners to break with this assimilative power and reconstitute certain works of art as occasions for transcendence, self-knowledge, and critique.

Jean-Paul Sartre reminds us that every writer presents a world he has in common with his readers, a world the writer "animates and penetrates with his freedom." Sartre writes that, "It is on the basis of this world that the reader must bring about his concrete liberation; it is alienation, situation, and history. It is this world which I must change or preserve for myself or others."[7] This possibility still exists for us today. The pedagogical task is to make the "worlds" in literature available. The works to be opened up might come from any tradition, but there appears to be a special value in the literature that belongs to the Western adversary tradition, largely because of what afflicts us today.

There are intimations to be found in this literature—intimations of discontents familiar to us all. Blake, Baudelaire, Dostoyevsky, and the others obviously did not live in advanced industrial societies and had no way of anticipating the growth of technology. They were experiencing, in some sense, the emergence of industrial economies and experiencing it against a remembered background of faith in and emphasis on the inviolable individual. Many had come to the city from the provinces or the rural areas; they had the option of abandoning, whenever they chose, the anonymity and confusion of urban life. Nevertheless, hypersensitive to pressure and domination, they mounted a passionate onslaught against whatever demeaned the existing person —hypocrisy, complacency, *ennui,* and lassitude. They mocked or lamented all attempts to thrust them (as individuals or as artists) into comfortable molds. They reacted, in distinctive ways, against prevailing norms and even what Jurgen Habermas now describes as "dependence on hypostasized powers."[8]

Modern readers, used to taking such dependence for granted, are likely to attribute what weighs down and limits them to the "nature of things." They overlook the fact that domination in the intellectual and social realm, unlike mortality, is alterable. They forget that norms and prohibitions and denials are functions of particular sets of interests at particular moments of time. In the 19th and early 20th century, this was evident, at least to some; the emerging constraints seemed unnatural. They were not easily internalized as they are today. Seeming to impinge on personality itself, they were reacted to personally and in the contexts of the artists' personal histories.

Alvin Gouldner has written about a "romantic" revolt against utilitarian culture in the 19th century, a significant challenge to achievement-seeking, material success, and "the values of conforming usefulness."[9] Whether romantic in the ordinary sense or not, many of the writers to be considered here shared (for diverse reasons) the antipathies Gouldner describes. Themselves members of the middle class, their standpoints were not those we would expect of workers conscious of actual exploitation and oppression. They were not political economists or social revolutionaries, and so they did not see things as did Marx and Engels, or even the liberal reformers of their time.

Nevertheless, in their own concern for personal valuing and for the moral condition of humankind, they seemed peculiarly sensitive to the utilitarian tendency to place primary emphasis upon the *consequences* of human actions, even if that meant excluding the question of values altogether. Gouldner writes that, "The question of whether an action is intrinsically 'right' is increasingly superseded by efforts to appraise its consequences and therefore by efforts to determine what these will be or are."[10] If, he seems to be saying, something "works" in the simplest sense, if it settles some difficulty or calms some unrest, it is an alternative (according to the view) that ought to be chosen. And it is indeed the case that, as the 19th century wore on, more and more courses of action were selected on grounds "independent of moral propriety or impropriety." We need only recall certain corporate decisions, decisions having to do with "manifest destiny" and conquest, decisions affecting the deviant and the sick. Stress was increasingly placed, as Gouldner points out, on what was useful for social stability and progress rather than on what might promote individual happiness. And this appears to be what the adversary writers *saw.* Foundations were being laid for the strange, amoral depersonalization of our own time. The "system" was already beginning to overwhelm the person without individuals being fully aware of what was happening to them.

In our own era, positivism and scientism seem to represent the latter-day working out of those tendencies. One writer describes positivism as "the decisive moving forward of a disciplined march" and talks about the way in which positivism discriminates "the initiator of speech" from the object of his speaking "as if they really were two discrete things. . . ."[11] Not only is there a separation between subject and object, but assertions and explanations seem to take on a life or status of their own. All knowledge becomes identified with empirical scientific knowledge. To be an enlightened person is to act in accord with technically correct strategies, with specific kinds of procedures—and to do so in the context of accepted values. So, as Merleau-Ponty said, does the present exceed the past in meaning, "although it recognizes itself in it."

But it is an emancipatory recognition for which we search. One means of undertaking the search is to identify what Jorge Luis Borges calls "precursors" in an essay called "Kafka and his Precursors." Borges talks about how he came to recognize Kafka's voice in texts from diverse periods in history. He identifies a number of heterogeneous works that resemble Kafka, even though they do not always resemble each other. Then he says that, "If Kafka had never written a line, we would not perceive this quality; in other words, it would not exist." He goes on:

> The poem "Fears and Scruples" by Browning foretells Kafka's work, but our reading of Kafka perceptibly sharpens and deflects our reading of the poem. Browning did not read it as we do now. In the critics' vocabulary, the word "precursor" is indispensable, but it should be cleansed of all connotation of polemics or rivalry. The fact is that every writer *creates* his own precursors. His work modifies our conception of the past, as it will modify the future.[12]

It is not simply that Thomas Pynchon,[13] Kurt Vonnegut,[14] Margaret Atwood,[15] Saul Bellow,[16] and other modern writers may well create their own precursors and, in so doing, change our views of certain earlier works. It is also that our half-articulated experiences with domination, with the pressure of technological rationality and the rest, may enable us to find foretellings when we look back. These, too, may alter our conceptions of our past and, in so doing, make the present disclose some of its buried forms.

Naturally, Blake, Flaubert, Distoevsky, and the others did not read their own writings as we are likely to do today. Literary meanings are concretized in distinctive ways in different historical periods; among other things, there is a "cumulative life of meaning"[17] that permits no leaps backward in time. Attending to the substance and shape of a text, we can only interpret it in the light of a present perspective. And we are free to seek out precursors as we do this, thereby attempting to modify our conceptions of past, present, and future as well. This is what I am suggesting, to the end that we achieve a firmer grasp on our self-formative processes and, if we are fortunate, the "concrete liberation" Sartre describes.

For a first example, let us turn to a segment of William Blake's "Proverbs of Hell," which deals with the emergence of an authority that tamps down religious energies. Blake is here pointing to the ways in which deities are externalized and objectified (as ideas often tend to be), until they become modes of control and enslavement. Most particularly, he is stressing the most terrible oppression of all—people's acquiescence in their own silencing, the separation of the "initiator of speech" from that which he has the right and the capacity to say.

> *The ancient Poets animated all sensible objects*
> *with Gods or Geniuses, calling them by the names*
> *and adorning them with the properties of woods,*
> *rivers, mountains, lakes, cities, nations, and*
> *whatever their enlarged & numerous senses could*
> *perceive.*
>
> *And particularly they studied the genius of each*
> *city and country, placing it under its mental deity;*
> *Till a system was formed, which some took advan-*
> *tage of and enslav'd the vulgar by attempting to*
> *realize or abstract the mental deities from their*
> *objects: thus began Priesthood;*
> *Choosing forms of worship from poetic tales.*
>
> *And at length they pronounc'd that the Gods*
> *had order'd such things.*
> *Thus men forgot that All deities reside in the*
> *human breast.*[18]

This is a working out, of course, of themes that appear and reappear in Blake's poetry: the multiple forms of authority and constraint (church, army, throne, school, "Satanic mills") that enslave human beings and thrust them into molds. Attentive modern readers cannot but be moved to self-confrontation by these poems, if they permit the imaginary mode of awareness to take over, even for a while. Recall the familiar "London":

> *I wandered thro' each charter'd street,*
> *Near where the charter'd Thames does flow,*

And mark in every face I meet
Marks of weakness, marks of woe.

In the cry of every Man,
In every Infant's cry of fear,
In every voice, in every ban,
The mind-forg'd manacles I hear.

How the Chimney-sweeper's cry
Every black'ning Church appalls;
And the hapless Soldier's sigh
Runs in blood down Palace walls.

But most thro' midnight streets I hear
How the youthful Harlot's curse
Blasts the new born Infant's tear,
And blights with plagues the Marriage hearse.[19]

Blake is summoning us into a city where monopolies have taken over the streets and even the free-flowing river. The inhabitants, manipulated and regimented, are chained by "mind-forg'd manacles." The power of wealth and property is bad enough; far more destructive is the internalized oppression, the hopeless and one-dimensional vision that governs human lives. To make the experience even more dreadful, there is the evocation of a chimney-sweep, sold as a stunted child to a company for a few guineas, forced up narrow chimneys repeatedly until he was cancer-ridden and crippled. No image could evoke exploitation and imprisonment so effectively: a naked, hungry child in a pitch-black flue. Then, to compound the horror in the clanging darkness, there are the specters of illegitimacy and syphilis associated with marriage and childbirth, the emblems of what is most valued, most reliable, even under tyranny. Yet we are not permitted to distance all this as a picture of London before social reforms. We are not because Blake talks of "mind-forg'd manacles." This is the constriction of meaning Marcuse speaks of, the ultimate in "false consciousness."

Those who read Blake in his own time and who looked at his engravings undoubtedly viewed him as a mystic, a radical foe of rationalism and mechanism, or a spokesman for fearful (perhaps demonic) energies (like the tiger "burning bright in the forests of the night"). He certainly was those things and more; much of what he said is still suppressed, because the crucial problems he was presenting are still not solved. He was, as it were, rediscovered in the decade of the 1960s, but it seems that we might be able to recreate him now as a precursor of emancipatory activity, of the buried desire for freedom in those with "marks of weakness" on their faces. He knew there had to be transmutations, new syntheses, if mutilations were to be ended and a higher human consciousness were to emerge. Perhaps we can only perceive this now, as modern writers sharpen and deflect our reading of him, as our own experiences force us to recognize ourselves in what he wrote.

Blake was profoundly different from William Wordsworth, but many of Blake's themes become visible in Wordsworth's work when we read with our modern predicaments in mind. What we discover repeatedly is a challenge to the constraints and violations of society, an insistence on the experiential ground of values and ideas, and a resistance to predefined norms and systems—whether embodied in the artificial order of the city or the neo-classic rules of poetry. *The Prelude*[20] is once again of particular interest, because it is a rendering of a human being's conscious effort to understand his own self-formation and to do so by reconstituting his own biography.

The speaker in Wordsworth's poem embarks on his journey because of a realization that the roles he has been playing, the burden of an "unnatural self," have kept him from his own authentic thoughts. When he goes back to the Lake Country, he determines to "make rigorous inquisition" through himself. He recaptures his home countryside as it was given to his childhood consciousness; he recalls his university days, time spent in France, his enthusiasm for and then disillusionment with the French Revolution, and the years in London that followed. What is crucial is the effort to recall not only the events in the public world, but the perceptual background against which the poet generated the meanings of his life. The purpose is to find his own voice, to express in "the common language of men" what he himself thought and felt. His orientation is to experienced reality, to a world into which an imaginative person can *release* value, a world in which "we half create what we perceive."

He writes about the roads being open schools, about "how little those formalities to which/ With overweening trust alone we give/ The name of Education, have to do with real feeling and just sense." He recalls the "oppression worse than death" that derives from poverty and excessive labor, about how hard it is for love to thrive "among the close and overcrowded haunts/ Of cities, where the human heart is sick,/ And the eye feeds it not, and cannot feed."[21] And then:

> —*Yes, in those wanderings deeply did I feel*
> *How we mislead each other; above all,*

> *How books mislead us, seeking their reward*
> *From judgments of the wealthy Few, who see*
> *By artificial lights; how they debase*
> *The Many for the pleasure of those Few;*
> *Effeminately level down the truth*
> *To certain general notions, for the sake*
> *Of being understood at once, or else*
> *Through want of better knowledge in the heads*
> *That framed them. . . .*[22]

"General notions," he is saying, tyrannize when they are given official sanction by the few, the same few who exploit the poor and impose an "oppression worse than death."

For this poet there can be no rational calculus. Values and facts are intertwined; we may become acutely conscious of this when we read it now. The poet struggles with explanatory systems, with "precepts, judgments, maxims, creeds," which he knows full well are made by men. He suffers terrible perplexities about right and wrong, especially about the grounds of obligations, sanctions, and rules:

> *till, demanding formal proof,*
> *And seeking it in every thing, I lost*
> *All feeling of conviction, and, in fine,*
> *Sick, wearied out with contrarieties,*
> *Yielded up moral questions in despair.*[23]

The despair is due to his effort to justify moral rules and principles logically, to overcome contradiction with reason alone. At length he finds an intuitive and imaginative resolution. He becomes aware of what Immanuel Kant had named a "realm of ends," of human beings becoming legislative through freedom of will and "subject to the will of no other." As someone in quest of his own history, the poet is creating himself as legislator of his own world, even as he is affirming in his own idiom that (as Kant put it) every individual "should treat himself and all others never merely as means but in every case also as an end in himself."[24] He stands, as Wordsworth puts it, in nature's presence, "A sensitive being, a *creative* soul." And, at the end, he writes of finding in man "an object of delight,/ Of pure imagination, and of love" and of a sharpened sense of excellence, "of right and wrong."[25]

If we are to enter such a created universe and disclose to ourselves a world of value, as the poet did, we cannot allow our imagination to be arrested by one-dimensional seeing. Opening ourselves as im-

aginative, intuitive, feeling, thinking beings, we may discover something about what it signifies to create our own meanings along with
other human creatures. We may be able to say with Wordsworth that
"what we have loved,/ Others will love, and we will teach them
how. . ."[26] The lake, the smoke from the cottage chimneys, the old
soldier wandering in the woods, St. Bartholomew's Fair in London: all
these may seem strange and remote from the contemporary moment.
They may not seem "realistic" or socially conscious. But this need not
prevent us from trying to recapture our own landscapes as we involve
ourselves in a poet's quest nor from posing questions to the marchers
under the positivist banner as we struggle to find a common language
and our sovereignty in a realm of ends.

To move from Wordsworth to Baudelaire is to move from a
spacious and often weighty consciousness to a tense, self-dramatizing
spirit going to every extreme just to feel alive. Baudelaire was the first
city poet, the reputed discoverer of "modernity." Writing in Paris in
the mid-19th century, he was more likely than the others to challenge
what he saw to be the cruel, implacable regularity of industry. He
perceived the domination of the machine to be "sanguinary,
sacreligious, and unnatural." At one point he said, "Mechanization
will Americanize us; progress will atrophy us." He meant an idea of
progress that excluded the self and made individual exertion unnecessary. Afflicted by *ennui,* like so many artists of the period, and by what
he described as "spleen," he struggled to live life as a problem, a
predicament.[27] Developing a repertoire of novel and often shocking
images (a "lustful pauper" biting the shrivelled breast of an old whore;
"hives of maggots" in human brains; "man's foul menagerie of sin";
an "ant-seething city, city full of dreams")[28], he wrote the kind of
poetry intended to arouse his reader—his "hypocrite reader"—from
complacency. Sentimentality, genteel illusions, and torpor of all kinds
horrified him. He raged often childishly at stupidity, at the
bourgeoisie, and at provincial life. He smoked hashish to achieve an
artificial paradise; he consciously imposed upon himself a sense of sin,
of the abyss, so that he would feel compelled to strain upwards
towards infinity.

What is especially significant from our perspective is this poet's
preoccupation with that which weighs down and dominates: the heavy
sky weighing "like a lid,"[29] "The clock, calm evil god that makes us
shiver,"[30] the Guardian Angel shouting, "You shall obey, do you
hear?"[31] He rebelled, certainly, but more important was the intense
devotion Baudelaire brought to the making of a pure art that would

encompass subject and object. Affirming the imagination's autonomy, he transmuted what he called "states of the soul"[32] into images, into a "forest of symbols," analogues pointing beyond themselves to a con-structed Reality. To do this, he had to break with rationalist coercion. He had to replace the traditional, objectively existent system, "the great chain of being" itself, with projections of human devising. Always a critic, always sensitive to technique, he used his art to dis-close unsuspected aspects of color, sound, city street life, and the many moods (including boredom) by which living beings encounter what is real. One way, after all, to react against objectification and domi-nation is to assert initiative as a consciousness capable of grasping a diversity of realities and releasing multiple meanings into the world.

Marcuse finds in Baudelaire suggestions of a liberated way of living "beyond the rule of the performance principle."[33] The poet knew that, "True civilization does not lie in gas, nor in steam, nor in turntables." It lay in wide-awakeness, in being grounded in situations, and in the possibility of perceiving the "multiform and multicolored" beauty that existed in the infinite spirals of life. The reader is not likely to find humaneness here, nor political concern, nor an interest in *praxis*. But many modern people may well be moved to self-confrontation, if they risk some readings of Baudelaire; they may discover new vistas of per-sonal vitality. The poet's "flowers of evil" can still arouse some of us from submergence; they can serve both as purge and critique.

The novels of Gustave Flaubert may have a similar effect upon us. Flaubert said he was concerned with the rectification of illusions. He did not simply mean the romantic illusions that distorted Emma Bovary's vision of reality; he meant the *idées fixes,* the formulas, the conventions that fixed and often falsified dimensions of life and art. To escape fixity, he thought, life ought to be seen fitfully, in its flow and fragmentation under the corrosions of time. The perverse desires of human beings, the irrational responses, and the irregular and banal rhythms of existence had to be captured in a language properly atuned to the phenomenal world. "I loathe anything compulsory," said Flaubert, as he struck out against the shams and distortions that char-acterized bourgeois and utilitarian thought. He tried to do so im-personally, without affective involvement, even though he was aware that *he* was Emma Bovary, that it was *his* consciousness thrusting towards the restless figures, the objects, the landscapes of the forever questionable world.

Modern readers, encountering his *A Sentimental Education,*[34] can-not but feel the tension between common sense or traditional conventions and the desire to render truly what is happening. It is a tension inescapable in social life and certainly inescapable in literature. How *are* we to express what happens to us except through the categories and formulations handed down to us? How are we to escape stereotypes, clichés, and commonplaces? How are we to teach the young to reject mere chatter, unthinking repetition of the "received"?

An initial confrontation with Frederic Moreau in *A Sentimental Education* may well bring the reader up against conventional expectations that have to do with character, plot, and theme. Frederic is a person who drifts pointlessly through life, who cannot make commitments, who cannot choose. And, indeed, because we look at what we read through received categories, it may seem that "nothing happens" in Flaubert's novel. The closer the movement of the book comes to the banal rhythms of the ordinary, the more "boring" it may appear to be. This is because we are so accustomed to the imposition of purposeful (logical, sequential) narrative orders on the flow of things that we confuse those orders with "reality."

Frederic refuses, from the beginning, to be what we understand a "hero" to be. Living by an array of juvenile illusions, he dreams of becoming a writer, a lawyer, a painter, and a revolutionary, but he is only a dilettante, incapable of commitment. One reason is his vacuous and blind idealism, expressed through his adoration of the unattainable Madame Arnoux, mother-figure and romantic image, "the luminous point towards which all things converged."[35] Another reason is his entanglement in half-understood networks of business, politics, and illicit love in 19th century Paris. He needs money. He wants patronage and support as well as fame. But he is fundamentally indifferent; there is nothing about which he deeply cares. Many readers, wanting him to strive, to act, find themselves rebelling against the dullness of such a life and the lack of concern all around, even during the great 1848 Revolution in France.

Political commitments are presented as illusions. Numerous characters suffer changes of heart, no matter how personally involved they seem to be. Because of their vagueness, their vacillations, they experience world-shaking events as things happening randomly in the distance. When, for example, the people begin marching and the National Guard is mustered, Frederic looks out of the window with his mistress, Rosanette, and tells funny stories. When they hear the discharge of muskets, he remarks calmly, "Ha! a few of the citizens are getting a crack."[36] The people sack the Tuileries. Someone remarks that, "Heroes have not a good smell."[37] The people throw an armchair from the palace window and, watching it fall, cry out, "The Ship of State is tossing about in a stormy sea! Let it dance the cancan!"[38] In another part of the city, M. Dambreuse (a businessman given to confusing Property with God) feels his fortune threatened, his experience deceived: "A system so good! A king so wise! Was it possible?"[39] Many young men die. When he cries out from behind the bars for bread, one is shot in the face by the respectable Père Roque. Others become doctrinaire little tyrants. Apathy takes over. All efforts are foiled.

Now the point is not nihilistic. Read from our vantage point, Flaubert's work is challenging abstract schemata of all kinds, particularly those not subjected to experiential test. Reality is problematic for him, multi-faceted. The artist Pellerin, in the novel, says, "Some see black, others see blue, most people see stupidly."[40] To see stupidly is to see one-dimensionally, to take a conventional opinion as if it were unquestionable. The fearsome figures in A Sentimental Education are not the drifters and the dabblers, although their indifference makes it easy for injustice to prevail. The fearsome ones are those who have made themselves into one-dimensional creatures with fixed ideas. Senecal, for instance, begins as a radical mathematician and ends as a man with "the faith of an inquisitor," an authoritarian who functions as a police spy. M. Dambreuse moves from easygoing social trust to the kind of fury at incipient socialism that makes him demand outright dictatorship. Like Sartre's anti-Semite,[41] each one takes on a rock-like self the more he identifies with a doctrine, a single idea. Lending them our lives as we read the novel, we cannot but confront, in some fashion, the meaning of a "disciplined march," the detachment it imposes and the damage it can do.

And we are moved to search for some alternative, even as we struggle against what the novel enacts and what it reveals. The alternative to fixity cannot be the lives lived by Frederic and his friend Deslauriers, charming and well-meaning though they may be. They are self-absorbed and undisciplined, fundamentally uninvolved. Nor can it be the corrupt life lived by the man of commerce, M. Arnoux, nor the hollow, glamorous existence of the courtesan, Rosanette.

It can only be the ordinary life of someone like the workman, Dussardier, who is rooted solidly and unromantically in the everyday. He chooses himself as a revolutionary simply because he has seen people brutalized, and he cannot endure it. He loves simple justice; he hates the police; so he fights for what he believes freedom to be. Slogans and abstractions are irrelevant for him, because he is grounded, situated in his own lived life. After the uprising, he is the only one clearly to see that the people have been flung back into a worse condition than ever, that there is no way to gloss over suffering and defeat. "If, however, we only made the effort! If we were only sincere, we might understand each other."[42] He is asking for something that is almost impossible, given the illusions and bad faith prevailing in his world. Perhaps inevitably, he is killed by the positivistic Senecal, who can tolerate neither free speech nor authenticity.

Frederic and Deslauriers go home to the provinces, whether or no. "They had both failed, one to realize his dreams of love, the other to fulfill his dreams of power. What was the reason?....Then they blamed chance, circumstances, the times into which they were born."[43] They look back on adolescent exploits (as pointless and ineffectual as what followed after). They say to one another, "That was the happiest time we ever had."

We are left with a thousand unresolved questions. Is it possible to transcend "chance, circumstances, the time...."? Can the individual human being overcome the alienation that accompanies middle-class life? Can a vital, authentic self be created in a society dominated by material interests, manipulations—lies? Flaubert wrote his novel near the end of the 19th century, in what is thought of as the heyday of middle-class power, a time of invention and progress and expanding reforms. Knowing what he appears to have known, he was not likely to take an optimistic view of mankind or the future. At the same time, he did not choose himself as a "social" novelist, nor was he a "realist" writer in the sense Balzac was a realist. He was not interested in uncovering the hidden forces that lead to social change.

Radical critics like Georg Lukacs[44] have treated Balzac's novels as superior because they suggest the economic and political forces that account for what human beings do. Even though Balzac was a political conservative, he was able to present men and women enmeshed in their social reality. Because he could show the dynamics of causation, his work has been thought of as revolutionary, and, at a certain time, it almost surely might have had that effect—at least for those with a traditionally Marxist point of view. In our own time, however, it is the problematic of the human self that has become crucially interesting. Socio-economic entrapments, while important, do not seem as significant to many observers now as do the impacts of mystification and the depredations of technique. That is why, when a writer like Flaubert moves us to look at our own illusions, at the myths that surround us, and at the abstractions that falsify our lives, the effect may be more revealing than a reading of Balzac. Can Balzac move us to question the everyday, as Flaubert does, or to look anew at our own predicaments with such stunned and wondering eyes?

It is, of course, the case that we can only become individuals within society and that the kinds of individuals we become cannot but be affected by our place within the social whole. This is a period, however, when the sense of the self, particularly, has become questionable. The self emerges in human experience over time as individuals engage with their social realities and as they communicate with others and internalize others' attitudes. George Herbert Mead, in his studies of the self, said that it has two components or aspects: the "I" and the "Me."[45] The "Me" refers to the cultural experience that has been internalized, to previous history, and to the matrix in which actions are carried on. The "I," on the other hand, refers to the spontaneity of the self, the sense of freedom and agency. The "I" is responsible for present choices, which are made against a background of past occurrences, that which constitutes the "Me." It is always tempting to identify oneself as what one has been or done in the past (how one was named, credentialled, defined), to become—as it were—a "me." The alternative is continually to create and recreate the self through the agency of the "I." To do this requires a considerable ability to look reflectively and critically at the "Me," to select future projects, and to gear actively into the world. It requires as well an ability to recognize openings in one's life situations, openings that permit some kind of action or transcendence, that allow one to go beyond what one has been.

In Balzac's novels people present themselves as explicable through the forces that shaped them. They play allotted roles; they are too entangled in meshes of cause and effect to make efforts to transcend. In realism and in naturalism, generally, as in much of Marxist writing, the "Me" dominates. The "I" is forever a function of the matrix; thus it is to a large extent determined. The social novelist, like the social critic, is concerned with exposing the drama of causation to the end of moving people to change the matrix, the social fabric.

There are others, actually more modern writers, who are preoccupied with the self and with characters who, as Michel Zeraffa writes, "can no longer be individuals—members of a social group." He goes on: "Their basic attachment to the 'self' as the sole authentic human value demonstrates that they are characters who are not the creatures of a Balzacian society, where the individual was related to society as a word is to a sentence." It is these characters who become the "instruments of revelatory shocks."[46] We need only think of Flaubert's characters again, or of Dostoyevsky's Underground Man,[47] or of Virginia Woolf's Mrs. Dalloway (who feels it is her "punishment to see sink and disappear here a man, there a woman, in this profound darkness, and she forced to stand there in her evening diress."[48]). We need only recall such precursors as Thomas Mann, who wrote the following about Hans Castorp at the beginning of *The Magic Mountain:*

> All sorts of personal aims, ends, hopes, prospects, hover before the eyes of the individual, and out of these he derives the impulse to ambition and achievement. Now, if the life about him, if his own time seems, however outwardly stimulating, to be at bottom empty of such food for his aspirations; if he privately recognizes it to be hopeless, viewless, helpless, opposing only a hollow silence to all the questions man puts. . .as to the final, absolute, and abstract meaning in all his efforts and activities; then, in such a case, a certain laming of the personality is bound to occur. . . .[49]

My point is that works of this sort have a special capacity to arouse us to wide-awakeness in our own time and that this kind of arousal is a necessity if there is to be transcendence, if the matrix is ever to be changed. Wordsworth somehow knew this, and that is why he put so much stress upon the recovery of his landscape; Baudelaire knew it, and that is why he fought so hard against *ennui* and lack of care. Flaubert worked, because of it, to goad his readers to break with illusions and find their own truth. In all of these, there were intimations of "a certain laming of the personality" that would afflict those who stayed on the flatland, those trying to make their way uncritically in the modern and post-modern world. Perhaps, in the end, Joseph Conrad said it most directly when his Marlow (in *Heart of Darkness*[50]) rages at the ones who take refuge, "surrounded by kind neighbors. . .stepping delicately between the butcher and the policeman, in the holy terror of scandals and gallows and lunatic asylums. . . ." And he goes on, aiming at the submerged ones, those who take no risks, who refuse to question, who evade critique:

> Of course you may be too much of a fool to go wrong—too dull even to know you are being assaulted by the powers of darkness. I take it, no fool ever made a bargain for his soul with the devil. . . . Or you may be such a thunderingly exalted creature as to be altogether deaf and blind to anything but heavenly sights and sounds. Then the earth for you is only a standing place—and whether to be like this is your loss or your gain I won't pretend to say. But most of us are neither one nor

the other. The earth for us is a place to live in, where we must put up with sights, with sounds, with smells too, by Jove!—breathe dead hippo, so to speak, and not be contaminated. And there, don't you see? your strength comes in, the faith in your ability for the digging of holes to bury the stuff in—your power of devotion, not to yourself, but to an obscure, backbreaking business.[51]

He is like Dussardier; he talks of falling back on a "capacity for faithfulness." He too is calling for a rootedness in the world. He is evoking something associated with all human efforts to confront fatality—and at once to remain in touch with "primordial perception,"[52] the original grasp on the world.

It seems clear enough that interpretive encounters with literature can, at least to some degree, lead to clarification of modern readers' lives. Turning our attention to our own life—worlds and our own situations—we ought—by coming in touch with a range of adversary artists —to find ourselves breaking with submergence, posing our own critical questions to reality. There have been many instances in Western literature, especially in the past century and a half, of struggles for emancipation from a domination much like what we experience today. To come in touch with those who articulated such struggles is to come in touch with people atune to deep currents in the culture, currents of feeling and thinking not yet visible on the surfaces of life. It may be that the official histories of progress, the optimistic treatments of increasing controls, have obscured certain fundamental wants and concerns. It may also be that engagements with artists who were critical, artists for whom the achievement of self was the most authentic human value, may reawaken us to fundamentals and make it possible to transcend.

Without that awareness and that hope, teachers find it unimaginably difficult to cope with the demands of children in these days. They may become drifters as a result, or authoritarians. If they undergo a purely technical training or a simplified "competency-based" approach, they are likely to see themselves as mere transmission belts—or clerks. The question of the freedom of those they try to teach, the question of their students' endangered selves; these recede before a tide of demands for "basics," "discipline," and preparation for the "world of work." Teachers (artlessly, wearily) become accomplices in mystification. They have neither the time, nor energy, nor inclination to urge their students to critical reflection; they, themselves, have suppressed the questions and avoided backward looks.

I am arguing against conventional wisdom. I am proposing

aesthetic encounters that are bound to disturb, if they do not simply confuse. I am asking that attention be paid to a literature that seems, on the face of it, irrelevant to teacher education, a literature whose critical elements have been effectively absorbed. The reason, again, is that literature may have an emancipatory function for people whose selves have become attenuated, who have forgotten the function of the "I." I do not see how individuals who know nothing about "the powers of darkness," who account for themselves by talking about "chance, circumstances, and the times," can awaken the young to question and to learn. Learning involves a futuring, a going beyond. Teachers who themselves are submerged, who feel in some sense "finished," like the desks before them or the chalkboards behind, can hardly move students to critical questioning or to learning how to learn.

Because teachers are living beings, they suffer objectification like other members of the society; they also are thrust into molds. They play roles in many ways defined by others, although their interpretations of these roles must, in some manner, be grounded in an understanding of themselves. Again, committed rationality also rests on the capacity for self-reflection. Boredom, lassitude, automatism, and abstractness; all of these erode self-awareness and the desire to make sense. It ought to be possible to bring teachers in touch with their own landscapes. Then learning may become a process of the "I" meeting the "I."

References

1. Jurgen Habermas, *Theory and Practice* (Boston: Beacon Press, 1972), p. 22.
2. Daniel Bell, *The Coming of Post-Industrial Society* (New York: Basic Books, 1973), p. 350.
3. Herbert Marcuse, *One-Dimensional Man* (Boston: Beacon Press, 1966), p. 208.
4. See Paulo Freire, *Pedagogy of the Oppressed* (New York: Herder and Herder, 1970).
5. Maurice Merleau-Ponty, "The Crisis of the Understanding," in *The Primacy of Perception* (Evanston: Northwestern University Press, 1964), p. 204.
6. Marcuse, *op. cit.,* p. 60.

7. Jean-Paul Sartre, *Literature and Existentialism* (New York: Citadel Press, 1965), p. 51.
8. Habermas, *Knowledge and Human Interests* (Boston: Beacon Press, 1970), p. 310.
9. Alvin Gouldner, *The Coming Crisis of Western Sociology* (New York: Basic Books, 1970), pp. 65-78.
10. Ibid., p. 69.
11. Alan F. Blum, "Positive Thinking," *Theory and Society,* Vol. 1, No. 3, Fall 1974, p. 247.
12. Jorge Luis Borges, "Kafka and His Precursors," in *Labyrinths* (New York: New Directions, 1964), p. 201.
13. See Thomas Pynchon, *Gravity's Rainbow* (New York: Viking Press, 1973).
14. See Kurt Vonnegut, *Slaughterhouse-Five or The Children's Crusade* (New York: Delacorte Press, 1969).
15. See Margaret Atwood, *Surfacing* (New York: Popular Library, 1970).
16. See Saul Bellow, *Humboldt's Gift* (New York: Viking Press, 1975).
17. Rene Wellek and Austin Warren, *Theory of Literature* (New York: Harcourt, Brace & World, 1956), p. 150.
18. William Blake, "Proverbs of Hell," in *William Blake, A Selection of Poems and Letters,* ed. J. Bronowski (Baltimore: Penguin Books, 1958), p. 99.
19. Blake, "London," *op. cit.,* pp. 52-53.
20. William Wordsworth, *The Prelude: Selected Poems and Sonnets,* ed. Carlos Baker (New York: Holt, Rinehart, and Winston, 1962).
21. Ibid., p. 419.
22. Ibid.
23. Ibid., p. 398.
24. Immanuel Kant, "Theory of Ethics," in *Kant* (Selections), ed. Theodore Meyer Greene (New York: Charles Scribner's Sons, 1929), pp. 311-315.
25. Wordsworth, *op. cit.,* p. 415.
26. Ibid., p. 438.
27. Sartre, *Baudelaire* (Norfolk, Conn.: New Directions, 1950), pp. 97-99.
28. Charles Baudelaire, "To the Reader" *The Flowers of Evil* (New York: New Directions, 1958), p. 3.
29. Baudelaire, "Spleen," *op. cit.,* p. 63.
30. Baudelaire, "The Clock," *op. cit.,* p. 73.
31. Baudelaire, "The Rebel," *op. cit.,* p. 147.
32. Baudelaire, "Correspondances," in *Paths to the Present,* ed. Eugen Weber (New York: Dodd, Mead, 1970), p. 204.
33. Marcuse, *Eros and Civilization* (New York: Vintage Books, 1962), p. 139.
34. Gustave Flaubert, *A Sentimental Education* (New York: New Directions, 1957).
35. Ibid., p. 22.
36. Ibid., p. 378.
37. Ibid., p. 387.
38. Ibid.
39. Ibid., p. 397.
40. Ibid., p. 546.
41. See Sartre, *Anti-Semite and Jew* (New York: Schocken Books, 1948).
42. Flaubert, *op. cit.,* p. 545.

43. Ibid., p. 546.
44. See Georg Lukacs, *Studies in European Realism* (London: Hillway Publishing Company, 1950).
45. George Herbert Mead, *Mind, Self & Society,* ed. Charles W. Morris (Chicago: University of Chicago Press, 1948), pp. 173-178.
46. Michel Zeraffa, *Fictions: The Novel and Social Reality* (New York: Penguin Books, 1976), p. 29.
.47. Fyodor Dostoyevsky, *Notes from Underground,* in *The Short Novels of Dostoyevsky* (New York: Dial Press, 1945), p. 152.
48. Virginia Woolf, *Mrs. Dalloway* (New York: Harcourt, Brace & World, 1953), p. 282.
49. Thomas Mann, *The Magic Mountain* (New York: Alfred A. Knopf, 1955), p. 32.
50. Joseph Conrad, *Heart of Darkness,* in *Three Great Tales* (New York: Random House, n.d.).
51. Ibid., pp. 272-273.
52. Merleau-Ponty, "The Primacy of Perception and Its Philosophical Consequences," *op. cit.,* p. 25.

3

Wide-Awakeness and the Moral Life

"**M**ORAL reform," wrote Henry David Thoreau, "is the effort
to throw off sleep." He went on:

> Why is it that men give so poor an account of their day if they have not
> been slumbering? They are not such poor calculators. If they had not
> been overcome with drowsiness they would have performed something.
> The millions are awake enough for physical labor; but only one in a
> million is awake enough for effective intellectual exertion, only one in
> a hundred million to a poetic or divine life. To be awake is to be alive.
> I have never yet met a man who was quite awake. How could I have
> looked him in the face? We must learn to reawaken and keep ourselves
> awake, not by mechanical aids, but by an infinite expectation of the
> dawn, which does not foresake us in our soundest sleep. I know of no
> more encouraging fact than the unquestionable ability of man to
> elevate his life by a conscious endeavor.[1]

It is of great interest to me to find out how this notion of wide-
awakeness has affected contemporary thought, perhaps particularly
the thought of those concerned about moral responsibility and commitment in this difficult modern age. The social philosopher Alfred
Schutz has talked of wide-awakeness as an achievement, a type of
awareness, "a plane of consciousness of highest tension originating in
an attitude of full attention to life and its requirements."[2] This attentiveness, this *interest* in things, is the direct opposite of the attitude of
bland conventionality and indifference so characteristic of our time.

We are all familiar with the number of individuals who live their
lives immersed, as it were, in daily life, in the mechanical round of
habitual activities. We are all aware how few people ask themselves
what they have done with their own lives, whether or not they have
used their freedom or simply acceded to the imposition of patterned
behavior and the assignment of roles. Most people, in fact, are likely

42

to go on in that fashion, unless—or until—"one day the 'why' arises," as Albert Camus put it, "and everything begins in that weariness tinged with amazement." Camus had wide-awakeness in mind as well; because the weariness of which he spoke comes "at the *end* of the acts of a mechanical life, but at the same time it inaugurates the impulse of consciousness."[3]

The "why" may take the form of anxiety, the strange and wordless anxiety that occurs when individuals feel they are not acting on their freedom, not realizing possibility, not (to return to Thoreau) elevating their lives. Or the "why" may accompany a sudden perception of the insufficiencies in ordinary life, of inequities and injustices in the world, of oppression and brutality and control. It may accompany, indeed it may be necessary, for an individual's moral life. The opposite of morality, it has often been said, is indifference—a lack of care, an absence of concern. Lacking wide-awakeness, I want to argue, individuals are likely to drift, to act on impulses of expediency. They are unlikely to identify situations as moral ones or to set themselves to assessing their demands. In such cases, it seems to me, it is meaningless to talk of obligation; it may be futile to speak of consequential choice.

This is an important problem today in many countries of the world. Everywhere, guidelines are deteriorating; fewer and fewer people feel themselves to be answerable to clearly defined norms. In many places, too, because of the proliferation of bureaucracies and corporate structures, individuals find it harder and harder to take initiative. They guide themselves by vaguely perceived expectations; they allow themselves to be programmed by organizations and official schedules or forms. They are like the hero of George Konrad's novel, *The Case Worker*. He is a social worker who works with maltreated children "in the name," as he puts it, "of legal principles and provisions." He does not like the system, but he serves it: "It's law, it works, it's rather like me, its tool. I know its ins and outs. I simplify and complicate it, I slow it down and speed it up. I adapt myself to its needs or adapt it to my needs, but this is as far as I will go."[4] Interestingly enough, he says (and this brings me back to wide-awakeness) that his highest aspiration is to "live with his eyes open" as far as possible; but the main point is that he, like so many other clerks and office workers and middle management men (for all their meaning well), is caught within the system and is not free to choose.

I am suggesting that, for too many individuals in modern society, there is a feeling of being dominated and that feelings of powerlessness are almost inescapable. I am also suggesting that such feelings can to a large degree be overcome through conscious endeavor on the part of individuals to keep themselves awake, to think about their condition in the world, to inquire into the forces that appear to dominate them, to interpret the experiences they are having day by day. Only as they learn to make sense of what is happening, can they feel themselves to be autonomous. Only then can they develop the sense of agency required for living a moral life.

I think it is clear that there always has to be a human consciousness, recognizing the moral issues potentially involved in a situation, if there is to be a moral life. As in such great moral presentations as *Antigone, Hamlet,* and *The Plague,* people in everyday life today have to define particular kinds of situations as moral and to identify the possible alternatives. In *Antigone,* Antigone defined the situation that existed after her uncle forbade her to bury her brother as one in which there were alternatives: she could indeed bury her brother, thus offending against the law of the state and being sentenced to death, or (like her sister Ismene) submit to the men in power. In *Hamlet,* the Danish prince defined the situation in Denmark as one in which there were alternatives others could not see: to expose the murderer of his father and take the throne as the true king or to accept the rule of Claudius and his mother and return as a student to Wittenberg. In *The Plague,* most of the citizens of Oran saw no alternative but to resign themselves to a pestilence for which there was no cure; but Dr. Rieux and Tarrou defined the same situation as one in which there were indeed alternatives: to submit—or to form sanitary squads and, by so doing, to refuse to acquiesce in the inhuman, the absurd.

When we look at the everyday reality of home and school and workplace, we can scarcely imagine ourselves taking moral positions like those taken by a Hamlet or a Dr. Rieux. One reason has to do with the overwhelming ordinariness of the lives we live. Another is our tendency to perceive our everyday reality as a given—objectively defined, impervious to change. Taking it for granted, we do not realize that that reality, like all others, is an interpreted one. It presents itself to us as it does because we have learned to understand it in standard ways.

In a public school, for instance, we scarcely notice that there is a hierarchy of authority; we are so accustomed to it, we forget that it is man-made. Classroom teachers, assigned a relatively low place in the hierarchy, share a way of seeing and of talking about it. They are used to watching schedules, curricula, and testing programs emanate from "the office." They take for granted the existence of a high place, a seat of power. If required unexpectedly to administer a set of tests, most teachers (fearful, perhaps, irritated or sceptical) will be likely to accede. Their acquiescence may have nothing at all to do with their convictions or with what they have previously read or learned. They simply see no alternatives. The reality they have constructed and take for granted allows for neither autonomy nor disagreement. They do not consider putting their objections to a test. The constructs they have inherited do not include a view of teachers as equal participants. "That," they are prone to say, "is the way it is."

Suppose, however, that a few teachers made a serious effort to understand the reasons for the new directive. Suppose they went out into the community to try to assess the degree of pressure on the part of parents. Suppose that they investigated the kinds of materials dispatched from the city or the state. Pursuing such efforts, they would be keeping themselves awake. They might become increasingly able to define their own values with regard to testing; they might conceivably see a moral issue involved. For some, testing might appear to be dehumanizing; it might lead to irrelevant categorizing; it might result in the branding of certain children. For others, testing might appear to be miseducative, unless it were used to identify disabilities and suggest appropriate remedies. For still others, testing might appear to be a kind of insurance against poor teaching, a necessary reminder of what was left undone. Discussing it from several points of view and within an understood context, the teachers might find themselves in a position to act as moral agents. Like Dr. Rieux and Tarrou, they might see that there are indeed alternatives: to bring the school community into an open discussion, to consider the moral issues in the light of overarching commitments, or to talk about what is actually known and what is merely hypothesized. At the very least, there would be wide-awakeness. The members of the school community would be embarked on a moral life.

Where personal issues are concerned, the approach might be very much the same. Suppose that a young person's peer group is "into" drugs or alcohol or some type of sexual promiscuity. Young persons who are half asleep and who feel no sense of agency might well see no alternative to compliance with the group, when the group decides that certain new experiences should be tried. To such individuals, no moral situation exists. They are young; they are members; whether they want to particularly or not, they can only go along.

Other young persons, just as committed to the group, might be able to realize that there are indeed alternatives when, say, some of their comrades go out to find a supply of cocaine. They might be able to ponder those alternatives, to play them out in their imagination. They can accompany their friends on their search; they might even, if they are successful, get to sniff a little cocaine and have the pleasure such sniffs are supposed to provide. They can, on the other hand, take a moment to recall the feelings they had when they first smoked marijuana—the nervousness at losing touch with themselves, the dread about what might happen later. They can consider the fact that their friends are going to do something illegal, not playful, that they could be arrested, even jailed. They can confront their own reluctance to break the law (or even to break an ordinary rule), imagine what their parents would say, try to anticipate what they would think of themselves. At the same time, if they decide to back away, they know they might lose their friends. If they can remember that they are free, after all, and if they assess their situation as one in which they can indeed choose one course of action over another, they are on the way to becoming moral agents. The more considerations they take into account, the more they consider the welfare of those around, the closer they will come to making a defensible choice.

A crucial issue facing us is the need to find ways of educating young persons to such sensitivity and potency. As important, it seems to me, is the matter of wide-awakeness for their teachers. It is far too easy for teachers, like other people, to play their roles and do their jobs without serious consideration of the good and right. Ironically, it is even possible when they are using classroom manuals for moral education. This is partly due to the impact of a vaguely apprehended relativism, partly to a bland carelessness, a shrugging off (sometimes because of grave self-doubt) of responsibility. I am convinced that, if teachers today are to initiate young people into an ethical existence, they themselves must attend more fully than they normally have to their own lives and its requirements; they have to break with the mechanical life, to overcome their own submergence in the habitual, even in what they conceive to be the virtuous, and ask the "why" with which learning and moral reasoning begin.

"You do not," wrote Martin Buber, "need moral genius for educating character; you do need someone who is wholly alive and able to communicate himself directly to his fellow beings. His aliveness streams out to them and affects them most strongly and purely when he has no thought of affecting them. . . ."[5] This strikes me as true; but I cannot imagine an aliveness streaming out from someone who is half-asleep and out of touch with herself or himself. I am not proposing separate courses in moral education or value clarification to be taught by such a teacher. I am, rather, suggesting that attentiveness to the moral dimensions of existence ought to permeate many of the classes taught, that wide-awakeness ought to accompany every effort made to initiate persons into any form of life or academic discipline.

Therefore, I believe it important for teachers, no matter what their specialty, to be clear about how they ground their own values, their own conceptions of the good and of the possible. Do they find their sanctions in some supernatural reality? Are they revealed in holy books or in the utterances of some traditional authority? Do they, rather, depend upon their own private intuitions of what is good and right? Do they decide in each particular situation what will best resolve uncertainty, what works out for the best? Do they simply refer to conventional social morality, to prevailing codes, or to the law? Or do they refer beyond the law—to some domain of principle, of norm? To what extent are they in touch with the actualities of their own experiences, their own biographies, and the ways in which these affect the tone of their encounters with the young? Teachers need to be aware of how they personally confront the unnerving questions present in the lives of every teacher, every parent: What shall we teach them? How can we guide them? What hope can we offer them? How can we tell them what to do?

The risks are great, as are the uncertainties. We are no longer in a situation in which we can provide character-training with the assurance that it will make our children virtuous and just. We can no longer use systems of rewards and punishments and feel confident they will make youngsters comply. We recognize the futility of teaching rules or preaching pieties or presenting conceptions of the good. We can no longer set ourselves up as founts of wisdom, exemplars of righteousness, and expect to have positive effects. Children are active; children are different at the various stages of their growth. Engaged in transactions with an environment, each one must effect connections within his or her own experience. Using whatever capacities they have available, each one must himself or herself perceive the consequences of the acts he or she performs. Mustering their own resources, each one must embark—"through choice of action," as Dewey put it[6]— upon the formation of a self.

Moral education, it would seem, must be as specifically concerned with self-identification in a community as it is with the judgments persons are equipped to make at different ages. It has as much to do with interest and action in concrete situations as it does with the course of

moral reasoning. It has as much to do with consciousness and imagination as it does with principle. Since it cannot take place outside
the vital contexts of social life, troubling questions have to be constantly confronted. How can indifference be overcome? How can the
influence of the media be contained? How can the young be guided to
choose reflectively and compassionately, even as they are set free?

The problem, most will agree, is not to tell them what to do—but
to help them attain some kind of clarity about how to choose, how to
decide what to do. And this involves teachers directly, immediately—
teachers as persons able to present themselves as critical thinkers willing to disclose their own principles and their own reasons as well as
authentic persons living in the world, persons who are concerned—
who care.

Many teachers, faced with demands like these, find themselves in
difficult positions, especially if they are granted little autonomy, or
their conceptions of their own projects are at odds with what their
schools demand. Today they may be held accountable for teaching
predefined competencies and skills or for achieving objectives that are
often largely behavioral. At once, they may be expected to represent
both the wider culture and the local community, or the international
community and the particular community of the individual child. If
teachers are not critically conscious, if they are not awake to their own
values and commitments (and to the conditions working upon them),
if they are not personally engaged with their subject matter and with
the world around, I do not see how they can initiate the young into
critical questioning or the moral life.

I am preoccupied, I suppose, with what Camus called "the plague"
—that terrible distancing and indifference, so at odds with commitment and communion and love. I emphasize this because I want to
stress the connection between wide-awakeness, cognitive clarity, and
existential concern. I want to highlight the fact that the roots of moral
choosing lie at the core of a person's conception of herself or himself
and the equally important fact that choosing involves action as well as
thought. Moral action, of course, demands choosing betwen alternatives, usually between two goods, not between good and bad or
right and wrong. The problem in teaching is to empower persons to
internalize and incarnate the kinds of principles that will enable them
to make such choices. Should I do what is thought to be my duty and
volunteer for the army, or should I resist what I believe to be an unjust
war? Should I steal the medicine to save my mother's life, or should I
obey the law and risk letting her die?

These are choices of consequence for the self and others; and they are made, they can only be made in social situations where custom, tradition, official codes, and laws condition and play upon what people think and do. We might think of Huck Finn's decision not to return Jim to his owner or of Anna Karenina's decision to leave her husband. These are only morally significant in relation to a particular fabric of codes and customs and rules. Think of the Danish king's wartime decision to stand with Denmark's Jewish citizens, Daniel Ellsberg's decision to publish the Pentagon Papers, or Pablo Casals' refusal to conduct in fascist Spain. These decisions too were made in a matrix of principles, laws, and ideas of what is considered acceptable, absolutely, or conditionally good and right. To be moral involves taking a position towards that matrix, thinking critically about what is taken for granted. It involves taking a principled position of one's own *(choosing* certain principles by which to live) and speaking clearly about it, so as to set oneself on the right track.

It is equally important to affirm that it is always the individual, acting voluntarily in a particular situation at a particular moment, who does the deciding. I do not mean that individuals are isolated, answerable only to themselves. I do mean that individuals, viewed as participants, as inextricably involved with other people, must be enabled to take responsibility for their own choosing, must not merge themselves or hide themselves in what Soren Kierkegaard called "the crowd."[7] If individuals act automatically or conventionally, if they do only what is expected of them (or because they feel they have no right to speak for themselves), if they do only what they are told to do, they are not living moral lives.

Indeed, I rather doubt that individuals who are cowed or flattened out or depressed or afraid can learn, since learning inevitably involves a free decision to enter into a form of life, to proceed in a certain way, to do something because it is right. There are paradigms to be found in many kinds of teaching for those interested in moral education, since teaching is in part a process of moving people to proceed according to a specified set of norms. If individuals are wide-awake and make decisions consciously to interpret a poem properly, to try to understand a period in English history, or to participate in some type of social inquiry, they are choosing to abide by certain standards made available to them. In doing so, they are becoming acquainted with what it means to choose a set of norms. They are not only creating value for themselves, they are creating themselves; they are moving towards more significant, more understandable lives.

Consider, with norms and self-creation in mind, the case of Nora in Ibsen's *The Doll's House.* If she simply ran out of the house in tears at the end, she would not have been engaging in moral action. Granting the fact that she was defying prevailing codes, I would insist that she was making a decision in accord with an internalized norm. It might be called a principle of emancipation, having to do with the right to grow, to become, to be more than a doll in a doll's house. If asked, Nora might have been able to generalize and talk about the right of *all* human beings to develop in their own fashion, to be respected, to be granted integrity.

Principles or norms are general ideas of that kind, arising out of experience and used by individuals in the appraisal of situations they encounter as they live—to help them determine what they ought to do. They are not specific rules, like the rules against stealing and lying and adultery. They are general and comprehensive. They concern justice and equality, respect for the dignity of persons and regard for their points of view. They have much to do with the ways in which diverse individuals choose themselves; they are defined reflectively and imaginatively and against the backgrounds of biography. When they are incarnated in a person's life, they offer him or her the means for analyzing particular situations. They offer perspectives, points of view from which to consider particular acts. The Golden Rule is such a principle, but, as Dewey says, the Golden Rule does not finally decide matters just by enabling us to tell people to consider the good of others as they would their own. "It suggests," he writes, "the necessity of considering how our acts affect the interests of others as well as our own; it tends to prevent partiality of regard. . . . In short, the Golden Rule does not issue special orders or commands; but it does clarify and illuminate the situations requiring intelligent deliberation."[8] So it was with the principle considered by Ibsen's Nora; so it is with the principle of justice and the principles of care and truth-telling. Our hope in teaching is that persons will appropriate such principles and learn to live by them.

Now it is clear that young people have to pass through the stages of heteronomy in their development towards the degree of autonomy they require for acting on principle in the way described. They must achieve the kind of wide-awakeness I have been talking about, the ability to think about what they are doing, to take responsibility. The teaching problem seems to me to be threefold. It involves equipping young people with the ability to identify alternatives, and to see possibilities in the situations they confront. It involves the teaching of principles, possible perspectives by means of which those situations can be assessed and appraised, *as well as* the norms governing historical inquiry, ballet dancing, or cooperative living, norms that must be appropriated by personns desiring to join particular human communities. It also involves enabling students to make decisions of principle, to reflect, to articulate, and to take decisive actions in good faith.

Fundamental to the whole process may be the building up of a sense of moral directedness, of oughtness. An imaginativeness, an awareness, and a sense of possibility are required, along with the sense of autonomy and agency, of being present to the self. There must be attentiveness to others and to the circumstances of everyday life. There must be efforts made to discover ways of living together justly and pursuing common ends. As wide-awake teachers work, making principles available and eliciting moral judgments, they must orient themselves to the concrete, the relevant, and the questionable. They must commit themselves to each person's potentiality for overcoming helplessness and submergence, for looking through his or her own eyes at the shared reality.

I believe this can only be done if teachers can identify themselves as moral beings, concerned with defining their own life purposes in a way that arouses others to do the same. I believe, you see, that the young are most likely to be stirred to learn when they are challenged by teachers who themselves are learning, who are breaking with what they have too easily taken for granted, who are creating their own moral lives. There are no guarantees, but wide-awakeness can play a part in the process of liberating and arousing, in helping people pose questions with regard to what is oppressive, mindless, and wrong. Surely, it can help people—all kinds of people—make the conscious endeavors needed to elevate their lives.

Camus, in an essay called "The Almond Trees," wrote some lines that seem to me to apply to teachers, especially those concerned in this way. He was talking about how endless are our tasks, how impossible it is to overcome the human condition—which, at least, we have come to know better than ever before:

We must mend "what has been torn apart, make justice imaginable again—give happiness a meaning once more. . . . Naturally, it is a superhuman task. But superhuman is the term for tasks men take a long time to accomplish, that's all. Let us know our aims, then, holding fast to the mind. . . . The first thing is not to despair.[9]

References

1. Henry David Thoreau, *Walden* (New York: Washington Square Press, 1963.), pp. 66-67.
2. Alfred Schutz, ed. Maurice Natanson, *The Problem of Social Reality,* Collected Papers I (The Hague: Martinus Nijhoff, 1967.), p. 213.
3. Albert Camus, *The Myth of Sisyphus* (New York: Alfred A. Knopf, 1955), p. 13.
4. George Konrad, *The Case Worker* (New York: Harcourt Brace Jovanovich, 1974), p. 168.
5. Martin Buber, *Between Man and Man* (Boston: Beacon Press, 1957), p. 105.
6. John Dewey, *Democracy and Education* (New York: Macmillan Company, 1916), p. 408.
7. Soren Kierkegaard, "The Individual," in *The Point of View for My Work as an Author* (New York: Harper & Row, 1962), pp. 102-136.
8. Dewey, *Theory of the Moral Life* (New York: Holt, Rinehart and Winston, 1960), p. 142.
9. Camus, "The Almond Trees," in *Lyrical and Critical Essays* (New York: Alfred A. Knopf, 1968), p. 135.

4
The Matter of Mystification:
Teacher Education in Unquiet Times

HERE are many modes of mystification. One is dramatized in Herman Melville's *Moby Dick*. Captain Ahab, in that novel, deliberately creates a surface reality, that of an ordinary whaling voyage, to mask the actuality of his personal manic quest. "To accomplish his object, Ahab must use tools; and of all tools used in the shadow of the moon, men are most apt to get out of order." The narrator remarks on his "superlative sense and shrewdness in foreseeing that, for the present, the hunt should in some way be stripped of that strange imaginative impiousness that naturally invested it; the full terror of the voyage must be kept withdrawn into the obscure background (for few men's courage is proof against protracted meditation unrelieved by action); when they stood their long night watches, his officers and men must have some nearer things to think of than Moby Dick."[1] Ahab offers rewards and prizes, therefore, to satisfy the crew's "common, daily appetites." He takes it for granted that the "permanent constitutional condition of the manufactured man . . . is sordidness" and he is careful not to strip his men of "hopes of cash—aye, cash."[2] At once, he keeps them constantly busy—watching out for whales, risking their lives in whaleboats, working over the try-pots, and stripping blubber from the carcasses. The point is to keep hidden a "private purpose" that takes no account of the crew's desires and needs. It is to delude them and use them by appealing to what they are made to think is their true self-interest. They are demeaned in consequence; in the end, they are destroyed.

Originally published in *Issues in Sociology, Politics and Education*. Nafferton, Driffield, England: Nafferton Books, 1977.

This strikes me as an exemplary mystification, certainly in the Marxian sense. Karl Marx used the term to describe the process whereby it becomes natural for workers of any kind "to feel completely at home in these estranged and irrational forms of capital-interest, land-rent, labor-wages, since these are precisely the forms of illusion in which they move about and find their daily occupation."[3] *Capital* eloquently describes the ways in which people overlook the fact that there are diverse forms of congealed human labor underlying such relationships as those apparent on Captain Ahab's ship, economic relationships distinctive of a capitalist society.[4] Ahab's ideology, like that of capitalism itself, depends upon a mystification that effectively obscures alienation—and the treatment of human beings as "tools."

Marx was not alone in exposing mystification. The phenomenological philosopher Paul Ricoeur calls Marx, Friedrich Nietzsche, and Sigmund Freud the great demystifiers. They are all "destroyers," Ricoeur says; they "free our horizon for a more authentic speaking, a new reign of truth, not only by means of a 'destructive' critique but by the invention of an art of *interpreting*."[5] Marxian thought deciphers the illusions fabricated by the ideologists of capitalism, by the Captain Ahabs of the world. Nietzschean aphorisms rip off the masks of moralism and self-deception. Freudian theory exposes the pretensions of the ego as it makes self-emancipation possible. Each mode of critique involves an interrogation of some surface reality. Each one is a demystification, the object of which is to liberate—for *praxis,* for self-fulfillment, for awareness, and a degree of happiness.

I want to propose that one of the responsibilities of teacher educators is to work for "a more authentic speaking," to combat mystification. Traditionally, teacher education has been concerned with initiating the "forms of life" R.S. Peters describes,[6] or the public traditions, or the heritage. Even where emphasis has been placed on the importance of critical thinking or experimental intelligence, there has been a tendency to present an unexamined surface reality as "natural," fundamentally unquestionable. There has been a tendency as well to treat official labelings and legitimations as law-like, to overlook the *constructed* character of social reality.[7]

My concern is with the creation of the kinds of conditions that make possible a critique of what is taken to be "natural," of the "forms of illusion" in which persons feel so "completely at home," no matter how alienated they are or how repressed. I am concerned as well with enabling individuals to reflect upon their own lived lives and the lives they lead in common with one another, not merely as professionals or professionals-to-be, but as human beings participating in a shared reality. It is not irrelevant that the crew members in *Moby Dick* are almost all island-men—"each *Isolato* living on a separate continent of his own."[8] Not only are most of them incapable of deciphering the meaning of the voyage; their separation from each other makes them susceptible to all kinds of delusions and manipulations. Captain Ahab knows full well that only one or two of them can squeeze another's hand.

Surely it is important for people who intend to work in education to feel that they inhabit some common continent, even as it is crucially important that they become capable of undertaking the kinds of *praxis* that might transform what they find deficient, surpass what they find inhumane. In the United States today, it seems particularly important for persons to achieve a wide-awakeness of this sort—not only for the sake of overcoming ignorance and warding off manipulations, but in order to resist the cynicism and powerlessness that silence as they paralyse.

I cannot but start with a conception of a technocratic society armed with awesome power, both technical and communicative. Americans have only begun to discover how adept their leaders are at what Hannah Arendt describes as "lying in public."[9] They have only begun to accept the picture of society that American literature has been presenting since the mid-19th century: a society lacking in trust and lacking in care; a society in which violence has been indigenous, and the pursuit of money an overriding concern. Scott Fizgerald's Jay Gatsby is in many ways the exemplification of this. His search for the green light, his use of any available means to gain the wealth he needs to win Daisy back, his radiance, even his innocence—all provide a telling metaphor for the American quest. Nick Carraway, the narrator in *The Great Gatsby,* explains: "He was a son of God—a phrase which, if it means anything, means just that—and he must be about His Father's business, the service of a vast, vulgar, and meretricious beauty."[10]

This is not the only novel to tell the story of American innocence and corruption. There are Mark Twain's *The Adventures of Huckleberry Finn* and *The Gilded Age.* There are Henry James's *Wings of the Dove* and *The Portrait of a Lady,* Melville's *The Confidence Man,* Theodore Dreiser's *The Titan,* and innumerable others, extending to the present day. One after another, American writers tell of people caught in the "cash nexus," made vulnerable by it, intoxicated with it, corrupted by it, struggling—usually vainly—to escape. And over it all, like a veneer, have been the visible surfaces of gentility, piety, high moral commitment, all masking what stirs below.

This has not been the standard documentation of American experience (in spite of Thorstein Veblen, Charles A. Beard, John Dewey, Henry Steele Commager, and their like); it has certainly not been the view promulgated by most American educators. Today, however, confidence in our institutions is declining; consumerism and wealth itself are being questioned. There is a half-articulated suspicion in many quarters that the surface reality may indeed be obscuring the true nature of the voyage, for all the satisfactions it has brought, for all the persisting hopes.

Much effort is expended in convincing people that the system does indeed satisfy not only common appetites but the artificial needs continually being created. When it does not, the dissatisfied are usually convinced that satisfaction will come in time. In spite of doubt and cynicism, the public appears to remain convinced that existing arrangements are perfectly "natural," even in their insufficiency, and geared to the eventual fulfillment of what people need and desire. The schools, like the mass media, play an important role in reinforcing this conviction. It is not that teachers consciously mystify or deliberately concoct the positive images that deflect critical thought. It is not even that they themselves are necessarily sanguine about the health of the society. Often submerged in the bureaucracies for which they work, they simply accede to what is taken for granted. Identifying themselves as spokespersons for—or representatives of—the system in its local manifestation, they avoid interrogation and critique. They transmit, often tacitly, benign or neutral versions of the social reality. They may, deliberately or not, adapt these to accommodate to what they perceive to be the class origins or the capacities of their students, but, whether they are moving those young people towards assembly lines or administrative offices, they are likely to present the world around as *given,* probably unchangeable and predefined.

One of the reasons for this is to be found in the long tradition of socialization through schooling. The rationale has been that public education in the United States is mass education, presumably making it possible for all children to find their places in an advancing industrial society. Children from all groups and classes are, therefore, to be granted an "equal opportunity" to pursue success in what have been described as "common schools." It has generally been assumed that effective socialization demands an affirmative approach to the *status quo.* This has meant a more or less uncritical acceptance of meritocratic arrangements, of stratifications and hierarchies. It has meant that in schools minimal attention has been paid to the insufficiencies of the culture—to inequity, racism, greed.

Some of this has been explained by the "anti-intellectualism" thought to be endemic in the culture and, most particularly, in schools.[11] Mounting attacks on this reached a climax when the Soviet Union launched its Sputnik rocket in 1957, and various authorities in the United States began cultivating a fear that the country was lagging in expertise. There was a "talent search"; an attempt was made to enlist university scholars in effecting a "curriculum revolution."[12] New attention was to be paid to mathematics and the hard sciences as well as to the traditional academic disciplines; but, for all the emphasis upon inquiry and discovery, little, if anything, was said about reflective social critique. In the sixties, as is well known, attention shifted to compensatory education for the poor and the "culturally deprived," on the assumption that the most equitable thing that could be done was to remedy the cognitive deficiencies caused by poverty and discrimination. It was a time of protest on several fronts, but teachers gave little sign of raising critical questions themselves. Conventional wisdom held that the structures could be opened in response to demand, that opportunities could be expanded, that equality could be realized at last. It was assumed that this could be accomplished within the existing system, for all the objections of de-schoolers and romantic critics, for all the scepticism with respect to "liberal" reforms.

At the present time, these liberal promises are generally conceived to have been hollow. The anti-poverty measures, like the compensatory efforts, are said to have failed. A new libertarianism has developed on the right, a point of view hostile to social spending and inimical to proposals for social justice and a welfare state. Radical critiques of public education have subsided as financial support has decreased. Schools are being directed to focus upon discrete "competencies," on basic skills. The focal preoccupations are with efficiency, with accountability in terms of what is measurable. There is continuing talk of behavioral engineering, of the values of management expertise. Less and less attention than ever is paid to emancipatory thinking or any type of critique. Technology and the free enterprise system are ascribed an implacable reality, along with explanations that legitimate them, even in economic decline. The most obvious concerns are with economic survival, with "making it" in the face of unemployment, inflation, oil crises, and presumably inexorable decay. Hopelessness is expressed; there is a grim cynicism with respect to possibilities of reform.

Teacher education, then, confronts a complex situation. Economic stress discourages educational reform in any traditional sense, but, at once, it makes schooling seem more necessary from an economic point of view. Research today points to the lack of correlation between schooling and economic success, but none of this persuades people *not* to put their faith in schools. When all else seems to fail, when people feel helpless about their own life situations, education is relied upon to prepare the children, at least, for mobility. Moreover, in what is rapidly being understood to be a "knowledge society,"[13] no other educational agency seems to offer as much as a school. Economic need, therefore, connects with free-floating anxiety about the future to keep alive some of the old illusions about public schools. And this reinforces the processes of mystification so important to capitalist ideology, processes reaching an ironic apotheosis most particularly in election years.

It seems clear that teachers cannot overtly attack or try to undermine the institutions in which their students plan to work. Nor can they, given their traditions and their scholarly commitments, simply train (and, in their own fashion, socialize) agents of the system, well-adapted clerks for bureaucracies. How, given the pressures of the times and the conservatism of educational institutions today, can they educate for interrogation and critique? How can they enable teachers-to-be to break with conceptions of the given, of the predefined? How can they equip them to decipher, to decode, and (if they are courageous enough) to surpass and to transform?

Mystification succeeds most dramatically when people believe that the expressed commitment to human freedom and human rights has been consistently acted upon throughout American history. Mystification succeeds when people take it for granted that democracy has been achieved. In fact, democracy is and has been an open possibility, not an actuality. The commitment to freedom and the rights of man has been a commitment to certain normatives, again, to possibility. Nevertheless, it is of extreme importance that values and commitments like these are in some sense latent in American experience. It is relevant that we have a written Bill of Rights and that we can refer to embodied principles having to do with the dignity of human beings.

There is no question but that these normatives in simplified or vulgarized form, have been used to fabricate a surface reality, to mask what has actually been occurring in the world. As we have learned from Hegel and other philosophers, however, the need for emancipation and for freedom is deeply rooted in human beings;[14] no deceptive claim can quite satisfy the longing people have to be self-determining, to be free. I believe, in fact, that the malaise so evident in American life today is as much a response to a sense of betrayal as to a loss of confidence in institutions. There is a feeling that promises have been broken, that possibilities have not been acted upon, and that untruths are being told. I find in all this a starting point for teacher educators interested in interpretation, the kind of interpretation that may lead to "destructive" critique.

Many students of teacher education have stressed the fact that more than technical or applicative knowledge is involved in the effort to function as a professional. They have stressed the importance of inquiry into the "interpretive context,"[15] meaning the ideational and socio-cultural contexts of teaching and learning as they proceed in schools. They have highlighted at times the advocacy role of educators and the policy orientation required in certain dimensions of the field. They have stressed the fact that teachers are not only obliged to become scholars and theorists in specialized fields but persons explicitly concerned with the polity and the kinds of action that make a difference in the public space. I would suggest that there must always be a place in teacher education for "foundations" specialists, people whose main interest is in interpreting—and enabling others to interpret—the social, political, and economic factors that affect and influence the processes of education. It is not of incidental interest that the proponents of the "competencies" orientation favor elimination of the "foundations" component in the teacher education curriculum and have already succeeded in eroding it.

The obligation of the "foundations" person is, of course, many-pronged. Teachers-to-be must be introduced to the concepts and principles that compose the relevant interpretive disciplines. They must be enabled to look through the perspectives opened by history, sociology, anthropology, economics, and philosophy; they must learn how consciously to order the materials of their experience with the aid of such perspectives. At once they must learn to understand the role of the disciplines, the role of organized subject matter in selecting out aspects of reality. This means a capacity (too seldom attended to) to engage in new kinds of questioning and problem-posing appropriate to an overly dominated human world.

It demands the kinds of dialogue that will involve all those engaged in the teaching-learning process in reflection upon their life situations *and* upon the constructs made available to schematize those situations. These constructs are component parts of what Alfred Schutz calls "the stock of knowlege at hand."[16] They derive from the cultural tradition; they are used for interpreting social reality; they make possible intersubjective communication. In many respects, they provide the substance of what is taught in schools. By the time they are incorporated in school curricula, however, they are reified, made part of "official knowledge," and given an objective life of their own. This is one reason it seems so important for teacher educators to stimulate critique— not solely of the constructs used to interpret and direct the educational process itself, but of the disciplines or the subject matters given instructional form at different levels of education. Without such critique, the disciplines are likely to be used for domination, for *fixing* the vision of young people on a reality others have defined.

Each discipline, each subject matter must be considered at some time in relation to the human interest that gave rise to it,[17] to the questions it was invented to solve. Knowledge structures of all sorts ought to be considered in their diverse expressions in relation to various communities of scholars and in terms of various group commitments. Thomas Kuhn provides a model when he considers paradigm-directed and paradigm-shattering research in the natural sciences.[18] This undertaking demands far more than revisionist thinking, more than mere iconoclasm. It is of special importance in the field of education, where it has been relatively easy to impart a law-like character to generalizations having to do with the role of public schools in "equalizing the conditions of men," promoting mobility, insuring democracy, and the like. In the relatively recent past, new generalizations have been defined, perhaps of even more consequence: those having to do with genetic inheritance, the distribution of talents, meritocracy, and hierarchy.

Educators and educational reformers have been continually tempted to test the rationality of what they have done by the effectiveness or efficiency of what has been accomplished, not by looking critically at their presuppositions. They have (partly because of their felt obligations to school boards, taxpayers, and the like) looked towards social consequences in their efforts to justify what has been done in schools. They have seldom looked at the question of whether their actions were intrinsically right. Facts have been easily separated off from values; decisions have been made on grounds independent of moral propriety (for all the ostensible moralism in the schools). Because public schools have dealt with the mass of children, the collective, what has been true about sociological positivism[19] has tended to be true about educational thought: consideration has been focused on what has promoted social stability and material progress rather than on what has promoted or might promote individual happiness and self-determination.

This is another argument for the need to look critically at what is understood to be theory in education and the need to encourage interpretation of structures and texts from the perspective of individual vantage points, individual backgrounds, and individual locations in the world. Nothing else, I am convinced, will effectively counter the fearful separation of facts from values that allows persons to claim that the knowledge they depend on is wholly neutral, even when used to dominate and impose controls.

I am proposing, of course, that self-reflectiveness be encouraged, that teacher educators and their students be stimulated to think about their own thinking and to reflect upon their own reflecting. This seems to be inherently liberating and likely to invigorate their teaching and their advocacy. Also, it may well help in delineating possibilities never seen before—in the processes of futuring and choosing in which individuals must engage in order to create themselves. Teacher educators have thought too little about the need to break with positivist notions, notions of the given. They have thought not at all about the need to expose mystifications; as a result, they have disseminated them and kept illusions of the "natural" alive.

The barriers to "authentic speaking" are, it must be stressed, enormous. Fifty years ago John Dewey described the new age of human relations that opened when the so-called "Great Society" emerged, the society created by steam and electricity. "The invasion of the community," Dewey wrote, "by the new and relatively impersonal and mechanical modes of combined human behavior is the outstanding fact of modern life."[20] Making the point that, while the impact of these new conditions was liberating for certain members of the middle class, the oppressive phase affected the silent ones, those (Dewey said ironically) "who did not count for much anyway," the ones who had always been oppressed. And then he made the relevant point that people thought "that there was something inherently 'natural' and amenable to 'natural law' in the working of economic forces, in contrast with the man-made artificiality of political institutions."[21] The industrial regime was being legitimated as entirely "natural," warranting the creation of artificial needs and wants as well as a changed direction of customs and institutions. Dewey wrote that, "Athenians did not buy Sunday newspapers, make investments in stocks and bonds, nor want motor cars." Yet today we not only take it for granted (and teach others to take it for granted) that these things are necessities, we are asked to take for granted the existing system in the same way, with all its manipulations of our tastes and expectations, with its disguised dominations, its channelling, and its controls.

Dewey's apparent understanding of mystification did not affect either teacher education or the schools. This may be because of his sustained belief that the phenomena he was describing could, in the long run, be dealt with by means of experimental intelligence. He made the point that there was "a social pathology which works powerfully against effective inquiry into social institutions and conditions"[22]; he knew that optimism, demands for conformity, and "riotous glorification of things 'as they are' " discouraged critical thought. But he seemed no more aware, in 1927, of the distortions of communication characteristic of the time than of the impact of technology on human consciousness.

Given his undying faith in cooperative intelligence, articulateness, and the scientific method, I am not sure how he would have responded to such contemporary descriptions of the post-industrial society as Daniel Bell's. Bell talks about a society in which the sources of innovation derive largely from research and development, the centralization of knowledge effects new relationships between science and technology, and the weight of society (measured in terms of the GNP and the proportion of employment) becomes increasingly a weight in the knowledge field. "In the social structure of the knowledge society," writes Bell, "there is . . . the deep and growing split between the technical intelligentsia who are committed to functional rationality and technocratic modes of operation, and the literary intellectuals, who have become increasingly apocalyptic, hedonistic, and nihilistic."[23] He thereby underlines the given-ness, the solidity of the "functional rationality and technocratic modes of operation" he believes will characterize our meritocracy as time goes on.

I take him to be suggesting that critiques grounded in subjectivity, even in despair, are in some manner destructive of what ought to be accepted as positive, indeed benign. If he is right, if he is also correct in saying that, in the future society, the central person will be "the professional, for he is equipped by his education and training to provide the kinds of skill which are increasingly demanded in the post-industrial society," then the invasion Dewey spoke of will not only be an invasion by impersonal forces or new customs and institutions, it will be an invasion by ways of thinking as well, ways of explaining, yes, of mystifying. If this is the case, the responsibility for critical understanding of the language of functional rationality, its premises, its origins, and its distortions falls heavily upon the educator. Perhaps it falls most heavily on the foundations specialists in teacher education, since they are distinctively obligated to equip teachers-to-be to reflect critically upon and identify themselves with respect to a formalized world.

The reductionist talk of "competencies," mentioned above, and the application of management science to considerations of teacher training are among the many indications of the effects of functional rationality upon educational thought and practice. Some of the proponents of efficiency talk openly about "the modern techniques currently employed in business and industry" and about the efficiency that will result if those techniques are used in quantifying the output of the schools. Playing into popular desires for economy and predictability at a time when there is so much slippage, the new cultists of efficiency, the would-be scientific managers, create their own mystifications by attempting to describe education as a technocratic operation, dependable because linked to what is most controllable and "real." This is one of the many indications of the importance of working against what Dewey called a "social pathology" and to do so with as much passion as can be mustered, with as much rigor and good sense. There must be concrete engagement with the situations in which education takes place, inside and outside the schools. Efforts must be made to reflect critically on the numerous modes of masking what is happening in our society—the numerous modes of mystifying, of keeping people still.

It may be useful to consider the official explanations for inflation for a moment, for recession, or for New York City's economic catastrophe. It is not simply that the public is lied to and deliberately deluded, it is that the explanations provided mystify and falsify by imparting an objective and a "natural" character to such phenomena as inflation, not to speak of social inequities, ethnic divisions, failure, and inferiority. Where inflation is concerned, it is interesting to see the degree to which desperation and fatalism are fostered. Carl Raschke, for one, makes the point that the average citizen has come to believe that no one can do anything to stop the erosion in the standard of living or the quality of life. People commonly talk fatalistically about the likelihood of a return of hard times, as in the 1930s. Convinced of the odds against them, they are resigning themselves. "Clutching for

scapegoats or comfortable explanations of their woes, they flex whatever sinews they have," writes Raschke, "in demanding a bigger
grubstake for themselves. 'I've got mine, Jack' becomes the watch-
word of their struggles."[24]

In the meantime, disenchantment over federal programs is exploited. The efforts to enrich the lives of little children through the
Head Start program might be recalled. Job-training programs, careers
for the poor, and other liberal and educational reforms might be con-
sulted as it is held in mind that most of them attempted (too briefly
and with inadequate support) to enable individuals to overcome the
deficits they suffered from—deficits which, as John Rawls has made so
clear,[25] were wholly undeserved. Special interest groups, each looking
out for themselves, lobby for their own panaceas. The public accepts
(for the want of something better) a devil theory "of massive and in-
domitable forces at work." "Mystification," says Raschke, "is the order of the day."[26]

Now my point is not that teacher educators should all become
economists and seek out model alternatives to the Keynesian or the
Galbraithian. My point is that teacher educators ought to work to
combat the sense of ineffectuality and powerlessness that comes when
persons feel themselves to be the victims of forces wholly beyond their
control, in fact beyond any human control. The explanations of inflation are not the only ones that breed powerlessness and self-interest.
They are not the only ones that turn people towards a kind of lifeboat
psychology that makes impossible any tuning-in relationship, any
sense of interdependence or common life.

This is not to suggest that individual human beings possess an efficacy that they do not recognize. Nor is it to suggest that, if they only
stood up and made demands, inflation and other ills would disappear.
Raschke himself proposes that we think in terms of new paradigms,
recognizing (for example) the legitimate claims of all persons in society
and placing barriers on how far and to what end wealth can be ob-
tained. He proposes that the new paradigms we develop rid themselves
of ethical unconcern. They should, he says, look to the role of government as a guarantor of social equity instead of merely a stake for a
faltering free enterprise system. Finally: "A new paradigm . . . must
shift the reference point for both theory and practice from ration-
alizing existing media of exploitation to *humanizing* the economic order altogether."[27]

I use this as analogy and example for those of us concerned with paradigms in education. I have already suggested some of what we have taken for granted over the years: utility, efficiency, stability, not to speak of equality of opportunity and meritocracy. We have seldom questioned the meritocratic paradigm, the notion that each individual, depending upon his or her capacity, has been thought to be free to move up the meritocratic ladder without prejudice or constraint. For too many years, we have accepted the idea that if a boy or girl were too unmotivated or inept to make the effort required, the system or the school could not be blamed. In some sense (we have traditionally liked to think) the individual could be thought to be choosing his or her own submergence or passivity. When Daniel Bell speaks of meritocracy, he argues that all that is necessary is for us to realize the traditional ideal of equality of opportunity fairly. If we do, he tells us, we can acknowledge that those who succeed have earned their authority. Recently, this acceptance of things as they are has been reinforced by the writings of the new libertarians, those who are calling for a minimal state and challenging what Robert Nisbet calls "the new equalitarianism." Nisbet, for example, asserts that, "In whatever degree or form, inequality is the essence of the social bond. The vast range of temperaments, minds, motivations, strengths and desires that exists in any population is nothing if not the stuff of hierarchy."[28] There is, he suggests, an objective tension between liberty and equality, even as there is a necessity in hierarchies.

Only recently have we been made aware of the limitations on equal opportunity, of the injustices and inequities that abound. Attention has only gradually been turned to the unfairness, indeed to the exclusiveness, of existing meritocracies. John Rawls has pointed out, for example, that meritocracy is unfair because, under meritocratic arrangements, equality of opportunity signifies an equal chance for the more fortunate to leave the less fortunate behind. He has also said (challenging what most Americans take for granted) that to be less fortunate is a matter of contingency. Disadvantages, deficits and inequalities due to birth and endowment are not only undeserved; they call for redress. In a just society (a cooperative arrangement for mutual advantage), social and economic inequalities would be so arranged as to benefit the least advantaged, to improve their long-term expectations and the quality of their lives. There is an implicit ethical concern in this approach to justice, even as there is an appeal to what Rawls calls "self-esteem."[29] And indeed, it would appear that the self committed to justice, or at least the self engaged sufficiently to know the "sense of injustice"[30] when damage is being done, is less likely to be an *Isolato,* less likely to be distant and indifferent than the one who never notices, who does not care.

There has been a concerned attack on Rawls in recent months. Philosophers like Robert Nozick,[31] sociologists like Daniel Bell and Robert Nisbet, and conservative journal commentators have raised challenges of varying degrees of validity. With the exception of Nozick's and Bell's, the attacks often take the form of defensiveness, a clinging to the taken-for-granted, to the old and comforting mystifications. There are, obviously, legitimate philosophic differences involved, but Rawls has inaugurated a type of critique that obviously troubles those sympathetic to the *status quo,* whether or not they feel themselves to be about their "Father's business." The very nature of the response at times suggests that intellectuals too are experiencing an unease.

Robert Heilbroner writes that there is a growing consciousness of a "civilizational malaise." It is one, he says, that "reflects the inability of a civilization directed to material improvement—higher incomes, better diets, miracles of medicine, triumphs of applied physics and chemistry—to satisfy the human spirit." He goes on to make the point that, "The values of an industrial civilization, which has for two centuries given us not only material advance but also a sense of elan and purpose, now seem to be losing their self-evident justification."[32] It does not follow that the industrial civilization or its institutions are fated to disappear nor that reliance upon technology is about to decline. The crucial point may be that even those who have benefited from the search for material improvement are finding themselves to be unfulfilled. What of those who have been asked to delay their gratifications? What of those who have been subjected (for economic reasons) to dominion and control? It becomes increasingly difficult to justify repression and manipulation by talking in terms of progress, productivity, efficiency, or any ulterior good. What has so long been treated as unquestionable must be questioned—from a human vantage point and on the ground of shared ethical concerns.

Teacher educators must ask themselves whether this kind of questioning can occur in teachers' colleges and schools. We are all well-acquainted by now with the so-called revisionist critique,[33] with the presumption that it was never the goal of the educational system to enable persons to question, anymore than it was to maximize each person's potential. Rather, we have been repeatedly told, it has been the goal of the school to induct the young into the industrial system, to stratify them to meet its requirements, to track, to exert dominion, to mystify. Knowing what we know about schools in social systems, I am not sure why we should have been surprised. Also, I am not sure what follows from the revisionist critique, since it carries within it no call for demystification, no call for cultural action on a meaningful scale. Most educators are by now aware on some level of the thousands upon thousands of young people who have been selected out of the system, the thousands rendered invisible, the thousands dehumanized and made mute. Even here, however, generalizations can be deceiving, in their own way mystifying. Numbers of persons did survive and did choose themselves within the system. Somehow or other, certain democratic values did remain alive in the American imagination, even as certain others were neglected and set aside. Open questions still confront us respecting schools: what they have made possible, what they may make possible today.

Walter Feinberg, calling the school "the social memory bank" of modern industrial societies, presents an unwarranted determinism, if not a demonology. The school serves, he writes, "not only to stamp into the young the correct attitudes, habits, and skills, but to stamp out others that are thought to be undesirable. Oftentimes what is stamped out is the result of 'dysfunctional' attitudes such as those of the family, the church, and the local community."[34] This, it seems to me, ascribes to the school an awesome power and a perhaps questionable effectuality. Also, like many revisionist views, it appears to be grounded in an appalling conception of humankind. Boys and girls, men and women, are presented as wholly malleable, wholly susceptible to victimization. They are the creatures of forces beyond understanding and control. What factors account for such total submission? What prompted the masses to sacrifice their freedom so acquiescently? I think of Dostoevsky's Grand Inquisitor when I read about stamping machines, about his declaration that people always want bread far more than freedom. He tells Christ, it will be recalled:

"In the end, they will lay their freedom at our feet and say to us, 'Make us your slaves, but feed us.' They will understand themselves at last, that freedom and bread enough for all are inconceivable together, for never, never will they be able to share between them! They will be convinced too that they can never be free, for they are weak, vicious, worthless, and rebellious. . . . I swear man is weaker and baser by nature than Thou hast believed him! . . . By showing him so much respect, Thou didst, as it were, cease to feel for him, for Thou didst ask far too much from him. . . . The flock will come together again and will submit once more, and then it will be once for all. Then we shall give them the quiet humble happiness of weak creatures such as they are by nature. We shall show them that they are weak, that they are only pitiful children. . . ."[35]

And I think of Paul Nizan's novel, *Antoine Bloyé*—of the railroad worker's son who is sent to a secondary school where he will be trained to take his place in the industrial system. When he graduates, he wins a prize. It is a book, and he reads in it:

> "Man is free—he is ever aware of his power not to do what he does do and to do what he does not do." Antoine reflects on these words . . . He ill understands them. Is his father free not to work nights, not to go where he does go? Is his mother free not to have her back ache from work, not to be tired out and old before her time? He himself—in what way was he free? To be free means simply not to be poor and not always ordered about. The rich enjoy a form of freedom. People with an income.[36]

This is an instance of a young person who has indeed been stamped— by his family, by his school—into someone alienated, helpless, unable to posit his situation as one in which there are alternatives. He is never helped to identify himself as self-determining, as an autonomous person equipped to choose class-consciousness, to choose himself as free. The entire novel bears within it a cry of outrage (because it is a novel written by the son of the fictional Antoine Bloye), not only at the mutilations imposed upon a human being by the system but at the mutilation an individual imposes on himself.

There is no need to be romantic; there is no need further to mystify. If teacher educators are to make a difference, they need to conceive of ways in which persons can be urged to assert themselves, to take their own initiative, to overcome their alienation. Trent Schroyer, in *The Critique of Domination,* talks about the relevance of a university setting for moving people to an understanding of domination and into the process of self-emancipation. He knows full well the limitations imposed by large institutions, but he writes, "Rather than assume that the meaning of 'radical education' is to subvert the education process, there is a need to actualize it by a serious engagement with the self-formation of a critical intelligentsia."[37] He speaks of free schools, clinics, community organizations, and of the need to reach beyond the formal institution. As I see it, teacher educators and teachers as well would not only be actualizing the educational process (and, in fact, promoting mastery) by working against mystification and for self-emancipation. They would be acting on behalf of a tradition of free institutions, acting on their freedom in the light of principle. For all the present pressures and aberrations within contemporary society, I cannot see this as anything but the enactment of what is thought of as democracy.

Working in this fashion with students, liberating them to understand that the social reality they inhabit is a constructed one, educators ought to avoid, if possible, the high-sounding voice of expertise. They and their students might well enter a conversation with one another, the kind of conversation that allows a truly human way of speaking, a being together in a world susceptible to questioning. Each one, including the one who is the teacher, might articulate his or her particular themes of relevance, might speak truthfully and simply about backgrounds and foregrounds, and what it means to be present, what it means to reach out and to question and to learn. It is indeed the case—or it ought to be the case—that formal inquiry, scientific thinking, and the rest are significant to the degree they nourish the human conversation.

The disciplines, the organized knowledge structures ought to be offered as possibilities to individual participants, each with the capacity to generate structures that relate to his or her concerns, that clarify what he or she wants to say. If this kind of conversation or dialogue were to be the model, positivist explanations might be put into perspective, distortions might be understood. Those conversing might learn to do their own "authentic speaking" about their life situations, their modes of sense-making, their futurings; talking together, being together, they might learn how to transcend.

No one is likely to enter into such a conversation without the capacity to turn his or her attention, not simply to the constructions of social reality, but to the dynamic process by which individuals enter into the shared agreements and understandings that constitute their cultural life. I believe that there must be an affirmation of a pluralist concern as this uncovering proceeds. Such an affirmation demands a new recognition of community. There must be a perception of the ways in which persons locate themselves in the world in the light of their own particular biographical situations, the experiences they have built up over time. Every individual interprets the realities he or she confronts through perspectives made up of particular ranges of interests, occupations, commitments, and desires. Each one belongs to a number of social groups and plays a variety of social roles. His or her involvements—the work he or she has done, the schools he or she has attended, his or her race and class membership—affect the way "the stock of knowledge at hand" is used. Particular persons make use of it to order, to interpret from particular vantage points; as they do so, a common meaning structure is built up among them; they share a common world.

The point, however, is that, because they come from different backgrounds and have sedimented their meanings differently, they intend the common meaning structure from diverse angles and vantage points. The schools, with their traditional presumption of a "normal" world and an official meaning-structure, have not only emphasized the givenness of what is taught, they have customarily neglected distinctiveness of viewpoint, unless it seemed desirable to tap into individual interests, the better to connect individuals with what was thought of as heritage, funded experience, or the accumulated experience of the race.[38] Doing this, they made the conversation described above impossible. Participation was not as important as accommodation, even in cases of explicit individualization.

In the past few years, we have been reminded of this repeatedly as we have been made to attend to the voices of persons inaudible in earlier times. We have heard the voices, often for the first time, of minority people, women, even children—members of what Paulo Freire called "a culture of silence,"[39]—whose perspectives were never taken into account. The interest in psychohistory, biography, and autobiography, in "history from the ground up," is in part a response to this. So is the interest in qualitative inquiry, if qualitative inquiry is taken to mean an effort to return to the perceptual ground of experience, to affirm the qualitative dimension of life. Whatever efforts can be made to enable teachers-to-be to speak for themselves and confront the concreteness of their lives ought to play into the critique that challenges mystification. And, in time, this might be carried into the classrooms of the schools or wherever such persons finally work.

The crucial problem, I believe, is the problem of challenging what is taken for granted and transmitted as taken-for-granted: ideas of hierarchy, of deserved deficits, of delayed gratification, and of mechanical time schemes in tension with inner time. A new pedagogy is obviously required, one that will free persons to understand the ways in which each of them reaches out from his or her location to constitute a common continent, a common world. It might well be called a democratic pedagogy, since, in several respects, the object is to empower persons to enact democracy. To act upon democratic values, I believe, is to be responsive to consciously incarnated principles of freedom, justice, and regard for others. If individuals can take such principles unto themselves and make them manifest in their confrontations with a concrete, an *interpreted* reality, the way may be opened for *praxis,* for bringing the world closer to heart's desire.

None of this is conceivable, of course, if persons are allowed to remain submerged. Democracy is inconceivable on Captain Ahab's ship, where the crew members remain island-men, deluded and dominated by someone else's mad idea. Nor is democracy conceivable in a society permeated by indifference, frozen in technological language, and rooted in inequities. So the concern of teacher educators must remain normative, critical, and even political. Neither the teachers' colleges nor the schools can change the social order. Neither colleges nor schools can legislate democracy. But something can be done to empower some teachers-to-be to reflect upon their own life situations, to speak out in their own voices about the lacks that must be repaired, the possibilities to be acted upon in the name of what they deem decent, humane, and just. "I am asking you to live in the presence of reality," wrote Virginia Woolf.[40] " 'There are pestilences, and there are victims,' " says Tarrou in *The Plague,* " 'and it is up to us not to join forces with pestilences.' "[41] These two statements suggest a summary. We can at least try to surpass what is insufficient and create conditions where persons of all ages can come together in conversation—to choose themselves as outraged and destructive, when they have to, as authentic, passionate, and free.

References

1. Herman Melville, *Moby Dick* (New York: Random House, 1930), p. 306.
2. Ibid., p. 308.
3. Quoted from *Capital III* in Richard J. Bernstein, *Praxis and Action* (Philadelphia: University of Pennsylvania Press, 1971), p. 65.
4. Karl Marx, *Capital.* ed. Frederick Engels (New York: Modern Library, 1906), chapters I and VII.
5. Paul Ricoeur, *The Conflict of Interpretations,* ed. Don Ihde (Evantston: Northwestern University Press, 1975), p. 149.
6. R.S. Peters, *Ethics and Education* (Glenview, Ill.: Scott, Foresman, 1967), p. 217.
7. Peter L. Berger and Thomas Luckmann, *The Social Construction of Reality* (Garden City, N.Y.: Doubleday, Anchor Books, 1967).
8. Melville, *op cit.,* p. 174.

9. Hannah Arendt, "Lying in Politics: Reflections on the Pentagon Papers," in *Crises of the Republic* (New York: Harvest Books, 1972), pp. 1-47.

10. F. Scott Fitzgerald, *The Great Gatsby* (New York: Charles Scribner's Sons, 1953), p. 99.

11. Richard Hofstadter, *Anti-Intellectualism in American Life* (New York: Alfred A. Knopf, 1963), pp. 299-390.

12. See Jerome S. Bruner, *The Process of Education* (Cambridge: Harvard University Press, 1960) and Robert W. Heath, ed., *New Curricula* (New York: Harper & Row, 1964).

13. Daniel Bell, *The Coming of Post-Industrial Society* (New York: Basic Books, 1963), pp. 262-265.

14. G.W.F. Hegel, *Philosophy of the Right* (Oxford: Clarendon Press, 1952), p. 53.

15. Harry S. Broudy, B. Othanel Smith, and Joe R. Burnett, *Democracy and Excellence in American Secondary Education* (Chicago: Rand McNally, 1964), pp. 54-55; 233-243.

16. Alfred Schutz, *The Problem of Social Reality:* Collected Papers I, ed. Maurice Natanson. (The Hague: Martinus Nijhoff, 1967), p. 38 f.

17. Jurgen Habermas, *Knowledge and Human Interests* (Boston: Beacon Press, 1971), pp. 301-317.

18. Thomas S. Kuhn, *The Structure of Scientific Revolutions,* 2nd ed. (Chicago: University of Chicago Press, 1970), pp. 144-210.

19. Alvin W. Gouldner, *The Coming Crisis of Western Sociology* (New York: Basic Books, 1970), pp. 88-108.

20. John Dewey, *The Public and Its Problems* (Chicago: The Swallow Press, 1954), p. 98.

21. Ibid., p. 102.

22. Ibid., p. 170.

23. Daniel Bell, *op. cit.,* p. 214.

24. Carl Raschke, "Demystifying Inflation," *Christianity and Crisis,* Vol. 24, No. 20, Nov. 25, 1974, p. 263.

25. John Rawls, *A Theory of Justice* (Cambridge: Harvard University Press, 1971), pp. 100-108.

26. Raschke, *op. cit.,* p. 264.

27. Ibid., p. 265.

28. Robert Nisbet, *Twilight of Authority* (New York: Oxford University Press, 1975), p. 238.

29. Rawls, *op. cit.,* pp. 440-446.

30. Edmond N. Cahn, *The Sense of Injustice* (New York: New York University Press, 1949).

31. Robert Nozick, *Anarchy, State, and Utopia* (New York: Basic Books, 1974).

32. Robert L. Heilbroner, *An Inquiry Into The Human Prospect* (New York: W.W. Norton, 1974), p. 21.

33. See, e.g., Clarence J. Karier, Paul Violas, and Joel Spring, *Roots of Crisis* (Chicago: Rand, McNally, 1973).

34. Walter Feinberg and Henry Rosemont, Jr., "Introduction," *Work, Technology, and Education,* eds., Feinberg and Rosemont (Urbana: University of Illinois Press, 1975), p. 8.

35. Fyodor Dostoyevsky, *The Brothers Karamazov* (New York: Modern Library, 1945), pp. 306-307.
36. Paul Nizan, *Antoine Bloyé* (New York: Monthly Review Press, 1973), p. 54.
37. Trent Schroyer, *The Critique of Domination* (New York: George Braziller, 1973), p. 252.
38. See John Dewey, *The Child and the Curriculum* (Chicago: University of Chicago Press, 1902), p. 17 f.
39. Paulo Freire, *Cultural Action for Freedom* (Baltimore: Penguin Books, 1972), p. 57.
40. Virginia Woolf, *A Room of One's Own* (New York: Harcourt, Brace & World, 1957), p. 114.
41. Albert Camus, *The Plague* (New York: Alfred A. Knopf, 1948), p. 230.

5
The Agon of "Basics":
Backward Looks
and Future Possibilities

I N his 1976 Nobel Lecture, Saul Bellow spoke of private disorder and public bewilderment. He talked of the visions of ruin with which we are constantly presented, the uproar around us, the daily dread. Convinced that we do not think amply enough about what we are, he reminded us that we remain able "to think, to discriminate, and to feel." And then he said:

> When complications increase, the desire for essentials increases too. The unending cycle of crises that began with the First World War has formed a kind of person, one who has lived through terrible, strange things, and in whom there is an observable shrinkage of prejudices, a casting off of disappointing ideologies, an ability to live with many kinds of madness, and an immense desire for certain durable goods—truth, for instance, or freedom, or wisdom.[1]

Like Bellow, many people today are trying to determine ("in confusion and obscurity," as he put it) whether they will endure or go under. They think of the precarious future, and fearful questions flood into their minds. When those questions touch upon the children and the children's future, they are likely to feel acutely the "immense desire" of which Bellow spoke: the desire for essentials, for something to counter disorder and uncertainty. Mystifications afflict them; they give up hope of truly understanding. They seek out panaceas wherever they can find them. They need, above all things, to believe.

Americans, more than other people, have turned towards the schools at moments like these. There are memories of promises made and assurances offered. Many would like, even today, to impose an almost sacred obligation on their schools. In the time of their founding, Horace Mann asserted that the experiment offered "the highest authority for its ultimate success." He said that its formula was "as legible as though written in starry letters on an azure sky. . ."Train up a child in the way he should go, and when he is old he will not depart from it."[2] He compared the free school system with the sun, shining "not only upon the good, but upon the evil, that they may become good. . . ." Like the rain, he said, "its blessings descend, not only upon the just, but upon the unjust, that their injustice may depart from them and be known no more."[3] Fifty years later, John Dewey called education "the fundamental method of social progress and reform" and said that "the teacher. . .always is the true prophet of God and the usherer in of the true kingdom of God."[4]

In the sixties, of course, there were many who discarded all this as myth and legend and diversion. Large sections of the public were convinced that the school was, after all, of only marginal importance when compared with other social institutions, especially when it came to promoting economic advancement for individuals or insuring economic equality.[5] Others, looking through diverse perspectives, were made to see the coerciveness of the schools, their credentialling functions, the ways in which they served the interests of the corporate society rather than those of growing boys and girls.[6] Paradoxically, these critiques were functions of a time of economic expansion and high expectation, even as they were responses to perceived brutalities at home and abroad. Those who were most eloquent in critique and exposure were those who assumed that there were options for most of the people who paid heed. Not only were there alternative life styles and ways of working, there appeared to be live possibilities for *praxis* and sweeping social change.

In the last few years, what with economic constraints and ravaging unemployment, the options appear to have narrowed for everyone; with the sense of diminishing possibility, there has been a diminution of protest and critique. Jean-Paul Sartre once made the point that it is only when we are able to conceive "of another state of affairs in which things would be better for everybody" that we acknowledge the harshness of our lived situations and find them in some way unendurable.[7] At the present moment, there appears to be little hope for improvement in our socio-economic conditions. There is no evidence that people are developing significant projects for changing those conditions; in consequence, a kind of dread resignation has taken over, a sense of powerlessness where meaningful reforms are concerned. Nostalgia follows, and a kind of empty dreaming—dreaming about old sustaining promises, about legends, about the sun and the blessings of the rain. And this begins to feed expectations, wishful expectations finding expression in demands. If no other institution can offer guarantees, surely the schools ought at least to prepare their charges for places in the system, no matter how faulty the system may appear to be, how disinterested the young. Educators, understandably, are abruptly held accountable, not only for what they have failed to accomplish, but for making present choices *for* their students in response to parent demand.

Obviously, there is an empirical ground for the dissatisfaction and for the demands. The public is constantly being instructed by the media that test scores are falling, that "output" is not keeping pace with "input." Taking the language and norms of technological culture for granted, middle-class taxpayers are willing to see things in management terms. The very idiom of the production ethos helps give legitimation even to weak knowledge-claims. To men and women trapped in poverty, even that legitimation is not needed. If the newspapers say that Johnny and Susie are not being taught to read, if it is assumed that reading has something to do (something important to do) with "making it," with success, they cannot but turn their anger and frustration against the schools. Images of closing factories assault them; they see long lines of young people waiting for non-existent jobs. The schools' advertised failures strike them as threats to their children's survival in this world. So they support demands that the schools move "back"—"back to basics," back to simpler and cleaner times. There is a desire for understandable answers, for clear and distinct ideas, for instance, the idea that the skills susceptible to testing are precisely those required by the capitalistic society. It probably helps that the "basics" are so often left undefined, or defined mainly in terms of what they are *not:* innovative teaching, permissiveness, free inquiry, or the arts. On some level, "basics" are used to refer to what teachers are thought perfectly capable of teaching—that is, if they are held accountable, if they live up to what is expected of them.

Some of this tendency of mind, of course, may be attributed to the habit of endowing one's own school days with a purposefulness and a clarity they can only retrospectively possess. A lawyer, say, or a department store buyer, a garage-owner, or a community leader may look back from his or her present vantage point and see early events as preparatory for what is happening now. He or she knows how to write a brief or a letter or a press release. This now seems a clear consequence of basic skills teaching and learning early in life (not to speak of strict teachers and staying after school). There were no open classrooms then, no innovations (at least as most people recall), and, if there were art classes, they met no more than once a week. It follows for many people that, if there were such distractions and innovations, the skills so well mastered would have been blandly ignored.

This kind of thinking is not unusual. Memory is naturally selective; in many respects, the justifications for such thinking are understandable, given the disorder of our times. It is all evocative of the beginning of E.L. Doctorow's novel, *Ragtime,* which starts with an account of what it used to be like in New Rochelle in 1902, or, at least, how Americans imagine it, how we believe it was.

> There seemed to be no entertainment that did not involve great swarms of people. Trains and steamers and trolleys moved them from one place to another. That was the style, that was the way people lived. Women were stouter then. They visited the fleet carrying white parasols. Everyone wore white in summer. Tennis racquets were hefty and the racquet faces were elliptical. There were a lot of sexual fainting. There were no immigrants. There were no Negroes.[8]

Any confrontation with the decline in skills must, in the first place, take into account some of what was hidden below the blandly swarming surfaces of the remembered world. Also, it must take into account the multiplying inequities, the pervasive malaise of the contemporary world. The barriers to learning erected by poverty and bad nutrition and inadequate housing remain. There are the barriers to be found in disinterest, boredom, and passivity. We know enough to attribute some of this to environmental attrition or to stimulus overload or to the blind quest for shocks and heightened sensations. We can attribute some of it to the recognition that "there are no causes anymore." Much of it is due to the sense that we are up against an object world others have interpreted and defined. Like an alien and immutable presence, it rests there, in no way susceptible to transformation or even to humanization. Like a wall, like a steel block, it presents no openings through which to pass. It resists interpretation; it is too inscrutable for critique.

In any case, all seems to have been said. Virginia Woolf gave a clue to the feelings this evokes or might evoke when she talked about things becoming "embedded in a kind of nondescript cotton wool,"[9] at moments when nothing makes any sharp impression and everything around seems muffled and bland and vague. There is a lassitude today that is almost palpable; there is a world-weary conventionality; there is a cynical willingness to play the game, no matter how absurd the game may seem. As never before, to use Mrs. Willy Loman's phrase, "Attention must be paid." It must be paid by all those engaged in or touched by the educational undertaking: members of the public, young people, parents, professionals, in their diverse roles and matrices, in their malaise and their uncertainty and their pain.

It can no longer be assumed that professional educators have the right or the authority to impose their own ethos without consent. Whether their commitments are "humanist," "academic," or primarily technical, they are in many ways dissonant with the preoccupations of many publics. When ordinary people are afraid and misinformed, when they are being conditioned by forces they cannot identify, they are bound to strike intellectuals and professionals as reactionary or ignorant. There is a consequent irony in the articulated liberalism of many of those at war with the "basics" movement. Their relatively emancipated thinking becomes oppressive in its own way. When it becomes entangled with vested interest (in maintaining, for example, a financially threatened school), it loses some of its polemic force. At once, there is no question that to agree to "go along" with what people are demanding is to accede to mystification, to support the delusion that properly defined competencies carry their own economic guarantees.

A conversation must be launched within communities, an educative conversation for the sake of enabling persons to see. It must be the kind of conversation in which diverse human beings play a part, "making sense together," as John O'Neill puts it.[10] O'Neill quotes Michael Oakeshott saying that, "Education, properly speaking, is an initiation into the skill and partnership of this conversation in which we learn to recognize the voices, to distinguish the proper occasions of utterance, and in which we acquire the intellectual and moral habits appropriate to conversation."[11] In the arguments and questionings that arise, the participants (non-professionals and professionals in dialogue) might be able to reconceive what we are doing in the spheres of education—and to discover what we ought to do. They might be able to ask themselves whether a significant cultural literacy is any longer possible in the post-industrial society or whether those ill-equipped for technical rationality[12] have to be considered Huxleyan Deltas or simply set aside. It is only in the *course* of such sense-making that literacy in any meaningful sense can be achieved: literacy linked to reflexiveness, listening, and *praxis;* literacy that might make possible new perceptions of walls and blocks of steel.

Joseph Schwab has written of "learning communities,"[13] in which persons can discover how to be vibrantly with one another and how to sustain one another as they reach out to understand and to make sense. In my view, the learning community ought to encompass the classroom and, at once, transcend it. It ought to reach out into the surrounding world to involve, on whatever grounds people choose, those who are uncertain and who have not yet found their own words. Learners, whoever they are, are persons who are "newcomers" in some human world, a world that was there before them, as Hannah Arendt once said, and that will continue after their death.[14] In one dimension, it is a constructed world stretching back in time, a world formed and interpreted by their predecessors and contemporaries. In another dimension, it is a particular, present community where, as Schwab says, teachers and learners both "require rewarding collaboration, communication, helping and being helped" toward goals they have set for themselves.[15]

It appears to me that many members of the public, like many young people, do not know what to make of their being in the world. Because it afflicts them as if it were objectively meaningless, they deny the need for thinking and look for technique in its stead. This does not imply that they are not, as all human beings are, "condemned to meaning,"[16] that they are not (on some level) seeking some kind of coherence, some way of unifying their lives. Nor does it imply that they do not yearn for openings in the wall confronting them, that they do not yearn for open possibilities.

They cannot be *told* this; they can only be given opportunities to come upon such ideas, opportunities to go in quest of meaning. That is what thinking is; according to Arendt, "men establish themselves as question-asking beings" by posing questions of meaning.[17] In the face of present fears and pressures, this is what ought to be held in mind when individuals think of educating in the post-industrial, technicized society. Martin Heidegger described it as a society sharply distinguished by hidden meanings and a widespread "flight from thinking,"[18] an avoidance of question-asking, a rejection of what ought to be food for thought. There ought to be places where questions are provoked, where people can begin to speak together in their own authentic voices, to learn how to engage in conversation and, at once, how to think with clarity and precision.

If this is to become possible at all, the idea of what is basic must somehow be enlarged into a conception of the kind of literacy that enables each person, from his or her own center, to interpret his or her experiences by learning to look through the multiple perspectives available in the culture: those provided by other human life experiences, those opened by the disciplines, those made possible by the several arts. Of course skill mastery is necessary; the schools have a great responsibility for enabling people to achieve it. But the demand for such mastery has somehow to be reconciled with the requirements of personal growth and futuring and with the requirements of critical thought.

There are suggestions to be gleaned from various people who have thought. Jean Piaget, who speaks on the basis of some demonstrable knowledge of how children think and children grow, has said that the principal goal of education ought to be "to create men and women who are capable of doing new things, not simply of repeating what other generations have done—men and women who are creative, inventive, and discovers"—who have minds which "can be critical, can verify, and not accept everything they are offered."[19] Other thinkers in the educational domain are laying renewed stress on the importance of educating for "new forms of learning and doing" that are quite at odds with what people generally have in mind when they talk of basics. Underlying much of what they have learned to say is a distinctively behaviorist conception of human nature. As in the case of competency-based teacher education and the various forms of the "cult of efficiency," the typical legitimation is found in a description of the human organism as malleable, responsive most of all to extrinsic motivation, if not to operant conditioning.

Piaget and others who speak of futuring and inventing and critique believe, on the contrary, that human beings are capable of autonomy and self-direction, that they possess the potential for seeing and for choosing in an open world. They seem to be saying that men and women both are capable of the kind of wide-awakeness that enables individuals to make life-plans for themselves. In this view, identity is created through conscious choice of action. People actually do identify themselves by means of their projects, by means of what they are interested in, by the work they want to do in the world.

It is easy enough to understand people talking about the "other" as passive and susceptible to molding (as Dostoyevsky's Grand Inquisitor speaks of "foolish children," or of "the quiet humble happiness of weak creatures such as they are by nature"[20]). But it is almost impossible to imagine people speaking of *themselves* or of those close to them as willing to exchange freedom for bread or happiness or what B.F. Skinner calls "cultural survival."[21] Indeed, this is another reason for enabling persons to come together for conversation or for dialogue. If they can be truly together in the "we-relation"[22] as grounded beings, aware of their existential realities, they are altogether likely to choose themselves as self-determined. They cannot but become aware that the very origin of their coming together was in a need to release their capacities somehow, to find their own words.

Finding their own words, perceiving the world around as problematic and susceptible to change, they might—as their conversation proceeds—articulate over-all purposes for what they conceive education to be. Over-all purposes (or what are sometimes called general objectives) are important, because they affect particular choices made and provide criteria against which immediate objectives can be weighed. They might help to determine what is basic in the education of persons in a deficient world—a world where inequities multiply daily, where depersonalization intensifies, where options continually close. What, after all, *is* basic in the education of individuals who are to become inventive, who can "be critical, can verify," who can engage in the acts of thinking, and who may try to transform the world?

An English professor, Elisabeth McPherson, has written:

> I think it's basic to be able to read with discrimination, to recognize unsupported generalizations and demand to see the specific evidence they're based on. . . .I think it's basic for people to know slant when they see it, and to be aware of double-speak. I think it's basic for people to recognize distortion in what they read and avoid it in what they write. . . . Above all, I think it's basic to remember that both reading and writing, at their best, are ways of sharing meaningful experiences with other people. . . .[23]

She is making a clear demand for thoughtfulness, critical awareness, *and* a mastery of fundamental skills. Obviously, the ability to read with discrimination, to write in a manner that communicates meaningfully, and to look for evidence depends upon prior learning; that prior learning involves the internalization of rules, as it involves practicing what Gilbert Ryle called "tricks of the trade," or ways of proceeding.[24] Also, it requires, on the foundation of a degree of rote learning, a considerable amount of self-teaching or making independent moves on one's own.

If all this is undertaken as a consequence of a series of conversations, of shared thinking about thinking, it may be envisaged as part of an ongoing *praxis. Praxis,* in this context, means a deliberate mode of action undertaken to bring about change. Those engaged, presumably, may be learning to transform their fears and their helplessness into indignation in the face of insufficiency. Not only may they want their children to transcend through reading, writing, and critical reflection; they themselves may want to master certain basics, if only for the sake of articulating the themes of their lives. It is, I believe, when members of the public are involved in this fashion that they can take note of the real deficiencies in an institution like a school. It is when they are initiated into a learning community and begin themselves to identify new possibilities, that they find the neglect of themselves and their children to be (in Sartre's sense) unendurable. And, indeed, they should find unendurable the presumed inability of some children to learn to read.

With the proper attention, with the necessary individualization, with the requisite attention to sequences and differential materials and grounding, all children (except for the most severely damaged) can be taught to read. Taken-for-grantedness must be eradicated, however. The situations in which ineffective schools exist must be problematized; those affected, even indirectly, must reflect critically upon them from as many vantage points as can be devised. Certainly, claims respecting inherent inferiority must be held questionable, along with claims respecting the inevitability of present allocations of educational goods.

Learning in the larger learning community ought to bring with it a new attentiveness to things in their linkages and interfaces, to the totalities and the concreteness of the world. It is not only that financial retrenchment where the schools are concerned relates to the absence of social utilities and services for the poor. Racism is as an aspect of it too; so is the traditional economic imbalance in society. The unemployment rate is relevant; so is the usually unacknowledged indifference to the condition of being poor. In addition to all that (and this the members of the community might also come to see), there are connections between the pressures on middle-class taxpayers (fearful for their children, bored with their lives, competitive with their neighbors), the insecurities of blue-collar workers, and the hopelessness of welfare families.

I am not suggesting that the larger social problems have to be dealt with before children are taught to read; nor am I suggesting that social action can take the place of intentional teaching when it comes to assuring mastery of skills. Obviously, there remains a place for professional teachers, especially those who can create the kinds of conditions that move diverse young persons to take their own initiatives and move beyond what they are taught. They need to be the kinds of teachers equipped to make practical judgments on the grounds of what they have learned in the realms of theory, what they have discovered from empirical research, what they understand about children and youth, and what they understand about themselves. They need to be the kinds of teachers who can make their own thinking visible to the young, to make manifest the ways in which the modes of procedure in each domain are put to work, to submit their own judgments to the critical scrutiny of those they teach,[25] to open perspectives, to open worlds.

It appears to me, however, that this kind of pedagogy only becomes meaningful when those who engage in it choose themselves as responsive to norms that go beyond purely professional standards. And it seems to me that the publics concerned with the learning process (even with skills and training and preparation) are only likely to support this type of teaching if their members see themselves as, in their own fashion, teachers and learners. There are persons in every community, for example, who are expert at grandmothering; there are those who are equipped to make understandable the anatomy of large institutions; there are those who can talk about the significance of sports or the meanings of community action or the potency of the arts. If all this enters into the ongoing conversation, if that conversation can relate to the lived worlds (and lived predicaments) of those involved, it is at least possible that the educational undertaking will appear differently to those who try to find out what it means. At once, it is possible that teachers will perceive their students differently: as persons who are not solely students or cases, but as individuals located in families, in clubs, in churches, sometimes in clinics, in museums, in movie houses, and on welfare agency lines.

The idea of networks and networking is not new these days; whenever school change of some sort is desired, there is an effort to bring together—*around* some existing enterprise—school people on various echelons, neighborhood representatives, and professional leaders. The arts may provide the occasion for networking, or the problems of supervision, or various problems having to do with school finances. I am suggesting, where the larger learning community is concerned, that the networks formed in these days of passivity and malaise also engage people in consideration, critical consideration, of the life situations they share. Thinking, the provoking of questions: these are the gains to be made. In my view, the basics movement too frequently has meant a "flight from thought," a turning to outside mechanisms to "fix" (in some sense, technologically) what persons themselves, working together, can only repair. I am not saying that learning communities, anymore than schools, can "change the social order."

But I *am* suggesting that the seeds of what Paulo Freire calls "cultural action"[26] can be sowed by means of conversation and shared activity—even if the activity simply is to arrange tutoring programs to reduce illiteracy in the neighborhood, to enable people to cope with bureaucracies, to give lost children or latchkey children somewhere to go after school. Such activities rarely happen if people are simply unable to reflect on their situations or to see what is needed, what is wrong. To come to reflect, to come to see is to learn. To be caught up in learning is to have something to say about the *point* of learning and what education ought to achieve. Perhaps the best of learning communities will continue to insist that it remains basic to prepare the young for security and jobs; even this need not invalidate an effort to engage persons in thinking together about how they live, about the deficiencies in their lived situations, and about how they might be repaired.

The backward look can only be altered by wide-awakeness, and there is no guarantee about what wide-awakeness can achieve. I would hope to see an expanding dialogue, as I would hope to see an intensified concern for the qualitative dimension of life and for the art experiences that make it possible to come in touch with emotional and imaginative perceptions, with what Merleau-Ponty called "the primordial"[27] and William James, the "lived reality."[28] This is because informed encounters with the arts at any age so often lead to disclosures of interior landscapes; they offer opportunities for persons to become present to themselves. It is only as more and more persons become present to themselves (to their worlds as authentically viewed and formed and listened to) that the talk in the conversation I have describe will be grounded talk, talk from the center, talk that provides food for thought. To look at Cezanne paintings, to read Tolkien or Melville, tlo listen to Mozart or Copland or jazz, to attend to *Romeo and Juliet* or *Colored Girls* or *The Cherry Orchard,* to watch *Swan Lake* or an Alvin Ailey ballet, to memorize a poem or to write a poem, to weave a rug, to shape a pot, or to watch a sculptor shape some clay:

all these are undertakings that demand our being there *in person,* that cannot (on some level) but open up new possibilities in our experiences, even as they confront us with ourselves.

The struggle against the simplifications attached to the call for basics cannot be simple. I have not been talking about total resolutions of the problems facing us; nor have I been talking about any assurance of success. I have been discussing, however, what Saul Bellow called "certain durable goods," goods that can only be secured, I think, if we conceive of open futures and open possibilities. For some of us, the world of risks and pursuits is far more appealing than the world of arrivals and assurances. The purpose of education, as many have seen it, is to open the way, as the young become empowered with the skills they need and the sensitivities they require in order to be human—to create themselves and to survive. Bellow wrote, near the end of his Nobel Lecture, about an immense, painful longing "for a broader, more flexible, fuller, more coherent, more comprehensive account of what we human beings are, who we are, and what this life is for. At the center, humankind struggles with collective powers for its freedom; the individual struggles with dehumanization for the possession of his soul."[29] We are all free to enter that center, if we wish to do so. Those concerned about and affected by the course of education in the United States are obligated to enter it, since it is part of *their* purpose to give an account of what we human beings are and what this life is for.

References

1. Saul Bellow, "The Nobel Lecture," *The American Scholar,* Summer 1977, p. 321.
2. Horace Mann, "Twelfth Annual Report (1848)" in *The Republic and the School: Horace Mann on the Education of Free Men,"* ed. Lawrence A. Cremin (New York: Teachers College Press, 1957), p. 100.
3. Ibid., p. 112.
4. John Dewey, "My Pedagogic Creed," in *Dewey on Education,* ed. Martin S. Dworkin (New York: Teachers College Press, 1959) p. 32.
5. Christopher Jencks et al., *Inequality: A Reassessment of the Effect of Family and Schooling in America* (New York: Basic Books, 1972).
6. See Edgar Z. Friedenberg, *Coming of Age in America: Growth and Acquiescence* (New York: Random House, 1965); Paul Goodman, *Compulsory Miseducation* (New York: Horizon Press, 1964); John Holt, *How Children Fail* (New York: Pitman Publishing Corporation, 1964);

Ivan Illich, *Deschooling in America* (New York: Harper and Row, 1961); Charles E. Silberman, *Crisis in the Classroom: The Remaking of American Education* (New York: Random House, 1970).

7. Jean-Paul Sartre, *Being and Nothingness* (New York: Philosophical Library, 1956), pp. 434-435.

8. E.L. Doctorow, *Ragtime* (New York: Random House, 1975), p. 3.

9. Virginia Woolf, *Moments of Being,* ed. Jeanne Schulkind (New York: Harcourt Brace Jovanovich, 1976), p. 70.

10. See John O'Neill, *Making Sense Together: An Introduction to Wild Sociology* (New York: Harper Torchbooks, 1974).

11. Ibid., p. 17.

12. Daniel Bell, *The Coming of Post-Industrial Society* (New York: Basic Books, 1973), pp. 350-351; p. 214.

13. Joseph J. Schwab, *Education and the State: Learning Community* (reprinted from *The Great Ideas Today,* 1976). (Chicago: Encyclopedia Britannica, 1976).

14. Hannah Arendt, *Between Past and Future* (New York: Viking Press, 1961), p. 185.

15. Schwab, *op. cit.,* p. 235.

16. Maurice Merleau-Ponty, *Phenomenology of Perception* (New York: Humanities Press, 1967), p. xix.

17. Arendt, "Reflections: Thinking 1," *The New Yorker,* November 21, 1977, p. 74.

18. Martin Heidegger, *Discourse on Thinking,* tr. John M. Anderson and E. Hans Freund (New York: Harper & Row, 1966), p. 45.

19. Quoted in Paul H. Sherry, "Editorial: Public Education Today and Tomorrow," *Journal of Current Social Issues,* Summer 1976, p. 3.

20. Fyodor Dostoyevsky, *The Brothers Karamasov,* tr. Constance Garnett (New York: Modern Library, 1945), pp. 300-301.

21. B.F. Skinner, *Beyond Freedom and Dignity* (New York: Alfred A. Knopf, 1971), p. 144.

22. Alfred Schutz, "The Dimensions of the Social World," in *Studies in Social Theory* Collected Papers II, ed. Arvid Brodersen (The Hague: Martinus Nijhoff, 1964), p. 25 f.

23. Elisabeth McPherson, "The Significance of the Written Word," in *Profession 77* (Selected articles from the Bulletins of the Association of Departments of English and the Association of Departments of Foreign Languages) (New York: Modern Language Association, 1977), p. 25.

24. Gilbert Ryle, "Teaching and Training," in *The Concept of Education,* ed. R.S. Peters (New York: Humanities Press, 1967), p. 114.

25. See Israel Scheffler, *Conditions of Knowledge* (Chicago: Scott, Foresman, 1967), p. 11.

26. Paulo Freire, *Pedagogy of the Oppressed* (New York: Herder and Herder, 1967), p. 131.

27. Merleau-Ponty, "Cezanne's Doubt," in *Sense and Non-Sense* (Evanston: Northwestern University Press, 1964), p. 13 f.

28. William James, *The Principles of Psychology,* Vol. II (New York: Dover Publications, 1950), pp. 299-300.

29. Saul Bellow, *op. cit.* p. 325.

⤳✿➤⤳✿➤⤳✿➤*⤳✿➤⤳✿

SOCIAL ISSUES

✽↬☺↬✽↬☺↬✽↬☺

6

Thoughts on Educational Policy

S AUL BELLOW and Richard Sennett suggest my starting points. In his 1976 Nobel Lecture, Bellow took issue with such received ideas as those "maintaining all the usual things about mass society, dehumanization and the rest." They represent us poorly, he told his audience. "We are much more limber, versatile, better articulated; there is more to us, we all feel it."[1] Sennett, in *The Fall of Public Man,* traces the roots of the "sanctification of personality" or what others are calling the "new narcissism." He discusses the growing split between the private and the public spheres, the erosion of interest in public life.[2]

It seems to me that any discussion of educational policy today must take this into account and begin with a determination to do what can be done to reconstitute a public space—or, perhaps, a political realm. A political realm is a realm of action that can only be called into being by human beings who feel themselves to be versatile enough, limber enough, and free enough to bring about differences in the world. Such a realm cannot exist, however, unless the individuals involved are able to make the kinds of judgments that transcend personal subjectivity. It cannot exist unless the participants see things as persons located in a concrete social reality—persons with the capacity to look through the perspectives of those around them and of those likely to be affected by what they say or do. For me, there is a peculiar importance in being able to take differing vantage points upon the common world, to hold as problematic what is taken for granted, and (perhaps, particularly, at this moment of history) to remain cognizant of alternative possibilities.

The retreat from the social goals enunciated in the sixties is not the only concern to those participating in such a political realm. There has been a dramatic shift of consciousness with respect to education since

89

the days in 1965 when the Elementary and Secondary Education Act was announced with the affirmation that, "Education is the first work of these times and the first work of society." A process of mystification seems to have taken place, a process so effective that people all over the United States seem convinced that problems of welfare, violence, street crime, urban decay, and human disability are in some sense insoluble.

There is a suspicion that inequity, discrimination, and failure are inherent in the nature of things and that social experimentation is ineffectual, if not absurd. Right-wing thinkers rationalize their own indifference with talk of laissez-faire and theories of inflation. Left-wing thinkers, insisting that injustices and insufficiencies are systemic in a capitalist society, find compensatory efforts to be manipulatory, disguises for the more efficient imposition of social controls. Libertarians and romantics murmur, "Small is beautiful" and object on principle to centralized planning, with the conviction that policies aimed at the aggregate inevitably injure the individual child, the "single one."

Messages of this kind (like the messages about the schools' "marginality") are mediated in various ways, but they frequently tend to reinforce public disinterest, as they justify privatist attitudes. It becomes a simple matter to say that Head Start, Follow Through, and the various Title I innovations were all discredited, even in the face of some acknowledgment that they were underfinanced and scarcely tried. It becomes a kind of ritual exercise to chant "back to basics," when there is almost no sign of a challenge to "basics" and when there are no serious efforts made to underwrite reading programs or related efforts to improve children's skills. It becomes almost fashionable to vote against school budgets and school bond issues; it is even possible to accept closings of the schools. Sometimes this has been attributed to "negativism"; sometimes, to distrust of school boards; sometimes, to pure selfishness; sometimes, to despair. A certain amount, of course, is due to explicit or an unexamined racism (when a poor or minority population lives nearby), but the diverse instances of disinterest when it comes to education also seem indicative of a kind of malaise, a sense that the schools are indeed "marginal," that they have little to do with making a better world, not to speak of a better life.

The "myth"—or the "legend"—of the common school is probably dead. By that I mean the faith that public education would create what Horace Mann called a "social balance wheel," eradicate class differences, equalize opportunity, and open the way (without distinction) for the pursuit of material success. It is certainly true that the children of many immigrant families were inducted into what was thought to be the mainstream and that mainstream attitudes and beliefs (largely Protestant and middle class) were kept alive by the work of the schools.

But I am not sure why so many kinds of people believed for so long that the schools had the power to cure fundamental social ills. Nor am I sure whether or not the prevalence of this belief deflected any revolutionary tendencies or distracted attention from the class struggle. It does seem, however, that it distracted attention from the need for social planning, public works, national health programs, and the rest. A virulent economic crisis, after all, was required before (in the Roosevelt era) the United States even began to catch up to Western Europe as far as social utilities were concerned. And there is no question but that reliance on the "promise" of the schools permitted people to deny the exclusion and suffering of minority groups, as it perpetuated their "invisibility." A widespread, militant civil rights movement was required before Americans even began to acknowledge that the "promise" of public education was empty for human beings who were segregated, exploited, and hopelessly poor.

In any event, the campaigns and articulations of the sixties should have convinced most of us that the demand for educational improvement must be linked to efforts to raise living standards, provide decent housing and medical care, and make available the kinds of recreational and art experiences that make life worth living in a technological age. It should be clear by now that there are countless linkages between learning ability and, say, good nutrition, a stable family life, and feelings of security and trust. We do not need quantitative research to demonstrate these things. We need to learn how to act upon what we know.

The fact that social phenomena are interconnected, however, does not invalidate efforts to focus on particular phenomena, to bring about improvements in particular dimensions of the field. Children who live in airless, unsanitary tenements should not be denied medical care because their environment militates against good health. The same children, deprived of privacy and family support, should not be denied a proper education because their home lives discourage them from trying. It may well be that the best Head Start program, the most skilled bilingual teaching, the most effective peer-teaching arrangements, and the most humane para-professional help cannot wholly compensate for the damage done to children by the world outside. But surely that is no argument for subjecting them to additional deprivation.

By that I mean the deprivation of what John Rawls calls "redress." The principle of redress, he writes, "holds that in order to treat all persons equally, to provide genuine equality of opportunity, society must give more attention to those with fewer native assets and to those born in the less favorable social positions. The idea is to redress the bias of contingencies in the direction of equality."[3]

As is well known, one of Rawls' signal contributions is the view that deficit or disadvantage (like superiority or advantage) is a matter of contingency—that disadvantage is not deserved. Even if his theory of justice remains problematic for many readers, the notion of contingency must be central in debate about educational policy. We have been for too long burdened with the Puritan idea that individuals are to be blamed for their insufficiencies, that deficit is a type of sinfulness. We have not yet succeeded in removing the onus from children where educational deficits are concerned nor in locating the responsibility where it belongs: in our social institutions, including our public schools.

Talking, then, about the right to a good education and the responsibility of the schools for providing it, we have to ask what we mean by "education" and whether an inequitable society is likely to provide one that is good. There is some agreement that the concept of "education" carries with it the idea that a person being educated is moved from a less to a more desirable state of mind, that he or she gains larger, more coherent perspective on his or her inhabited world. But there is also a considerable body of thought that suggests an alternative notion of the desirable, especially where the underprivileged are concerned. The assumption is made that education, in this society as in most others, is undertaken to fulfill the requirements of the economic system, no matter what the requirements of idiosyncratic, personal growth. More often than we like to admit, we are told, it is thought desirable to track children in the interests of a stratified, hierarchical structure, to distribute knowledge unequally, to impose the kinds of social control that tamp down initiative and questioning—to maintain social order at any cost.

Many critics of the schools consider their oppressiveness an inevitable consequence of their function in the larger system. Certain ones assert that nothing far-reaching can be done until the system itself is changed. Some believe that it ought to be possible to work within the system for the kinds of critical understanding that will feed into *praxis* and bring about change. Others believe that it is necessary to work outside the bureaucratic structures if the consciousness of either teachers or students is to be transformed. Thus, there are those who argue for de-schooling, those who work for "free schools," those who see some solution in voucher systems or equivalent arrangements to allow for pluralism and free choice. Then, of course, there are the people mainly concerned with "mindlessness" or simple ineffectuality, educators desirous of making the schools more effective by rendering them more relevant and humane. They are the ones who call for "humanization," who have established open classrooms here and there, set up mini-schools and satellite schools within the larger systems, and promoted learning centers, "confluent" education, and schools without walls.

In some sense, and for all the differences among them, these groups and individuals constitute the opposition to the behaviorists, the "competencies" specialists, the management engineers, and the exponents of technological control. It appears evident, however, that most educators act in the light of managerial norms. School boards in smaller communities around the country make decisions with economic efficiency in mind; school administrators feel required to perform accordingly. In big cities and in poorer communities, the demand is that the school equip young people, not to actualize themselves or to become critical thinkers, but to *perform* in appropriate ways. At community school board meetings, at the large assemblies of Jesse Jackson's PUSH supporters, in state and city administrative offices, the talk is the same: the objective of the public schools is to provide young people with the competencies they need to function productively in the economic system. The "promise" of the school is understood to be the promise of credentialling and the gaining of some kind of status as a result. Humanistic values or the values associated with a radical critique appear to be of consequence only in a few middle-class enclaves. What Daniel Bell says about the "fissure between the ethos of self-realization and the functional rationality that governs technoeconomic activities"[4] applies most dramatically to the world of the schools.

How then do we proceed? How do we counter the mystification that occasions disenchantment and distrust? How do we come to terms with the radical and humanist critiques? How can we reconstitute a realm in which people will feel free enough and effective enough to fight for an educational cause? How can we recapture the fervor of the sixties and convince people once again that, "Education is the first work of these times"? And how, if resources are provided once again, if indifference and privatism are overcome, can we render education something more than a process of credentialling, a process of imposing social controls?

References

1. Saul Bellow, "The Nobel Lecture," *The American Scholar,* Summer 1977, p. 324.
2. Richard Sennett, *The Fall of Public Man* (New York: Alfred A. Knopf, 1977), pp. 3-27.
3. John Rawls, *A Theory of Justice* (Cambridge: Harvard University Press, 1972), pp. 100-101.
4. Daniel Bell, *The Cultural Contradictions of Capitalism* (New York: Basic Books, 1976), p. 15.

7
Pedagogy and Praxis: The Problem
of Malefic Generosity

S ARTRE, in "A Plea for Intellectuals," talks about the contradiction suffered by the intellectual who is "a middle man, a middling man, a middle-class man":

> He has been a "humanist" from his earliest childhood—which means that he was taught to believe that all men are equal. Yet, if he considers himself, he becomes aware that he is living proof that all men are *not* equal. He possesses a measure of social *power* by virtue of his knowledge become skill. This knowledge came to him, the son of a civil servant or manager or member of the liberal profession, as a *heritage:* culture resided in his family even before he was born into it. Thus to be born into his family and to be born into culture were one and the same thing for him. And if he happens to be one of the few who have risen from the ranks of the working class, he will have succeeded only by traversing a complex and *invariably unjust* system of education which has eliminated most of his comrades. He is thus always the possessor of an unjustified privilege even, and in a certain sense above all, if he has brilliantly passed all the tests. This privilege, or monopoly of knowledge, is in radical contradiction with the tenets of humanist equalitarianism. In other words, he ought to renounce it. But since he *is* this privilege, he can only renounce it by abolishing himself, a course which would contradict the instinct for life that is so deeply rooted in most men.[1]

The predicament described is not only that of the intellectual; it is the predicament of many wide-awake professionals, including those who teach. It cannot but be exacerbated when such people become aware of what is now described as "domination," or distorted com-

munication, or the multiple manipulations in the technological society
they are asked to serve. The alternative? One of the few I can think of
is that chosen by Kyo Gisors in Andre Malraux's *Man's Fate*. He is
also a middle-class intellectual, but there is a difference.

> But with Kyo everything was simpler. The heroic sense had given him
> a kind of discipline, not a kind of justification of life. He was not
> restless. His life had a meaning, and he knew what it was: to give to
> each of these men whom famine, at this very moment, was killing off
> like a slow plague, the sense of his own dignity. He belonged with
> them: they had the same enemies. A half-breed, an outcast, despised
> by the white men and even more by the white women, Kyo had not
> tried to win them: he had sought and had found his own kind. "There
> is no possible dignity, no real life for a man who works twelve hours
> a day without knowing why he works." That work would have to take
> on a meaning, become a faith. Individual problems existed for Kyo
> only in his private life.[2]

It is not only that he is (because of his birth) an outsider. What concerns him is the alienation associated with labor in a capitalist society.
There is an assumption that, if the conditions of exploitation could be
eradicated, dignity would follow for each human being. In the contemporary situation, there is indeed a concern for meaning and dignity, as
there is for freedom and autonomy. But today, given the cataclysmic
changes that have taken place in the advanced technological society,
we recognize that more is demanded than an alteration of objective
relationships to the means of production or to the machine. Human
subjects have to be attended to; human *consciousness* must be taken
into account, if domination is to be in any way reduced. This is one
reason for the central importance of pedagogy in these days: once
pedagogy becomes crucial, the splits and deformations in those who
teach or treat or administer or organize take on a political significance
never confronted in time past.

There is, first, the matter of well-intentioned middle-class professionals who have no real faith in the capacities of the students (or
clients, patients, community members) with whom they work, but who
are nonetheless committed to transforming an unjust social order in
their behalf. In some sense, such persons resemble Kyo: they also want
to give to those who are exploited a conviction of their own dignity.
Throughout the struggles for liberation, as Paulo Freire says, these
people have played important roles. In spirit, at least, they have abandoned the oppressor class and its values. Like many disillusioned
young people, like a number of ostensibly radicalized intellectuals,

they are scornful of the success drive, the hunt for status and possessions, the preconceptions of meritocracy. Freire writes:

> It happens, however, that as they cease to be exploiters or indifferent spectators or simply the heirs of exploitation and move to the side of the exploited, they almost always bring with them the marks of their origin: their prejudices and their deformations, which include a lack of confidence in the people's ability to think, to want, and to know. Accordingly, these adherents to the people's cause constantly run the risk of falling into a type of generosity as malefic as that of the oppressors. The generosity of the oppressors is nourished by an unjust order, which must be maintained in order to justify that generosity. Our converts, on the other hand, truly desire to transform the unjust order; but because of their background they believe that they must be the executors of the transformation.[3]

Not trusting the people, incapable of entering into communion with them, these converts (although they believe they are doing something liberating) do their part in denying freedom—and in treating those with whom they work as cases, victims, or little more than objects or things.

Closely related to the problem of generosity is the problem of the converts' language. I have in mind not only what Murray Edelman calls "the political language of the helping professions," important though I believe it is to understand the ways in which that language extends and maintains authority and the ways in which it manipulates "the discontented into conformity and docility."[4] I have also been struck by what Alvin Gouldner describes as the characteristic language of intellectuals—reflexive, critical, and situation-free. Like such intellectuals, many professionals tend to set up hierarchies, to distinguish between precise and imprecise talk and between "good talk and lesser kinds."[5] Inhabiting a universe of discourse presumed to be all-inclusive (at least to the extent of including most rational, well-informed women and men), they are as likely as intellectuals to distance themselves from those who appear wordless, who speak in dialect or in restricted linguistic codes. They may express concern for the linguistically impoverished; they may do research into the causes of such impoverishment in the hope of curing what is wrong; they may even try to master a particular *lingua franca* or ghetto English, the better to convey their messages to those in need. But none of this produces a lessening of the distances between professional specialists and those they are attempting to help. Gouldner writes:

To be a modern intellectual. . .means to participate in a world-wide culture increasingly separable from specific local contexts. Those trained to a culture of a relatively reflexive discourse variant are capable of readier communication with others so trained, whether they are a technical or a humanistic intelligentsia, even though they have shared no common lived-history. They may be brought together, then, not by common histories or memories but by a common language and its grammar. Intellectuals, then, may be at home almost anywhere. Or they may be *homeless* anywhere, feeling an alienation from all particularistic, history-bound places, and feeling separated from everyday life unintelligible except to those sharing the same tacit assumptions.[6]

As I see it, those converts who are radicalized professionals today are much like the so-called "revolutionary intellectuals." They are likely—*because* of their language, their commitments, even their interest in critique—to exert a new kind of domination, a new mode of control. We need only imagine a confrontation between ourselves and someone who speaks in media-influenced colloquialisms or who says "Right?" and "Yea, Man!" and "Like radical, man," and "Wow!" We need only picture a well-intended meeting with, say, a Mary Hartman. How can we avoid malefic generosity? How can we learn to span the distances—to trust?

The third dimension of the predicament I am describing has to do with the place of *praxis* in the pedagogy many of us hope to undertake, perhaps particularly in schools. The contemporary notion of *praxis* probably stems from Karl Marx's writing. Recall his *Theses on Feuerbach:* "The coincidence of the changing of circumstances and of human activity or self-changing can only be grasped and rationally understood as revolutionary *practice.*"[7] Or, a few paragraphs later: "All social life is essentially *practical.* All the mysteries which lead theory towards mysticism find their rational solution in human practice and in the comprehension of this practice."[8] Paulo Freire quotes Georg Lukacs on the importance of clarifying and illuminating the action of the masses, "both regarding its relationship to the objective facts by which it was prompted, and regarding its purposes."[9] As Lukacs and Freire both see it, there must be a critical intervention in reality by means of *praxis. Praxis,* in fact, signifies a thinking about and an action on reality. Freire writes:

Men will be truly critical if they live in the plenitude of the praxis, that is, if their action encompasses a critical reflection which increasingly organizes their thinking and thus leads them to move from a purely naive knowledge of reality to a higher level, one which enables them to perceive the *causes of* reality.[10]

It is important to stress the fact that *praxis*, while emancipatory in its purpose, is not a purely therapeutic exploration of consciousness. It is more than what Sartre describes as a negation of a refused reality in the name "of the reality to be produced."[11] Merleau-Ponty has objected to Sartre's view of *praxis* because he views it as another rendering of "the vertiginous freedom, the magic power that is ours to act and to make ourselves whatever we want. . ."[12] He turns to Lukacs's notion that *praxis* cannot be viewed as the project of any single individual. Rather, it is "the cluster of relations of an ideology, a technique, and a movement of productive forces, each involving the others and receiving support from them, each, in its time, playing a directive role that is never exclusive, and all, together, producing a qualified phase of social development."[13]

Merleau-Ponty himself, responding to the question of whether it is the theoretician who creates proletarian praxis or whether it arises spontaneously, writes:

> For a philosophy of praxis, knowledge itself is not the intellectual possession of a signification, of a mental object; and the proletarians are able to carry the meaning of history, even though this meaning is not in the form of an 'I think.' This philosophy does not take as its theme consciousnesses enclosed in their native immanence but rather men who explain themselves to one another. One man brings his life into contact with the apparatuses of oppression, another brings information from another source on this same life and a view of the total struggle, that is to say, a view of its political forms. By this confrontation, theory affirms itself as the rigorous expression of what is lived by the proletarians, and, simultaneously, the proletarians' life is transposed onto the level of political struggle.[14]

With our Deweyan past, our familiarity with participant knowing, with learning as "the reconstruction of experience,"[15] we are sometimes tempted to treat the concept of *praxis* as an elaborated form of Deweyan knowing. Like Dewey, we acknowledge the social involvements of the human being; we acknowledge that the content of that human being's consciousness is always social, even though he or she thinks in his or her "singularity."[16] But this tends to make us overlook the fact that critical reflection, in Dewey's context, is intended to clarify and effect connections in experience, to make possible a widening perception of meanings, to promote growth.

100

Educationally significant though this may be, it is not to be confused with *praxis*. As I have suggested, *praxis* involves critical reflection—and action upon—a situation to some degree shared by persons with common interests and common needs. Of equal moment is the fact that *praxis* involves a transformation of that situation to the end of overcoming oppressiveness and domination. There must be collective self-reflection; there must be an interpretation of present and emergent needs; there must be a type of realization.

How, if at all, can this take place in educational institutions within the constraints we currently feel? Bowles and Gintis speak of the insuperable difficulty of reconciling the need for "a school system dedicated to greater equality and fuller human development" with the requirement that the schools be used "to perpetuate the capitalist system and its structure of wealth and power."[17] To what degree can professionals work with persons in such schools to help them come in contact, as Merleau-Ponty says, with the "apparatuses of oppression" and the shape of "the total struggle"? How, indeed, can they move those who want, above all things, to move upward through the structure of wealth and power, to achieve material success?

These, then, are the three aspects of the predicament I see confronting the critical educator and the radical professional: the temptations of malefic generosity, the distancing by means of language from the culture of everyday life, and the implicitly revolutionary meaning of *praxis*, no matter what the context or the frame. My interest is in trying to determine how these problems can be coped with by educators now in schools and universities, particularly those educators committed to cultural transformation and farflung social change. I am not assuming that the persons they work with are oppressed in the way Brazilian peasants are oppressed, nor am I assuming that there exists in the United States a "culture of silence" comparable with what Paulo Freire perceived among the poor. The oppression and the domination I have in mind are the kind that breed "false consciousness"—what Herbert Marcuse has called "the repression of society in the formation of concepts. . .an academic confinement of experience, a restriction of meaning."[18] They are the kind that lead to passive gazing —the gazing, according to Lefebvre, that becomes "the prototype of the social act."[19] They are, most crucially, the kind that subject human beings to technical systems, deprive them of spontaneity, and erode their self-determination, their autonomy.

There is no need here to review what critical theorists have said about the linkages between technology and power, the relation be-

tween knowledge and human interests, and the distinctions to be
drawn among human interests, especially the three primary ones
which, according to Habermas, govern most human activities.[20] There
is no need to argue for the importance of understanding the instrumental or rational-purpose interest that provides the framework
for the empirico-analytic sciences and the technical controls to which
they lead. Most of us are familiar by now with the kinds of knowledge
gained in response to the hermeneutic interest, as we are with the
modes of self-reflection determined by the emancipatory interest. Assuming that each one sets the conditions for entering a particular province of meaning, that each one suggests the specific cognitive style
required for constituting a particular kind of reality, I shall try to
make use of this orientation as I consider what it means to be a critical
educator today.

I want to concentrate on the confrontations and insights required
of the teacher who chooses himself or herself to be a convert to the
critical cause. I say that rather than following Freire on the matter of
conversion because it seems to me that the significant conversion, in
the North American context, is to a mode of negative thinking with
respect to taken-for-granted values and needs and with respect to certain lawlike statements used to explain and legitimate what happens in
the socio-economic world. To move from a so-called "oppressor
class" to the side of the oppressed—the disinherited, the minorities,
the submerged working class—is not necessarily to experience a shift
in consciousness.

An upsurge of questioning and critique must first occur; I believe
this is most likely to occur in response to what Alfred Schutz calls the
"experiences of shock," which compel people to break through the
limits of one province of meaning and shift "the accent of reality to
another one." Schutz says, for example, that when such experiences
befall individuals in daily life, they show them "that the world of
working in standard time is not the sole province of meaning but only
one of many others accessible to my intentional life."[21] Clearly, the
same remark might be made about the world described as objectively
real by the sciences, the province of meaning defined by empirico-
analytical rules.

The point is, however, that experiences of shock are necessary if the
limits or the horizons are to be breached. There must be a feeling akin
to that described by Albert Camus when he speaks of the "stage sets"
collapsing."[22] Indeed, many persons recall such experiences at crisis
moments in modern history: the 1968 Democratic convention, the

Kent State and Jackson State killings, the disclosure of the murders at My Lai, or the so-called "Saturday night massacre" in the Nixon days. But more often than not, whatever shock there was soon gave way to cynicism or to a reaching out for "positive images" as screen and over-lay. There was no problematizing, no effort to comprehend linkages, no effort to intervene.

Freire writes eloquently about the importance of reflection at such moments, when people discover themselves—or try to discover them-selves—in a situation, as too few suceeded in doing in the recent past:

> Only as this situation ceases to present itself as a dense, enveloping reality or a tormenting blind alley, and men can come to perceive it as an objective-problematic situation—only then can commitment exist. Men *emerge* from their *submersion* and acquire the ability to *intervene* in reality as it is unveiled. *Intervention* in reality—historical awareness itself—thus represents a step forward from emergence. . .[23]

Conscientization makes this possible, a "deepening of the attitude of awareness." It is important to see that such awareness is only available to those capable of reflecting on their own situationality, their own historical existence in a problematic world.

It seems to me that this type of reflectiveness is essential if teachers are indeed to choose themselves as critical. Just as in the case of Freire's converts, there are deformations and prejudices that have to be overcome. Only as they are overcome, can the malefic generosity that demeans under the guise of redeeming be confronted and under-stood. Those engaged in teacher education (if they are aware of their *own* situationality) face a particularly difficult problem because of the constraints and the promises associated with the teacher's role. Not only are teachers asked to mediate the taken-for-grantedness of cul-tural reality in the name of the larger society; they are assured that, by doing so, they will release young people's capacities, open up op-portunities, and contribute to the democratic way of life. On the one hand, convert-teachers must develop perspectives on the structures that condition and manipulate; on the other hand, they must withstand the seductions of self-righteousness, the pull of institutional bad faith.

For all these reasons, it is profoundly important that those who hope to be critical educators remain in touch with their lived worlds, their pre-understandings, their perceptual landscapes. Like Merleau-Ponty, I believe that a perceptual reality underlies the structures of rationality in every human biography and that to remain in touch with that reality is to be present to the self. Each one's life-history, in fact, is a history of emergences and transformations. Consciousness itself arises, writes Merleau-Ponty, in the realization that "I am able," meaning the realization that one can reach beyond what is immediate, make horizons explicit, and transcend what is first a field of presences towards other future fields. What were once perplexing shapes and fragments on the fringes of the perceptual field are thematized, transmuted into symbolic forms. Naming occurs; interpretations occur; meanings are built up; intersubjective relations entered into; gradually, the embodied consciousness constitutes a world.[24]

In a sense, transcendences and interrogations provide a leitmotif in human experience as persons become increasingly able to thematize, to problematize, to interpret their own lived worlds. Merleau-Ponty says that what defines the human being "is not the capacity to create a second nature—economic, social, or cultural—beyond biological nature; it is rather the capacity to go beyond created structures in order to create others."[25] To me, this has enormous relevance for teaching— the kind of teaching that moves persons to reflection and to going beyond. Only, however, if educators can remain in touch with their own histories, their own background consciousnesses, can they engage with others who are making their own efforts to transcend.

It is obvious enough that an educator's own capacity to interpret what is happening, in the form of written texts or human actions viewed as texts, depends upon his or her ability to remain in touch with pre-understanding. Habermas says: "Hermeneutic knowledge is always mediated through this pre-understanding which is derived from the interpreter's initial situation. The world of traditional meaning discloses itself to the interpreter only to the extent that his own world becomes clarified at the same time."[26] And this, in turn, relates to "action-orienting mutual understanding," which may be fundamental to dialogical teaching and to the communication, the exchange of messages that ought to be the consequence.

I do not know if the ability to be present to oneself and to one's initial situation can guarantee authenticity in being present to others or make less likely malefic generosity. It does appear, however, that attentiveness to one's own history, one's own self-formation, may open one up to critical awareness of much that is taken for granted, as it may to the importance of breaking with created structures—including the prejudices and deformations of which Freire speaks. And there is no question but that the creative interpretations associated with hermeneutical knowledge nurture and enrich communication. The need for this is highlighted in a now well-known article, Nell Keddie's "Classroom Knowledge," which discusses the ways in which "educational deviants are created and their deviant identities maintained" by a differentiated curriculum.[27] If you recall, Keddie reports on the kind of student behavior assumed to be appropriate, the kind of pupils assumed to be "normal, the kind of socio-economic system that is taken for granted—and, without questioning, taught. She makes the point that it is the very "failure of high-ability pupils to question what they are taught in schools that contributes in large measure to their educational achievement." Then she talks about the organization of knowledge in schools in such a way as to make eminently clear the importance of understanding the instrumental interest that prevails:

> It seems that one use to which the school puts knowledge is to establish that subjects represent the way about which the world is normally known in an 'expert' as opposed to a 'common-sense' mode of knowing. This establishes and maintains normative order in and within subjects, and accredits as successful to the world outside the school those who can master subjects. The school may be seen as maintaining the social order through the taken for granted categories of its superordinates who process pupils and knowledge in mutually confirming ways. The ability to maintain these categories as consensual, when there are among the clients in school conflicting definitions of the situation, resides in the unequal distribution of power. . . .In particular, there is a need to understand the relationship between the social distribution of power and the distribution of knowledge, in order to understand the generation of categorizations of pupil, and categories of organization of curriculum knowledge in the school situation.[28]

In her conclusion, Nell Keddie emphasizes the necessity for the categories used by teachers to undergo a fundamental change. It is my view that this is unlikely if teachers are unacquainted with the interests that govern the distribution of knowledge, if they are ill-equipped to problematize and question and if they have lost touch with themselves.

The problem of the language used by teachers, as well as by intellectuals, is as crucial as the problem of the categories devised for organizing what is known. It is clear enough that the language used in many classrooms is a type of school language—presumably standard English—at odds with and often alien to the "natural language" of those who are there to learn. A good deal has been written about the ways in which dialect speakers or, say, Hispanic speakers are alienated from the languages associated with home and heritage, and about how those languages are effectively undervalued and demeaned. There are many critics who see the imposition of a more public, situation-free language to be coercive and who would prefer that teaching be carried on in the idiom of those most concerned. There are others who believe that people can only be liberated if they are initiated into the critical, reflexive talk carried on by intellectuals and that this can be accomplished without the imposition of new controls.

It seems to me that, if we take seriously the accounts of contemporary domination, young people cannot be left innocent of the manipulations taking place. The demystifications required, for example, demand a degree of hermeneutic competence. Some reflexivity is needed if people are to break with the structures of what is presented as "normal," if they are to develop perspective on their social reality. The fact that educators are likely to speak a language of a sort different from many of their students and the fact that that language is in many senses (as Sartre suggests) part of themselves, does not necessarily entail the "cultural invasion"[29] Freire describes. If educators are committed to the possibility of autonomy, if they themselves have reason to understand the arbitrariness of hierarchies, they may come to see that there are many ways of talking, many ways of making oneself understood. This awareness relates in part to the awareness of multiple realities, of the sub-provinces of meaning, each of which depends upon a particular language for its constitution, as well as upon a particular cognitive style. Looking into their own everyday lives, many educators can understand this; they know they speak differently to their families, their colleagues, their superiors, and people on the street. Surely it ought to be possible to understand it when they move among the symbolic forms available to them—from a novel to a work in a social science, from an account of the DNA molecule to a newspaper article about an event in the scientific world.

Gouldner writes about the importance of opening up relationships of dominance, the kind associated with distrust of ordinary people; he seems to me to suggest another way of reducing malefic generosity when he writes:

Critical theory aims at transforming society into self-governing persons who value and who have a large variety of speech variants; who understand each variant as suitable for different purposes and for different but, quite possibly, equal kinds of lives; and who work toward a free community of multiple language speakers who have neither the need nor the power to impose themselves or their culture on others. It would be an essential function of a proper critical theory of intellectuals. . .revolutionary or otherwise—to make this invisible pedagogy a more visible one, thereby inhibiting the manipulation of the proletariat. An object of such a critical theory would be to demystify the role of intellectuals and intelligentsia, while giving no encouragement to anti-intellectualism.[30]

What might follow from this for teachers, I believe, is a deliberate effort to expand (in sympathetic dialogue with students) the languages available to all who are involved. What might follow, in addition to heightened mutual understanding, is a conscious attempt to examine together the implicit manipulativeness in classroom life—such matters as Sartre talks about when he asserts that all men are *not* equal, or the problem Nell Keddie discusses when she talks about the unequal distribution of power.

I mentioned literature tangentially before, but I wish to stress the uses of literary and other aesthetic experiences in stimulating the kinds of reflectiveness necessary for the pedagogy most of us wish to see. It is not simply that a work of art like *Moby Dick* or *A Sentimental Education* or *War and Peace* has the capacity to engage human beings with the range of human communication, as well as with the multifarious efforts to pursue individuality and meaning, to interrogate and to transcend. Nor is it simply that paintings like Monet's renderings of Rouen Cathedral or Cezanne's landscapes confront observers with the power of perspective viewing and re-presenting in the forming of what is felt and perceived. Informed encounters with art works can lead those involved in pedagogy to new kinds of self-confrontation, to recoveries of the pre-reflective background, and to fresh understanding of being in the world. In addition, such encounters may make present to those who teach the role of traditions in their own lives, the need for understanding of those traditions, and the need to make accessible to others the heritages of the past.

Like Paul Ricoeur, I would like (particularly in the case of teachers) to emphasize the complementarity of the hermeneutic and the emancipatory interests—and to try, within classrooms as well as outside, to render emancipatory the "reinterpretation of the tradition of the past." Talking about the manipulation of cultural life by a science and technology that have assumed an ideological function, Ricoeur stresses the need to distinguish constantly between what philosophers have described as the good life over the generations and "the purely quantitative growth of material goods." He writes:

> It seems to me that only the conjunction between the critique of ideologies, animated by our interests in emancipation, and the reinterpreta-

tion of the heritages of the past, animated by our interest in communication, may yet give a concrete content to this effort. A simple critique of distortions is just the reverse side and the other half of an effort to regenerate communicative action in its full capacity. If we had no experience whatsoever of an effective communication—even if this comes from the narrow sphere of interpersonal relations—the regulative idea of communication without frontiers and without constraint would remain a kind of wishful thinking. . . .[31]

I mention this here because it suggests to me the need to attend to the uses of subject matter in expanding the range and content of communication and the possibility of finding emancipatory interest in what we think of as the disciplines. In addition, and equally important, is turning attention to history, to a shared knowledge of the past. Merleau-Ponty speaks of history as "permanent interrogation"[32] as he speaks of man as an historical being participating in a human condition represented to others as his cultural tradition. This tradition can never be completely realized, but it may provide a ground for commonalities, a recognition of "men's intersubjective relationship, not only to his present lived reality but also to his past, to other men in other ages, with whom present man has a common bond."[33]

These commonalities, this common bond, are always future, to be constituted, to be achieved. This brings me, finally, to the notion of *praxis* and to what can be done to encourage *praxis* within the classroom. Bowles and Gintis accept the idea of the long march through the institutions; I find it hard to see an alternative. They talk, however, of socialist teachers and the creation of a working class consciousness, of revolutionary educators being in the forefront of the movement to create a unified class consciousness:

> We must fight for curriculum which is personally liberating and politically enlightening; we must reject our pretentions as professionals—pretentions which lead only to a defeatist quietism and isolation—and ally with other members of the working class. We must expand their demands to include the use of educational resources by parents, workers, community groups, and the elderly; and finally, we must fight for egalitarian educational practices which reduce the power of the schools to fragment the labor force.[34]

I have no real objections to this, but I would supplement it with an emphasis upon conscientization and the need to develop among teachers a conscious and grounded critique. Like Merleau-Ponty, I would lay stress upon talking together, upon the mutual exchange that expresses lives actually lived together, that forges commonalities. I would work for the kind of critical reflection that can be carried on by persons who are situated in the concreteness of the world, by persons equipped for interrogation, for problematization, and for hermeneutic interpretation of the culture—of the present and the past.

Andrew Arato talks of posing the problem of *praxis* "in terms of consciousness, needs, and constraints." New needs are emerging in the culture, he suggests, needs made evident in the work of the women's movement, in revaluations of family life, and in the multiple signs of worker discontent in factories. Needs of this kind have not yet been interpreted in such a fashion that they become unified and located "in the context of the over-all reproduction of the system." He sees a necessity for an increase in self-consciousness and for a conscious recognition of these needs and the constraints on their realization. And he too speaks of "a collective self-reflection" in the name of human liberation—and of a "consciously unifying struggle."[35]

The classroom has its distinctive constraints even as it responds to a restiveness and disinterest on the part of students, many of whom are experiencing the bite of needs much like those of dissatisfied workers, frustrated ghetto residents, and oppressed women. This may be shown in the degree of absenteeism, violence, drug addiction, and in the recurrent demands for student rights. Alternative schools and free schools have not provided the safety valves some people expected, because, in fact, the malaise and the sense of insufficiency are linked to tendencies in the society at large. If they choose to confront the incipient unease, educators must expose some of the mystifications having to do with educational institutions and what they can accomplish in the United States. If they are radical educators, they must engage their students in the process of demystification as they must work with them to interpret what is presently happening with regard to education and to schools. The constraints involved can be set forth in the course of conversation: each student, in his or her own language, can tell what ebbing support of education means in his or her experience, how it connects with deprivations outside the school, how his or her needs relate to those he or she perceived on the near horizon and on the fringes of his or her lived world. At once, both teachers and students can deal with such challenges as the "back to basics" movement, the return to tracking, and the decline of liberal arts emphases, especially for the poor.

There is more to be said; but I shall just point to the need for educators to work with their students for the kinds of synthesis and awarenesses that open the way, the *praxis,* as those students explore their common condition and work to transform what is given to them as inexorable. I believe that educators may gain the capacity to overcome the pessimism that so often accompanies critique. They, after all, are condemned to action as historical beings. Their problem—once they have overcome the generous intellectuals in themselves—is not simply to interpret the world in various ways. The point, as Marx wrote long ago, is to *change* it.

References

1. Jean-Paul Sartre, "A Plea for Intellectuals," in *Between Existentialism and Marxism* (New York: Pantheon Books, 1974), pp. 239-240.
2. Andre Malraux, *Man's Fate* (New York: Modern Library, 1936), p. 70.
3. Paulo Freire, *Pedagogy of the Oppressed* (New York: Herder and Herder, 1970), p. 46.
4. Murray Edelman, "The Political Language of the Helping Professions," Institute for Research on Poverty Discussion Papers (Madison: University of Wisconsin, 1974), p. 23.
5. Alvin W. Gouldner, "Prologue to a Theory of Revolutionary Intellectuals," *Telos,* No. 20, Winter 1975-76, p. 33.
6. Ibid., pp. 19-20.
7. Karl Marx, "Theses on Feuerbach," in *Marx & Engels: Basic Writings on Politics & Philosophy,* ed. Lewis S. Feuer (Garden City, Anchor Books, 1959), p. 244.
8. Ibid., p. 245.
9. Freire, *op. cit.,* p. 38.
10. Ibid., p. 125.
11. Sartre, *Search for a Method* (New York: Alfred A. Knopf, 1963), p. 92.
12. Maurice Merleau-Ponty, "Sartre and Ultrabolshevism," in *Adventures of the Dialectic* (Evanston: Northwestern University Press, 1973), p. 132.
13. Merleau-Ponty, "Western Marxism," *op. cit.,* p. 49.
14. Ibid., p. 50.
15. John Dewey, *Democracy and Education* (New York: MacMillan Company, 1916), pp. 89-92.
16. Dewey, *The Public and Its Problems* (New York: Henry Holt, 1954), p. 24.
17. Samuel Bowles and Herbert Gintis, *Schooling in Capitalist America* (New York: Basic Books, 1976), p. 263.
18. Herbert Marcuse, *One-Dimensional Man* (Boston: Beacon Press, 1966), p. 208.
19. Henri Lefebvre, *Everyday Life in the Modern World* (London: Penguin Press, 1971), p. 96.
20. Jurgen Habermas, "Knowledge and Human Interests: A General Per-

spective," in *Knowledge and Human Interests* (Boston: Beacon Press, 1971), pp. 301-317.

21. Alfred Schutz, "On Multiple Realities," in *The Problem of Social Reality*, Collected Papers I, ed. Maurice Natanson (The Hague: Martinus Nijhoff, 1967), p. 231.

22. Albert Camus, *The Myth of Sisyphus* (New York: Alfred A. Knopf, 1955), p. 12.

23. Freire, *op. cit.*, pp. 100-101.

24. See Merleau-Ponty, "Vital Structures" and "The Human Order," in *The Structure of Behavior* (Boston: Beacon Press, 1967), pp. 145-184.

25. Ibid., p. 175.

26. Habermas, *op. cit.*, pp. 309-310.

27. Nell Keddie, "Classroom Knowledge," in *Knowledge and Control*, ed. M.F.D. Young (New York: Collier-Macmillan, 1971), p. 133.

28. Ibid., p. 156.

29. Freire, *op. cit.*, pp. 150 ff.

30. Gouldner, *op. cit.*, p. 35.

31. Paul Ricoeur, "Ethics and Culture," in *Political and Social Essays* (Athens: Ohio University Press, 1974), p. 267.

32. See Merleau-Ponty, *Adventures of the Dialectic, op. cit.*, pp. 23, 31-32, 78.

33. Joseph Bien, "Translator's Introduction" to *Adventures of the Dialectic*, Merleau-Ponty, *op. cit.*, pp. xxviii-xxix.

34. Bowles and Gintis, *op. cit.*, p. 287.

35. Andrew Arato, "Notes on *History and Class Consciousness*," *The Philosophical Forum*, Vol. III, Nos. 3-4, Spring-Summer 1972, p. 399.

8
Steamboats and Critiques

We could hear her pounding along, but we didn't see her good till she was close. She aimed right for us. Often they do that and try to see how close they can come without touching; sometimes the wheel bites off a sweep, and then the pilot sticks out his head and laughs, and thinks he's mighty smart. Well, here she comes, and we said she was going to try and shave us; but she didn't seem to be sheering off a bit. She was a big one, and she was coming in a hurry too, looking like a black cloud with rows of glowworms around it; but all of a sudden she bulged out, big and scary, with a long row of wide-open furnace doors shining like red-hot teeth, and her monstrous bows and guards hanging right over us. There was a yell at us, and a jingling of bells to stop the engines, a pow-wow of cussing, and whistling of steam—and as Jim went overboard on one side and I on the other, she came smashing right through the raft.[1]

T HIS is one of the crucial scenes in Mark Twain's *The Adventures of Huckleberry Finn*. Huck and Jim have just drifted past Cairo in the fog and find themselves moving downstream into slave country again. The weather is so thick they can neither make out the shape of the river nor judge the distances. They hear the steamboat coming unexpectedly upstream; they light a lantern in the belief that the pilot will see it and turn the boat aside. But the boat plows through the raft and starts up her engines "ten seconds after she stopped them. . . ." Why did she aim right for them? Why did she not stop to find out what happened to them? Huck, accustomed to indifference, says simply that, "They never cared much for raftsmen." All he can do is listen to the boat go churning up the river, while he and Jim thrash about in the water and try helplessly to find each other again.

Writing this in what he called the "Gilded Age" some years after the Civil War, Mark Twain (intentionally or not) proved a metaphor that captured the predicament of democracy face to face with technol-

111

ogy—or, in this case, the machine. Huck may be considered to be a version of the "American Adam," described as "miraculously free of family and race, untouched by those dismal conditions which prior tragedies and entanglements monotonously prepared for the newborn European."[2] He is the unspoiled individual, inheritor of the tradition of freedom and self-determination. Jim, the runaway slave, is pursuing *his* freedom, his natural rights, including the right to be a husband and a father in a sustaining world. Together, Huck and Jim enter into a kind of voluntary community for companionship and mutual respect. It is a relationship that enables each one of them to grow; indeed, it has been undertaken to help each one attain his own particular territory, to become what he has the capacity to be. Jim, feeling himself coming closer to freedom, sheds his superstitions and his humility; he becomes a type of sage, insightful and protective, a father to the boy. Huck, learning to consider Jim as he makes his own choices, continues to grow as they journey together up the river. He becomes increasingly skillful at the practical tasks raftsmen must perform. He become increasingly moral as he learns to regard Jim as a fellow human being, to respond to his feelings, to look through his eyes. Freedom and mutuality, personal choice and shared authority; these are the touchstones of a democratic community, and these are what the voyagers temporarily achieve.

The difficulty is that the education made possible within that small community is irrelevant in the settlements on the riverbanks. Huck meets frauds of many kinds—hypocrisy, violence, and appalling indifference. His candor and spontaneity lead, more often than not, to his or someone else's undoing. The steamboat's action, then, like the boatmen's utter lack of concern, is both summary and emblematic. It refers backward and forward to the violations and depredations that stud so many of Huck's adventures and endanger his relationship with Jim. It becomes a symbol for the cruelties implicit in the existing society, even as the hopeful, futile lighting of the lantern becomes a symbol for innocence and artlessness, for an inability to cope with the complexities of the world. But there is an even larger significance in the choice of a mechanical image, "big and scary," a monstrous presence with doors like red-hot teeth. Its very *weight*, its fearful connotations hold intimations of what John Dewey was to describe as an "invasion of the community by . . . new and relatively impersonal and mechanical modes of combined human behavior."[3] The raftsmen's plight holds intimations of the plight of individuals counting for less and less, as Dewey also put it, "at a time when mechanical forces and vast impersonal organizations were determining the frame of things."[4]

At his pre-technological moment of time, Mark Twain was already suggesting that community was endangered by the manipulations and restrictions of organized society. It could only appear, if at all, at a distance from the riverbanks—apart from the greed, the brutality, even the pieties. It could only exist outside the "civilized" relationships among men and women, free citizens and slaves. The education Huck and Jim experience, therefore, is appropriate for an older, now receding world. It cannot keep them from being disarmed by their simplicity, their very "goodness." It leaves them powerless on the river they know so well, just as it leaves them powerless on shore. "I sung out for Jim about a dozen times, But I didn't get any answer. . . ." Run down by the "big one," their community—for the moment at least—was destroyed.

When we consider democracy and education today, we cannot set aside the ironies involved. Nor can we underestimate the difficulties of equipping individuals to cope with oncoming steamboats while encouraging their freedom and spontaneity. Looking back over the years, we see little evidence of educational thinkers coming to terms with the impact of "mechanical forces and vast impersonal organizations" on human lives and associations. Taken for granted as inexorable, as normal manifestations of what has been called "progress" in America, these forces and organizations have seldom been subjected to questioning. Young people have not been helped to reflect critically on what dominates and often overwhelms. They have not been enabled to identify their shared concerns as human beings or to challenge, in the name of those concerns, what dehumanizes and compels.

The dominant preoccupation, from the days of the founding of the public schools to the present moment, has been with what Horace Mann called "dominion and supremacy over the appetites and passions—during the docile and teachable years of childhood."[5] There have been exceptions, of course, but contemporary observers, like Charles Silberman and others, still find life in classrooms characterized by "values of docility, passivity, conformity, and lack of trust."[6] The call for a return to "basics," the dismay over presumably falling test scores, and the troubled preoccupation with "discipline" are likely to lead to more passivity as new kinds of "order" are imposed.

The pendulum has moved back and forth, of course, from time to time; the pole opposite the pole of dominion and control has ordinarily been the pole of permissiveness, a type of *laissez faire*. The children have been set free to explore their own interests, to light their own lanterns. Far too infrequently has cooperative activity been encouraged, the kind of activity "whose consequences are appreciated as good by all singular persons who take part in it, and where the realization of the good is such as to effect an energetic desire and effort to sustain it in being just because it is a good shared by all. . . ."[7] In other words, there has been almost no serious consideration of democracy and all that it might entail. Dewey has said that democracy is characterized by the "widening of the area of shared concerns, and the liberation of a greater diversity of personal capacities. . . ."[8] Emphasizing the democratic society's repudiation of the "principle of external authority," he thought it would find a substitute in "voluntary disposition and interest." Education, he believed, could create that substitute, so long as it made possible "conjoint communicated experience." It is at least likely that the critical reflection necessary for detecting steamboats depends on such shared experience and on the ability to communicate. Yet, given the organization and the values of too many schools, the young appear to have two alternatives: to submit or to break free, which means going it on their own.

This does not mean that the schools have never tried to stimulate critical thinking or to promote personal efficacy. A complex society requires echelons of people with problem-solving abilities, technical knowledge, and administrative skills. Schools, both public and private, have inevitably tried to meet that need. There is, however, a more consuming and compelling need to prepare people for work on assembly lines, behind counters, in more or less menial service jobs, in offices, and on farms. Fundamental literacy is required; so are good work habits, a decent conformity, respectability, and compliance with traditional norms. The schools, working along with families and churches and media of various kinds, have exerted great effort to supply what has been required. It has not been easy. There have been many incorrigible people, untrainable ones, "delinquent" ones. These have customarily been "selected out," their failures not officially attributed to schools. This distribution of people, on the face of it, would appear to be at odds with American ideals, but the presumption of equal opportunity has traditionally made it (when noticed at all) acceptable. Each person, depending upon his or her capacity, has been thought to be free to advance himself or herself, to move up the meritocratic ladder without prejudice or constraint. If a boy or a girl seemed too inert, too unmotivated, too inept to make the effort required, the system (or the school) could not be blamed. On some level, the individual could be thought to be *choosing* his or her own submergence and passivity.

Only recently have we become aware of the limitations on equal opportunity, of the injustices and inequities that still abound. Attention has only gradually turned to the unfairness, indeed to the exclusiveness of existing meritocracies. People are only beginning to realize how much those arrangements interfere with the possibility of community. At once, they are beginning to suspect that the demands made upon individuals by the structures we have created are in some way antithetical to existential needs. There is, Robert Heilbroner writes, a growing consciousness of a "civilizational malaise." It is a malaise that "reflects the inability of a civilization directed to material improvement—higher incomes, better diets, miracles of medicine, triumphs of applied physics and chemistry—to satisfy the human spirit." And then he says that, "The values of an industrial civilization, which has for two centuries given us not only material advance but also a sense of *elan* and purpose, now seem to be losing their self-evident justification."[9]

It does not follow that the industrial civilization is fated to disappear nor that reliance on technology is about to decline. The crucial point may be that even those who have benefited from the search for material improvement are finding themselves to be unfulfilled. What of those who have been asked to delay their gratifications? What of those who have been subjected (for good economic reasons) to dominion and control? We can no longer justify exclusion, repression, and manipulation by talking in terms of progress, productivity, or some other ulterior "good." What has for so long been treated as unquestionable must be questioned—from a human vantage point and on the ground of explicitly shared concerns.

People (school people included) who take the world and the system for granted as finished, objectively *there,* overlook the fact that reality is socially constructed.[10] Whatever the reality contains—political arrangements, educational institutions, movie houses, physics laboratories, television commercials—is known by means of shared schemes of relevance and shared interpretations. Alfred Schutz has written about the "intersubjective world which existed long before our birth, experienced and interpreted by Others, our predecessors, as an organized world." Were it not for such interpreting, such constructing, we would not *know* a social reality; there would only be a chaos of unrelated perceptions; what surrounded us would not make sense. It is given to us, however, transmitted to us in an organized form; "It is given to our experience and interpretation," as Schutz put it. "All interpretation of this world is based upon a stock of previous experiences of it, our own experiences, and those handed down to us by our parents and teachers, which in the form of 'knowledge at hand' function as a scheme of reference."[11] To deny the role of *"our* experience and interpretation" is to separate oneself as subject from a world made into an object. It is to give up the responsibility for critical reflection, to take an absolute and one-dimensional view. Also, it is to accede to predefinition by conventional wisdom or by "official" spokesmen for the culture, whether representative or not. In some sense, it is to be submerged, to give up hope of transformation and control.

We need but recall the long years in which people took it for granted that failure was the fault of the individual pupil or that certain minority groups were content with their lot. We need but recall the "invisibility" imposed upon poor persons, members of various ethnic communities, even upon what we now know as the "third world." The attitudes taken, the points of view held (often by those who were themselves oppressed) were reflections of a naming of the world by unknown Others. It occurred to few people that there had *been* a naming. A climactic event now and then—a My Lai massacre, a Watergate— might shock some individuals into a kind of awareness. But, generally speaking, most have assumed that the world was as conventionally described; no matter who looked at it (from another land, another planet), it would appear the same.

The inability to reflect upon vantage point and perspective has greatly affected views of public education. It has been taken for granted for an astonishingly long time that public schools, as Horace Mann had promised, would "equalize the conditions of men."[12] It has been assumed that the appeal and the attractiveness of schools were somehow given; since, after all, the schools were the crucibles in which ordinary children were transformed into citizens, candidates for the American success. More seriously and more consistently, the schools (thought to be the single deliberately educative institutions in society[13]) were believed to be the primary agents of social change. Their functions as change agents, as liberators, as facilitators, and redeemers were ascribed an independent existence, like the other facets of the social world.

This attitude appears to be viable if we take but one perspective on the schools; this is what we have tended to do for many years. That perspective is derived from the rhetoric of 19th century school reform, perhaps best exemplified by Horace Mann's:

In a social and political sense, it is a *Free* school system. It knows no distinction of rich and poor, of bond and free, or between those who, in the imperfect light of this world, are seeking, through different avenues, to reach the gate of heaven. Without money and without price, it throws open its doors, and spreads the table of its bounty for all the children of the State. Like the sun, it shines, not only upon the good, but upon the evil, that they may become good; and like the rain, its blessings descend, not only upon the just, but upon the unjust, that their injustice may depart from them and be known no more.[14]

To take this for granted as an empirical fact is to screen out the inequities, the contradictions, and the unanswered questions that must be confronted if schooling is ever to be effectively transformed. Frequently, the assumption of a "bounty for all children" is accompanied by a view that democracy itself is a given, for all the fact that the early schoolmen did not utilize the term. And that view makes it impossible to realize that democracy must be continuously *enacted,* created and recreated in the wake of onrushing steamboats, in the flux of a changing world.

A new kind of dialogue with the past may be needed, the kind of dialogue that clarifies vision and pushes back the boundaries of thought. It may be a dialogue founded in a recognition that the past is multivocal—that there are and have always been diverse perspectives on the valuable and the real. To recognize that and, at once, to look through a variety of perspectives at particular historical situations is to come to realize that what Jacob Bronowski called "the ascent of man" involves a continuing constitution of meanings. "Man is," Bronowski said, "a shaper of the landscape"[15]; there are always new ways of seeing and asserting coherence. No one-dimensional viewing can encompass changes over time. This is as true of the educational domain as it is of any other. The reality of American education is an interpreted one, a constructed one; so is the educational tradition; so is the context we inhabit today.

With Horace Mann's promise in mind, we might turn to the work of two other observers of the 19th century scene: Michel Chevalier and Robert Owen, both newcomers to Jacksonian America from across the sea. Chevalier noted the prevalence of social disorder in the country and the lack of mutuality and concern. He described the burning of a Catholic convent in Massachusetts, for instance, "in sight of a city of 70,000 without a drop of water thrown upon the flames and without it being possible to find a jury that would convict the authors of the cowardly outrage." He told of how the destruction of blacks'

schoolhouses in New York were "looked upon as a show."[16] He saw
contempt for law all around him, a dread reliance on expediency. Robert Owen, the utopian socialist, wrote that it would be impossible to
educate people to become rational creatures in a society so divided
"into sects, parties, and classes." Since existing external circumstances
were forcing people into irrationality, he said, the only solution was
"gradually, peacefully, and with the kindest feelings to all" to in-
troduce "a new, scientific, and very superior combination of external
arrangements. . . ."[17]

Both were identifying (from entirely different vantage points) grave
deficiencies in what was being described as "democracy." Both were
finding the kind of inequities that in some manner dehumanized; they
were seeing intimations of the "invasion" Dewey was later to disclose
—an overcoming of what had been cherished as community. Organization seemed already to be taking over. It was no wonder, as
Emerson wrote, that there was "a gradual withdrawal of tender consciences from the social organization."[18] Like Huck and Jim, alienated
from the towns on the riverbanks, the tender one, the idealistic hero,
was likely to find himself to be a solitary—alienated, cast out into a
hostile universe. The alternative, as in the case of Robert Owen, was
to set up a short-lived utopian community or, as in the case of
Thoreau, to take to the woods in search of authenticity.

Mann, Henry Barnard, and other reformers reacted differently. It
may be said that, for all their intense public spirit, their consciences
were less "tender"; it may be that they denied the oncoming darkness.
They responded to perceived insufficiencies by calling for an education
that would control the terrible propensities and the multiplied human
energies released by the social system. Gambling, ambition, "an un-
bridled, unchastened love of gain"; such things could be—indeed, had
to be—dealt with by means of schooling and the infusion of duty into
youthful minds. There was no necessity, as they saw it, for changing
external arrangements, There was no necessity to pose questions regarding the "cash nexus" in which so many were entangled. Nor was
there any reason to stimulate a critical reflection that might give rise
to dangerous questioning of the status quo. The solution to be sought
was "educational": training people in such a way that they would accommodate, even as they learned the skills of coping with competition,
making a living, and (if they were lucky) creating wealth. It was taken
for granted that, if enough individuals were properly trained and as-
similated, there would be national cohesion as well as social peace.
Inequities would be eventually overcome; the divisions that troubled

Owen would become irrelevant; lawlessness would give way to voluntary compliance; prosperity would be ensured and liberty guaranteed. The lacks so apparent to all who looked would be repaired in time through the agency of public schools. The United States would become the traditional "community" writ large, sustained by and empowered by the steamboat or the "locomotive in the garden,"[19] by industry and the machine.

The point is that this construction of reality, rather than one or another of the alternatives, prevailed in the public space. We can leave open the question of whether society would have been different if less had been claimed for the public schools. We can even leave open the question of whether individual powerlessness would have been allayed if the forces invading the existing communities had been confronted and made susceptible to critique. In doing history, however, in trying to make our own sense of what happened (*and* what ought to be), we can no longer look through a single perspective. We can no longer assume that the proper function of the school is (or was) as the reformers identified it. This does not necessarily involve us with the radical revisionist view that the domination was inexorable, a necessary consequence of industrial progress, and a requirement of capitalism. Nor does it necessarily involve us with certain anthropological views having to do with enculturation and socialization. These views may well disclose structural aspects of our schools and society never made evident before; they may extend our understanding of the impact of cultural and economic institutions, codes, languages, rituals, and the rest. But we must remember that all such schemata are in some sense provisional, that *we*—engaging in our own informed dialogues with the past—need consciously and deliberately to constitute that past as meaningful. As we do so, as we pose our questions to what has been held to be unquestionable, we need to consider how to transcend, how to alter what is insufficient and dehumanizing. And we need, as Maurice Merleau-Ponty has put it, to form the events we uncover in the past into an "intelligible series," the events that sediment meanings in us, "not just as survivals or residues, but as the invitation to a sequel, the necessity of a future."[20]

As we attempt to make sense in this way, to identify those events that have sedimented such meanings in us, we might well look through some of the perspectives provided by literature and the other arts. This is partly because an engagement with an imaginative form can lead, as no other engagement can, to a recapturing of our authentic perspectives on the word. It may enable us to discover which of the mean-

ings we have accumulated have indeed become invitations to a future
and which have not. We can only, after all, read *The Adventures of
Huckleberry Finn* or *The Scarlet Letter* or *The Great Gatsby* by shaping the stuff of our experience in accord with each work's demands.
We can only enter such illusioned worlds by lending Huck and Hester
and Nick Carraway "our life."[21] The illusory reality was in the first
place created out of the stuff of a writer's perceptions of, encounters
with, or insights into the social reality of which he was a part. We do
not, therefore, confront someone else's innerness when we engage with
a book; we confront a writer's consciousness of (or grasping) a moment of historical time. But we confront it by means of an act of consciousness on our part, an act of imagining, or bringing into being in
absence, as it were, absence from that to which the writer's original
ordering referred.

Encountering, say, Nathaniel Hawthorne's Ethan Brand, we find
ourselves engaging with a Berkshire mountain lime-burner in the early
19th century. A plain laborer, he desires a wisdom he does not have;
so he goes off, for purely humanitarian reasons, to pursue learning and
uncover what he calls "the Unpardonable Sin." He returns years later,
a shattered man. He has found the sin in his own breast; he is no
longer a "brother-man." And what has he done? He has become "a
cold observer, looking on mankind as the subject of his experiment."[22]
It is not merely that the story may make us conscious of our own
knowing of what it is like to distance other people, to make objects of
them. Without such a direct confrontation of ourselves, we would not
understand what we were reading. Having experienced the confrontation, we are likely to recognize the human consequence of exploitation
and manipulation in a more intense and immediate way than ever
before.

In addition, however, we are aware on some level that Hawthorne
was embodying certain responses to the perversities of his own time as
well as that time's possibilities; it is of some interest that he was a
contemporary of Horace Mann, in fact, his brother-in-law. Ethan
Brand, as magnificent as Mann in his desire to do good, goes off on his
original quest in a mood of "holy sympathy." When he attains the
knowledge he was seeking, he uses it exploitatively, because (as
Hawthorne suggests) his intellect has outpaced his "moral nature." In
context that can only mean that he no longer feels like a fellow-
creature when he encounters another human being. Having reached a
high place, he is forever alienated—from himself as well as others. If
given the opportunity, he would decide *for* his fellow-beings; he would

show himself to be unable to look through others' eyes. He is, of course, an American Faust, tempted to overreaching by the American experience, by an open world. Hawthorne, being an artist, did not offer a solution. His obligation was only to make people see. And so he provided another perspective for those of us attempting to constitute our past—a perspective upon an eroding community, upon the dangers of the "scientific mentality," upon the need for a new kind of brotherhood and sisterhood among fallible human beings. This, too, may be an invitation to a sequel, perhaps a democratic sequel. In one of his novels, Hawthorne wrote, "The world owes all its onward impulses to men ill at ease."[23]

Unease of this sort can be a function of breaking with what has been taken for granted. It is a necessary—and, as Hawthorne implied, a *futuring*—mood. Although it can be understood in many ways, its impact may be most immediately felt in the course of personal explorations in art. We need but think of Herman Melville's story, "Bartleby the Scrivener," as an instance. It is a tale of a Wall Street office in the 19th century, of walled-in human beings, of a formulated and organized world. The lawyer-narrator, whose exemplary office it is, has his clerks and his life under control. Each person is judged by his contribution to the business, whatever his limitations or distinguishing marks. Each one says, "With submission, sir," when he addresses his employer; the employer has a "natural expectancy of instant compliance"; no one uses the term "prefer" or the word "choose." When the new scrivener, pallid young Bartleby, begins saying (for no apparent reason), "I prefer not to," the lawyer's altogether "natural arrangement" begins to be disturbed. Afflicted by Bartleby's passivity, his pallor, and his negations, the prudent man is aroused to a tragic awareness he has never experienced before. He feels a strange "fraternal melancholy" at the end when Bartleby has died in the Tombs. He cries out, "Ah Bartleby! Ah humanity!"[24]

Again, we may achieve a perspective by means of our own presentness to ourselves. We may achieve it by means of our own perceptions of what it is to be categorized in a society bent on material gain, our own perceptions of what it might mean to "prefer not to," our own recognition of how a stranger's preferring not to might shake our certainties.

There are many fictional realities to set beside the official versions of what progress has meant to this nation and what the schools can and cannot do. There is the bulldozer gnawing away at the wilderness in William Faulkner's "The Bear." There are the valley of ashes and the foul dust in F. Scott Fitzgerald's *The Great Gatsby*, the tractored dust bowl in John Steinbeck's *The Grapes of Wrath*, the chaotic streets and the underground room in Ralph Ellison's *Invisible Man*, the gunshots at the Morgan Library in E.L. Doctorow's *Ragtime*. On the one side, passion and incipient chaos; on the other, impersonal power, conventions, and controls. For a long time, it all seemed worth the trials; even the acceptances seemed warranted. It was the Dream, after all; we were the sons and daughters of God—and, like Jay Gatsby, we felt we were about our Father's business. Only slowly, as in Gatsby's case, did we begin to suspect that we were in the service of "a vast, vulgar, and meretricious beauty." To what future does this invite? And how do we educate for this?

This is not to suggest that the literary vision yields some higher or more dependable truth nor that what it reveals is in some sense "right." The perspective gained is in the imaginary mode of awareness, one that releases a reader into his or her own subjectivity as it enables him or her to break with the routine and the mundane. It can make possible a distancing of the routine, a new vantage point on everyday interpretations, an awareness of alternative possibilities. None of this invalidates or corrects empirical descriptions. There are unveilings; there are openings to alternatives; but, even in the darkest visions, there is no necessary obliteration of our norms nor of our democratic ideal. The point is that, when we look through multiple perspectives, we come to see that liberty, equality, fraternity, and civility are not pre-given. Like democracy, they must be continually enacted, continuously achieved. To achieve them, in and out of schools, demands more than the lighting of lanterns, more than a raftsman's education, certainly more than a reliance on dominion and control.

There must be critical understanding of the post-industrial society, run as it is by technical men and women "committed to functional rationality and technocratic modes of operation."[25] Individuals must be equipped to reflect upon the knowledge structures we provide, to identify themselves with respect to them, to penetrate their mystiques. They must be equipped as well to reflect upon the erosion of community in this society. "Community, in a normative sense of that term," writes Kenneth Benne, "as an association of people, mutually and reciprocally involved with each other, caring for each other, aware of the human effects of their action . . . committed to being responsible for these effects, is dangerously missing both in our institutions of formal education and in the society which environs these institutions."[26] People are too seldom *with* one another, even in schools; they are alongside one another, and they take this for granted too. It is as if we are prone to respond with Huck Finn's childlike fatalism: "They never cared much for raftsmen." We seldom go so far as to interrogate the "they."

What, then, of democracy? Dewey wrote that democracy "will have its consummation when free social inquiry is indissolubly wedded to the art of full and moving communication."[27] Free social inquiry signifies more today than the use of social scientific techniques and protocols. It entails the kind of critical reflection that is turned to our own life situations, our own realities. It entails the kind of knowing called *praxis,* a knowing that becomes an opening onto what has not yet been. "A flight and a leap ahead," writes Sartre, "at once a refusal and a realization. . . ."[28] There must be a disclosure of the reality to be surpassed—surpassed because it afflicts living persons as insufficient, mutilating, and inhumane. There must be a refusal of such a reality and a gathering of the forces needed to transform.

It must always be remembered that the reality in question is a constructed one. Only as people come to understand that they need not accede to the world as demarcated and named by others, will they acknowledge that things can be different. Acknowledging that, they will be free to point to insufficiencies of the kind the school reformers, among others, so easily obscured. Acknowledging that, they may also be free to engage in the modes of dialogue needed for reconstituting what exists. Here is where the "art of full and moving communication" comes into play. The communication must be of the kind that enables each participant to find his or her own singular and authentic voice in the process of identifying values common to all, ideals that are shared. Existing with each other, committed to realizing a good shared by all, men and women, girls and boys, may be empowered to constitute democracy.

This cannot, of course, happen solely within the schools and through the agency of the schools. There are open spaces to be created in living rooms, on playgrounds, in workplaces, studios, and waiting rooms; there are communities to be made. Dominion must be rejected if this is to occur; manipulation must be refused if dialogue is to take place, along with inquiry and critique. Moving in and out, from neighborhoods to classrooms, from classrooms to the surrounding world, from the world to the localities again, individuals must seize their opportunites for communication and concern. Taking social structures as well as knowledge structures as objects of study—steamboats, welfare centers, assembly lines, television programs, academic disciplines

—they must be helped to move towards wide-awakeness as they gain their conceptual skills. They need to learn how to interrogate together and help each other to see.

There is no fatality in the steamboat "pounding along," not if we try to "see her good" and pose our questions and try seriously to understand. Individuals can still link hands and enact democracy. They can still establish their own dominion and supremacy by rejecting the givenness of the mechanical and the impersonal. Working together, reflecting together, forging community together, they may at last surpass what is intolerable; they may yet transform their world.

References

1. Mark Twain, *The Adventures of Huckleberry Finn* (New York: New American Library, 1959), p. 98.
2. R.W.B. Lewis, *The American Adam* (Chicago: University of Chicago Press, 1959), p. 5.
3. John Dewey, *The Public and Its Problems* (Chicago: Swallow Press, 1954), p. 98.
4. Ibid., pp. 96-97.
5. Horace Mann, "The Necessity of Education in a Republican Government," in *Ideology and Power in the Age of Jackson,* ed. Edwin C. Rozwenc (Garden City, N.Y.: Anchor Books, 1964), p. 150.
6. Charles Silberman, *Crisis in the Classroom* (New York: Random House, 1970), p. 323.
7. Dewey, *Democracy and Education* (New York: Macmillan Company, 1916), p. 101.
8. Ibid.
9. Robert Heilbroner, *An Inquiry into the Human Prospect* (New York: W.W. Norton, 1974), p. 21.
10. See Peter L. Berger and Thomas Luckmann, *The Social Construction of Reality* (Garden City: Anchor Books, 1967).
11. Alfred Schutz, *Studies in Social Theory,* Collected Papers II, ed. Arvid Brodersen (The Hague: Martinus Nijhoff, 1964), p. 9.
12. Horace Mann, "Twelfth Annual Report (1848)" in *The Republic and the School: Horace Mann on The Education of Free Men,* ed. Lawrence A. Cremin (New York: Teachers College Press, 1957), p. 87.
13. See Dewey, *Democracy and Education, op. cit.,* pp. 20-21.
14. Mann, *op. cit.,* pp. 111-112.
15. J. Bronowski, *The Ascent of Man* (Boston: Little, Brown, 1973), pp. 19-20.
16. Michel Chevalier, *Society, Manners and Politics in the United States,* ed. John W. Ward (Garden City, N.Y.: Doubleday, 1961), pp. 371-381.

17. Robert Owen, "Rational Education for the New Moral World" in *Uto-pianism and Education: Robert Owen and the Owenites,* ed. John F.C. Harrison (New York: Teachers College Press, 1968), p. 122.

18. Ralph Waldo Emerson, "New England Reformers," in *The Prose Works of Ralph Waldo Emerson* (Boston: Houghton, Mifflin, 1870), Vol. I, p. 550.

19. See Leo Marx, *The Machine in the Garden* (New York: Oxford University Press, 1967).

20. Maurice Merleau-Ponty, *Themes from the Lectures at the College de France, 1952-1960* (Evanston: Northwestern University Press, 1970), pp. 40-41.

21. See Jean-Paul Sartre, *Literature and Existentialism* (New York: Citadel Press, 1965), pp. 50-51.

22. Nathaniel Hawthorne, "Ethan Brand," *Selected Short Stories of Nathaniel Hawthorne,* ed. Alfred Kazin (Greenwich, Conn.: Fawcett Publications, 1966), p. 233.

23. Hawthorne, *The House of Seven Gables. The Complete Novels and Selected Tales* (New York: Modern Library, 1939), p. 428.

24. Herman Melville, "Bartleby the Scrivener," *Billy Budd, Sailor and Other Stories* (Baltimore: Penguin Books, 1967), pp. 59-99.

25. Daniel Bell, *The Coming of Post-Industrial Society* (New York: Basic Books, 1973), p. 214.

26. Kenneth D. Benne, "Technology and Community: Conflicting Bases of Educational Authority," in *Work, Technology, and Education,* ed. Walter Feinberg and Henry Rosemont, Jr. (Urbana: University of Illinois Press, 1975), p. 156.

27. Dewey, *The Public and Its Problems, op. cit.,* p. 184.

28. Sartre, *Search for a Method* (New York: Alfred A. Knopf, 1963), p. 92.

❀↬✿↬❀↬✿↬❀↬✿

9

Equality and Inviolability: An Approach to Compensatory Justice

AMERICAN society is pluralist; American citizens are ineluctably diverse. We vary in temperament, talent, and capacity within all groups and categories, including those of sex and race. We locate ourselves in the world in the light of our own particular biographical situations, in the light of experiences we built up over time. We interpret the realities we confront through perspectives made up of particular ranges of interests, occupations, commitments, and desires.

Each of us belongs to many social groups and plays a great variety of social roles; our involvements affect the ways we use "the stock of knowledge at hand"[1] to make sense of the social scene. The stock of knowledge, the disciplines, the schemata made available to us not only give our culture its identity, they enable us to participate in a common meaning structure, to inhabit a common world. Even as we do so, however, we maintain our individual perspectives; we make personal interpretations of what is shared. Each of our undertakings, therefore, each of our projects remains distinctive; each vantage point is unique, despite all the association and communication essential to communal life.

I begin this way because my concern is as much with persons and their life-worlds as it is with equity in the social system. I am as interested in personal emancipation as I am in equality and justice. At once, I am entirely aware that the traditional liberal reliance on a mo-

Originally published in *Social Justice & Preferential Treatment: Women and Racial Minorities in Education and Business*, William T. Blackstone & Robert D. Heslep, eds. (Athens: University of Georgia Press, 1977)

rality based upon individual rights has not resulted in equal opportunity for many, many individuals—namely, females and members of minority groups, who continue to suffer from disadvantages that are undeserved. I want to try to develop an approach to equality and justice that rests upon a conception of individual inviolability and critical self-consciousness, one that takes into account the way inequity and exclusion actually afflict individuals struggling to define themselves in the world. I want to try to develop an approach that allows me to move back and forth between the objective arrangements made by the social system and the experiences people have with opportunities, both provided *and* withheld.

It is important, for instance, to hold in mind the idea that, "An individual experiences what we have defined in the objective sense as an opportunity, as a possibility for self-realization that stands to his choice, as a chance given to him, as a likelihood of attaining his goals in terms of his private definition of his situation within the group."[2] It is important to hold in mind the differences between what equality means to the one who feels discriminated against and what it means to those whose status an outsider wants to attain. It is important, also, to hold in mind the split created in consciousness when an individual is identified in terms of group membership, even when he or she is convinced that only through alliance with groups can individuals overcome inequities.

One of the crucial issues that confronts us, of course, is the matter of group rights and the break with pluralistic liberalism that an emphasis on group rights entails. Another has to do with preferential treatment and the relationship of such treatment to social justice. Still another has to do with the problem of collective compensation to groups and the ways in which such compensation is distributed to individual members of such groups. Does "affirmative action" mean, as one critic believes, an "erosion of legal principle"?[3] Can reverse discrimination be carried on in accord with principles that are relevant from the point of view of justice? What does justice, what does fairness entail?

None of these issues can be addressed without a clarification of concepts like "rights," "equality," "justice," and "compensation." It seems to me that no one of them can be clarified except within specific contexts, in reference to what Alfred Schutz calls prevailing "systems of relevance." The system of relevance that has won most social approval over the years in our culture is the one associated with meritocracy. We are so familiar with it, we take it so much for granted that we are likely to forget that the meritocratic reality is a constructed one, like every other example of social reality.[4] The explanations and legitimations connected with meritocratic thinking represent one mode of interpreting economic and social relationships, a mode so hallowed by tradition that we tend to confuse it with objective reality. Fundamental to the construct is the idea that human beings are to be judged and rewarded on the basis of individual merit. Achievement rather than ascription is to determine success. The assumed purpose of social and political arrangements is to enable diverse individuals to compete for places open to persons of comparable talent and ambition. From the point of view of the meritocratic system, this satisfies the requirements of efficiency. Equality of opportunity can be taken for granted because barriers of birth and wealth are not permitted to bar the way. In the last decade, as we know, efforts were made to help certain persons overcome specific deficiencies and thus compensate for previously unregarded disadvantages. Once this was done, it was believed, each individual would have a fair chance to realize his or her potentialities, to satisfy his or her desires. Natural rights (to life, liberty, and the pursuit of happiness) were assumed to be secured. Because everyone would be offered the same chance, the system was described as just.

Recent historic events and disclosures have made clear to many people that, even with compensatory arrangements, the meritocracy does not provide equal chances for all individuals, nor does it protect everyone's natural rghts. Many have come to realize that true equality of opportunity is, in any case, impossible. R.S. Peters says flatly:

> The obvious fact is that, descriptively speaking, there is no equality of opportunity and never can be unless equalitarians are prepared to control early upbringing, size of families, and breeding. Without taking such steps, there will always be ineradicable differences between people which will affect how any system works in practice. Were there not such differences the principle of equality would have little point.[5]

To speak of a principle of equality is to speak of equality of consideration, of equity in the treatment of persons whose skills, strengths, and talents are necessarily diverse. Peters is concerned with justice in the making of distinctions, when it is important that distinctions be made. "The notion basic to justice," he writes, "is that distinctions should be made if there are relevant differences and that they should not be made if there are no relevant differences or on the basis of irrelevant differences."[6] The interesting question has to do with the criteria of relevance. Are considerations of efficiency, for example, more important than considerations of self-development? Is a concern for interests as important as respect for persons? Is achievement more significant than self-respect? It is easy enough to say that sex and race are not relevant when choices are made in hiring. What does determine relevance? What warrants distinctions being made?

John Rawls, in *A Theory of Justice,* has devised a formal system that takes into account what he considers to be the most profoundly relevant differences: between the most and the least favored in a society. His approach explicitly challenges the meritocratic view; his prime considerations are equality and self-esteem. He believes that meritocracy is unfair because, under meritocratic arrangements, equality of opportunity signifies an equal chance for the more fortunate to leave the less fortunate behind. To be less fortunate, he says, is a matter of contingency. Disadvantages, deficits, and inequalities due to birth and endowment are undeserved and call for redress. Clearly, this breaks fundamentally with what is taken for granted in our culture. People all too often confuse success in the meritocratic hierarchy with individual worth; there is no question but that self-esteem in this culture is a function of the ability to achieve. Individuals are held responsible for their failures as well as their successes. Offered an equal chance, a person who does not "make it" is considered to be less valuable as a person—and has little chance to develop self-esteem. He or she may be undisciplined and aggressive or uninterested in learning to read. He or she may be poorly fed or unclean; his or her test scores may be appallingly low. All these, suggests Rawls, are deficits and undeserved.

The social ideal Rawls develops is one in which equality, for reasons of justice, is given priority. Justice, he writes, is the primary virtue of social institutions. It provides a standard for determining whether the distribution of goods in a given society is fair or unfair. The conception most rational men would accept, he says, is one that requires social and economic inequalities to be so arranged that they benefit the least advantaged in the society.[7] Not only is there to be redress for deprivation; there is to be a "difference principle" requiring that resources be allocated in such a way as to improve the long-term expectations of the least favored.[8] In connection with all this, "positions of authority and offices of command must be accessible to all"; inequalities in general must be attached to offices open to all in such a fashion that everyone benefits.

Prior, however, to the principles regulating inequalities is a principle of liberty. Rawls asserts that every member of society has an inviolability founded on justice "which even the welfare of everyone else cannot override." He believes that no proper conception of justice or fairness can affirm that "the loss of freedom for some is made right by a greater good shared by others."[9] He is not a leveler; he is not asking that handicaps be evened out nor that individuals be denied the freedom to achieve. He is saying that higher achievement and greater advantage are to be justified not by the individual satisfaction they produce (nor by the net balance of satisfactions) but by the contribution they make to the welfare of the least advantaged.

How, guaranteed inviolability and freedom, can human beings be expected to attend to those born into less favorable social positions or into less advantaged groups? Why would anyone who is better endowed and more advantaged concern himself with the life prospects and expectations of the least favored? Rawls, positing a rational and rule-governed society, speaks of mutual benefits and the capacity of human beings to treat others with respect. The principles that support self-respect and make social cooperation more effective are that, "Each person is to have an equal right to the most extensive total system of equal basic liberties compatible with a similar system of liberty for all" and that the arrangement of inequalities should be to the benefit of those least favored. No longer is equal opportunity to be used mainly to unleash energies for the pursuit of wealth and power. The higher expectations of the gifted and better situated citizens are to be considered just "if and only if they work as part of a scheme which improves the expectations of the least advantaged members of society."[10]

Self-respect is the primary good in this system; indeed, it is the primary motivation. Self-respect, for Rawls, refers to a rational individual's sense of his or her own worth and to his or her conviction that the life plan he or she has developed is worth carrying out. In addition, there is a confidence in the ability to fulfill whatever his or her intentions are. Justice supports such self-esteem, Rawls says; life itself has more value if we are appreciated by others whom we ourselves esteem. So a sense of their own worth must be sought for the least favored as well. The point of education, in fact, is to enrich personal and social life even more than to train productive abilities.

Daniel Bell finds all this extremely radical; he sees Rawls's theory, in fact, to be a "socialist ethic." It should be pointed out, however, that Marxists would disagree in almost every particular with Rawls. For one thing, most of them believe that class struggle is necessary if inequalities are to be effectively reduced, especially since the most favored class in society is a ruling class with a need for wealth and power and little desire for social cooperation based on a difference principle.[11] Marxists would object vehemently to Rawls's neglect of the problem of class interest; they would find meaningless the concern for self-esteem within the free competitive society that is assumed. Bell's charge of radicalism is primarily based on the belief that Rawls makes the disadvantaged identifiable in group terms. Therefore, says Bell, he is making a claim for group rights that "stands in formal contradiction to the principle of individualism, with its emphasis on achievement and universalism."[12] Why not, he asks, provide for greater incentives "for those who can expand the total social output and use this larger 'social pie' for the mutual (yet differential) advantage of us all?"[13]

Granting the fact that few people yet conceive society "as a cooperative venture for mutual advantage," granting the fact that Rawls's social ideal may be unrealizable, I find it difficult to see how Bell's "just meritocracy" deals with the inequities confronting us today. He says that all we have to do is to realize the traditional ideal of equality of opportunity fairly; he is convinced that questions of inequality have little to do with meritocracy, which is made up of those "who have earned their authority."[14] Is it the fact that women and blacks remain relatively disadvantaged because they have *not* earned the right to success and authority?

When I consider the empirical realities of the hiring situation as it pertains to women and blacks, I find it less than satisfactory to be told to wait for the advent of a "just meritocracy." I find it frustrating to read again that, "We must insist on a basic social equality in that each person is to be given respect and not humiliated on the basis of color, or sexual proclivities, or other personal attributes." The social equality Bell has in mind is not the kind that leads to democratization in every sphere of life. It is qualified by his conviction that, in the technocratic society, there must be a regard for intellectual authority, significant achievement, and earned status confirmed by a person's peers. The question is whether these considerations exclude a concern for the plight of those discriminated against or kept (by accident, prejudice, thoughtlessness, or neglect) from developing themselves and attaining a sense of worth.

The Educational Testing Service recently conducted a study on persons awarded Ph.D.s and Ed.D.s in 1950, 1960, and 1968. The study concluded that, "Women, having often subordinated their careers to family responsibilities, have consistently received lower pay, less prestigious jobs, and fewer employment opportunities" and that this has changed little over the years. The report goes on to state that disparities in income between men and women with doctorates increase with years of experience. Because of marriage and motherhood, many women have had to work part-time. "Men with full-time positions received the grants, published the research, and got the promotions."[15] Is this required by a just meritocracy? Is it, from any point of view, fair?

Unnecessary though it may be to review the details, I must emphasize that, in 1970, only 18 percent of the professional staffs of institutions of higher education were women.[16] The proportion of women professors has decreased since 1920, despite the increased number of women in the labor force. It is well known that after the change in the character of that labor force during World War II, 51 percent of all mothers with children aged 6-17 were employed, and a middle-class woman was as likely to be working as one from the working class. This fact is one of many that account for the growing ambivalence of women in all classes towards traditional family roles. Their ambivalence, yes, and restlessness, along with rapidly increasing access to higher education, have led to an expanding pool of potential female participants in the work life and the professional life of this country.

These factors are countered, to a significant although decreasing degree, by women's culturally conditioned fears of success.[17] They are countered as well by an educational system that reflects society's values and therefore imposes expectations on women that differ from those imposed upon men. From the beginning of school, little girls learn from textbooks, toys, and teachers that they are inferior in important respects to little boys.[18] Efforts are being made to alter the toys and textbooks made available to girls to help release expectations and promote self-respect in what is still regarded as a man's world, but the injustices, whether intended or not, remain. It ought to go without saying that black women, most particularly black women professionals, suffer even more when it comes to status and salary differentials. The sprinkling of black women assistant deans and heads of recruitment programs should not obscure the fact that, in 1973, only 1,073 black females were employed as teaching and administrative personnel in 1,764 two- and four-year colleges and universities—less than one per institution. And the statistics show as well that black women professionals were clustered in the low-status schools.[19]

Where blacks in general are concerned, there can be no argument with the claim that too many have been casualties. The long years of exclusion, humiliation, poverty, persecution, and inadequate training have left a fearsome mark. Job discrimination, despite the improvements of the last decade, still abounds. (After all, unemployment in the male black population is twice what it is in the white.) Feelings of "nobodyness" and "invisibility" still afflict many members of minority groups, for all the increase in self-esteem derived from new-found pride in identity. The disadvantages with which they are burdened are of a different order from those holding women back from self-realization and feelings of worth. The color blindness that was supposed to result from anti-discrimination legislation has not helped as much as the reformers hoped.[20]

The matter of poor qualification still has to be confronted, along with the problem of rising expectations and the bitter sense of unmet needs. Using an old Aristotelian idea, some critics say that, since white society has enslaved and exploited blacks for so long (and been enriched by doing so), justice demands that the victims be compensated. This, they assert, is commutative justice and only right. We have, we are told, a long way to go in achieving a society where race is as irrelevant as eye color and where minority groups are judged on individual worth alone. When we reach that point, "Their history will have left them so educationally, economically, and psychologically disadvantaged that unless they receive special preference, they and the vast majority of their children will be condemned by our now color blind society to perpetual deprivation in the midst of surrounding affluence."[21]

More arguments could be amassed to indicate the extraordinary problems involved in the effort to achieve fair employment policies in a basically inequitable society. Affirmative Action programs, developed largely in response to pressures by women's organizations, are understood to be the consequence of a lack of enforcement of executive orders preventing discrimination. Once the Civil Rights Office of the Department of Health, Education and Welfare took over the responsibility for holding colleges and universities accountable, the controversy over group rights and preferential hiring began. J. Stanley Pottinger, then Director of the Office for Civil Rights, said at the time the regulations were devised that the Executive Order had never been intended to set aside professional qualifications as the primary standard for hiring. He "never understood academic freedom to deny a qualified person an opportunity for appointment or advancement because of race or sex, or the right to pay one person less than a person of another race or sex performing the same job,"[22] and it is difficult to argue with that belief.

The problem has been the vagueness of the language used in the directives. Many persons have understood them to call not only for quotas but for preferential hiring. One reason for this is that universities have been asked, not simply to declare themselves against discrimination, but to take positive action to remedy inequities according to timetables worked out in advance. They have also been asked to appraise what their schedules are likely to yield in the future. According to regulations, those predictions must be expressed as statements of goals, which are to be used in measuring the efforts made. One writer says that it may be useful "to look upon the use of goals—and their attendant timetables—as a management information device to allow both ... the colleges and the regulatory agency (HEW) to monitor more effectively and evaluate the progress being made towards the achievement of actual equal employment opportunity."[23] Others, however, have said that the effort to prove "good faith" has led many universities to spell out their goals numerically. Virginia Black, who finds it logically impossible to show the effectiveness of special treatment mandates, is convinced that affirmative action programs must be discriminatory. Enumeration is necessary, she says, to demonstrate that an organization is in compliance, and this inevitably implies a quota system.[24]

The point has also been made that, even though the goals demanded are to operate in favor of minorities and not as ceilings, a numerical requirement in favor of any group must become a restrictive ceiling for others. Although no one defends quotas in the restrictive sense, many of the arguments against Affirmative Action are based on the assumption that the requirements of the Executive Order make quotas inescapable. Vernon Jordan writes in rejoinder that quotas are "a phony issue, a red flag to divert attention from the real issue of discrimination by falsely categorizing reasonable numerical *goals* and generalized intentions as rigid mathematical formulae. Nevertheless, if numerical goals and timetables are not formulated, as one commentator has stated, 'the future will resemble the past.' "[25]

Shifting the ground somewhat, Sidney Hook and others have responded by insisting that the effect of Affirmative Action is to force institutions to hire unqualified members of preferred groups and discriminte against qualified members of majority groups.[26] Daniel Bell, viewing the setting of "target" figures as equivalent to quotas, says this means that "standards are bent or broken."[27] Most recently (although probably not conclusively) the present director of the Office of Civil Rights has issued a memorandum on college hiring policies that explicitly orders colleges to hire the best qualified and asserts that sex and race must play no part. "The affirmative action process must not operate to restrict consideration to minorities and women only. . . . Job requirements must be applied uniformly to all candidates without regard to race, color, sex, ethnicity. . . ."[28]

The aim of those who called for Affirative Action in the first place was to take steps to overcome preferential treatment of the white male and to allow groups to compete with all others on the basis of individual merit. As we can see, the issue is in no sense resolved because of the danger of new inequities, once special treatment for particular groups is required. The prevailing belief seems to be that unqualified people should not, under any circumstances, be hired; preferential treatment of any sort is taken to mean that something other than individual merit will determine who is chosen.

Underlying this is a view of a "natural" distribution of talents that free, unhampered competition makes possible. There must be, according to this view, no arbitrary interference with what is thought to be the "bell-shaped curve" according to which talents are distributed in any society. The presumption that such a curve has some objective existence is profoundly questionable. It is a presumption integral to the knowledge structure that sustains and legitimates what Bell calls the "post-industrial society," but we need to understand that it is a construct developed over time to serve particular human interests,[29] certainly not all. The very idea of an unequal distribution of talents almost always assumes a conception of single talents, those of most utility to the social system. It becomes all too easy to overlook "the range and variety of human capacities: intelligence, physical strength, agility and grace, artistic creativity, mechanical skill, leadership, endurance, memory, psychological insight, the capacity for hard work—even, moral strength, sensitivity, and the ability to express compassion."[30]

Granting the fact that college or university hiring policies must now be geared to a selected range of capacities, I still would emphasize the ways in which the notion of merit is linked to a conception of the "given," of the conventional and unquestionable. The requirements universities have in mind when they hire are frequently defined to correspond with what is taken to be the distribution of talents. Yet they are granted an objective status that makes us overlook the fact that they too were created by human beings in the light of interests interpreted over time.

My interest, as I have said, is to develop an approach to equality founded in a commitment to inviolability and critical consciousness.

Such an approach requires that we break with either/ors as we break with what we blandly take for granted where fairness, merit, and efficiency are concerned. It also requires that we pay heed to the self-respect and the life plans of many different members of our society with the idea that each one is entitled to act upon what she or he chooses, to question, to become what he or she has the capacity to be. If each one is entitled to equality of consideration, as I believe to be the case, the claims of injured groups for compensation cannot override the rights of the white male to act upon his life plan.

I am unable to discover principles relevant from the point of view of justice that sanction arbitrary discrimination in favor of certain victims of discrimination, nor am I able to justify preferential hiring if it restricts opportunity for members of the majority group. I am concerned, among other things, about the individual in the nonpreferred group who may have been maltreated for reasons other than sex or race. I am concerned as well with the unfairness of holding the group of young white males responsible for the injuries done blacks and women, even though the individuals in the group may neither have done injury nor profited from exploitation.[31] Like John Rawls, I do not believe that the better situated white male ought to be held back in the name of justice. It seems at least possible that his advantages may be acted upon in such a fashion that they benefit those who are not as well situated as he. In any case, as I shall try to make clear, it seems to me that that should be the focus of our discussions of compensatory justice. My interest is primarily in what individuals, freed from discrimination and domination, can do together to create a more equitable world.

The terrible fact is that social injustice still characterizes this society. In addition, equal attention is not being paid to the individuality of every man and woman. Even when plans are devised for compensating injured groups as groups, there is little concern for the dignity and self-esteem of the persons involved. There is, admittedly, some recognition that amends should somehow be made for unjust discrimination over time, that some compensation is due the victims of inequity. It may be useful to think in terms of what Edmond Cahn calls "the sense of injustice," meaning a response to real or imagined instances of injustice. He writes that all human beings possess the capacity to see injustice to others as personal aggression against themselves. Much depends, however, on whether there can be imaginative identification with the persons who are oppressed. If not, if individuals are "tethered" and remain at a distance from those being victimized, their awareness is dulled. The sense of injustice, then, is a compound of reason and empathy.[32] I believe that it is only as we keep this in mind that something can be done to increase equality while protecting inviolability, taking personal vantage points into account, and extending self-esteem.

Cahn seems to me to be quite right when he says that people do not become outraged when a decision violates some dialectical pattern or an analytic conception of justice. They become outraged when they feel themselves—or someone they can identify with—being treated unfairly. Indeed, ever since the philosopher Hegel pointed it out,[33] there has been a recognition in Western philosophy of the human need to criticize constraints upon experience and to struggle against what is felt as unnecessary domination. At the height of the civil rights campaigns, many white citizens were able to empathize with black people because of the way such great leaders as the Reverend Martin Luther King, Jr., were able to present the struggles to them. They could identify with other human beings who were being brutalized, imprisoned, demeaned, and oppressed. They became capable of reading black literature as well; the novels, the poems made it more and more difficult to remain "tethered," to be indifferent to what was happening to other human beings.

Somewhat the same thing has happened, although far more slowly and ambivalently, where women are concerned. Some men have read such poetry as Dilys Laing's ("Women receive/the insults of men/with tolerance. . . .")[34] or Muriel Rukeyser's ("Praise breakers,/praise the unpraised who cannot speak their name.").[35] They can identify with the potential editor condemned to being a typist, with the woman who cannot get a bank loan, or with the woman refused a job because she might some day have a child. Certain men can even recognize the domination by household tasks, convention, and routines. There developed, therefore, a sense of injustice through imaginative connection with persons being recognizably oppressed. And out of this came a certain willingness to make amends.

Recent preoccupation with the possibility of preferential hiring has changed the focus of the sense of injustice for many people. Tales are told of young male graduate students unable to secure jobs or even interviews for jobs in colleges and universities. They are being passed over, we are told, by women and blacks, often (we are told) far less qualified. To retain their federal contracts, institutions of higher education try to prove their "good faith efforts" by writing fixed numerical goals and then hiring with those goals primarily in mind. The public consequence has been an outraged response to a new kind of victimization. The sense of injustice is now aroused, not by the plight of blacks and women, but by the plight of the young white male—who (more than all others, it is still assumed) *deserve* the fair treatment superiority demands. This accounts for some of the passion aroused by the Bakke case. Yet the fact is, as more and more observers are discovering, that white males are neither being effectively excluded nor removed from faculties. Nor have the percentages of blacks and women risen sufficiently to suggest that the effects of discrimination have been overcome.

Certainly the facts should be made clear. At once it should be recognized that the assumptions and the constructs of our culture are such that injustices cannot be overcome through numerical balancing, nor can they be overcome by means of limited compensations to groups. Whatever costs are involved in attaining equity in hiring should be born by a population larger than the group abruptly non-preferred. Some have suggested that senior and tenured professors should contribute to the cost by agreeing to early retirement or, perhaps, to reductions in salary. This would not only take the onus off the "innocent bystander," who is the white male,[36] it would, to an extent, enlarge the pie. It would, in other words, provide more opportunities and more financial resources, and a few more members (although not all) of the preferred groups might benefit. The question of how this would help the members not hired, or how it would help the entire group, remains open. The question of what this would do to the consciousness and self-esteem of the one hired as a member of a group remains open and troubling as well, even if the one hired is perfectly qualified. And finally there is the life plan of the senior professor; there is the matter of the contribution he or she is capable of making at the moment of full maturity; there is the crucial issue of his or her dignity and self-esteem.

None of the compensatory mechanisms appear to be fair, since each one violates some person's freedom or interferes with a choice of a life. I do not, however, believe that we can return to the kind of color blindness and apparent disregard for gender that perpetuated inequities for so long. Colleges and universities do have to be held accountable in some way. Those responsible for hiring do have to make deliberate efforts to select candidates from every group in the community for interviewing and assessment, even as they maintain what they conceive to be their standards. Personnel and hiring committees such as search committees must be organized with care, so that what has so long been taken for granted does not prevent them from recognizing promise and distinctive quality. Interview questions must be sensitively evaluated so that individuals who have not been members of the "network," not even members of the dominant class, are provided a fair chance to say who they are and what they can do. If at all possible, candidates must be permitted to perform in classrooms so as not to be judged on credentials or appearance alone. All this suggests an increase in self-consciousness on the part of all the persons involved and a capacity to think about what they are doing, to offer good reasons for the decisions they make, to work in accord with principles.

I am not convinced that indirect coercion by federal agencies nurtures this kind of consciousness. Nor am I convinced that intervention by federal agencies is appropriate in academic life. Virginia Black, arguing strongly against reverse discrimination, warns against "short-term policy implants whose function is to coerce the correction of an observed economic imbalance. Social change comes about gradually," she says, "and the only laws that are economically feasible or morally tolerable are those laws that people are ready spontaneously to obey."[37] Not as troubled as Professor Black by the prospect of a rigid class structure emerging from preferential treatment, I am impressed with the notion of people being *ready* to obey, because this suggests the change in consciousness and attitude I believe is required if justice is to be attained. People are "spontaneously ready" when the sense of injustice is aroused. They do not need coercion from without when they can freely identify with individuals endowed in diverse ways and grant them the respect each one requires. Granting such respect, acknowledging the worth of the other, people may be expected to criticize and to refuse unwarranted domination. Seeking their own realization and self-esteem, some may be expected to choose equity and social justice.

But, first, perspectives must change; people must break with what they take for granted. I do not have in mind only traditional notions of merit, hierarchy, and bell-shaped curves. It also seems to me that we must rethink our attitudes towards differential economic rewards. Thomas Nagel, writing on "Equal Treatment and Compensatory Discrimination," says that it may be unjust for larger rewards to be provided for tasks that require superior intelligence. "This is simply the way things work out in a technologically advanced society with a market economy. It does not reflect a social judgment that smart people *deserve* the opportunity to make more money than dumb people." And later:

Justice may require that we try to reduce the automatic connections between material advantages, cultural opportunity, and institutional authority. But such changes can be brought about, if at all, only by large alterations in the social system, the system of taxation, and the salary structure. They will not be achieved by modifying the admissions or hiring policies of colleges and universities. . . .[38]

I am as aware as Dr. Nagel is of the unlikelihood of this degree of change in a competitive society like ours. Nevertheless, it is important for people to examine their assumptions about the relation between money and merit. Do individuals actually deserve the financial rewards they receive for what they do? Does the exchange value given a job of work always match its intrinsic value? Are there not other values for which work can be exchanged—respect, for example, the sense of having contributed to others' welfare?

It seems to me that the question of economic justice ought to be separated from the question of equity in the distribution of employment. If this could be accomplished in fact, it would be possible to think in terms of multiple criteria of relevance where equality of consideration is concerned. There are multiple contributions non-credentialed, *relatively* unqualified persons might make to the lives of universities. Not only is there skill-teaching, there are experiences in the several arts that might be opened up in distinctive ways by persons whose unique perspectives have been too long ignored. There are sociological insights to be shared; there are coping capacities to be taught. I am suggesting that, were it not for the linking of money to levels of traditional achievement, a great range of occupations might become significant possibilities. If there were greater uniformity of reward, many of these occupations would appear more worthy than they presently do and new opportunities for self-definition and self-esteem might be created.

I am not talking about a kind of second-class citizenship within the system, nor am I suggesting that qualified members of minority groups not compete with other qualified individuals for traditional university posts. I am suggesting that the opportunities made available be diversified in the light of an expanded vision of merit and competency, an altered approach to rewards. There is, theoretically, no limit to the kinds of services that might be offered in this society, no limit to the need for services. Whether the capacities tapped are those of an elderly woman able to care for disturbed juveniles, a neighborhood block leader, a blues singer who can tell tales about the past, a ham radio operator, or a motorcycle repair man, they all might be conceived as valuable, just so long as they were valued by persons interested in what they have to give. If, in this society, we can create such openings for those who are now among the least favored, if we can make it possible for them to gain self-esteem, we might come far closer to attaining justice.

I realize that there would still be the appeal of status, even if rewards were equalized; I am quite aware that the colleges and universities would still have to make unprecedented efforts to overcome the biases for which they are now made to pay. I believe, however, that legitimate compensation can only be made if living individuals of all kinds are enabled to contribute to the society's store of talents in the manner most appropriate for each one. But this can only happen, as I have said, if we can break with meritocratic conventions and make self-development a criterion of relevance. It can only happen if, through education and work experiences, consciousness can be altered in our culture—and people can begin opting for diversification, for the end of domination and constraint.

Given the need for attentiveness on the part of colleges and universities where the hiring of qualified women are concerned, I believe that here, too, preferential hiring and reverse discrimination will do harm. I think that institutions should indeed define their goals in this domain, and it may be necessary that these be sometimes numerical goals. But this will not solve the larger problems confronting qualified women whose lives encompass more than their careers. Jill Conway, writing in *Daedalus,* talks about increasing differentials between rewards for male and female work and about the fact that access to higher education has not had real impact on the pattern of female employment. The major problem is, she says, for women to find places at the center of academic institutions that create and transmit the culture of the West.

> On the one hand, to be in command of that culture women must master skills in mathematics and the hard sciences which have traditionally been defined as unfeminine and neglected in the education of females. On the other hand, if these skills in abstract reasoning are to be applied in a manner which draws upon the inner springs of creativity, they must be acquired in a way which is no threat to the female identity. This can be achieved by an educational experience which is critical of many of the assumptions of a male-controlled culture and which takes the female as the norm rather than the deviant exception to the life of the mind. One pre-condition for such a view of intellectual life is a sense of solidarity with female colleagues.[39]

Women's studies will be necessary, she suggests, and cooperative efforts to transform male definitions of scholarly roles. Only, in fact, as male faculty members come to see women as potential leaders who can play a part in reshaping institutions will women begin participating consequentially in decision-making bodies. Dr. Conway sees a danger in government efforts to force affirmative action programs on universities. Forced compliance can lead to purely formal action, like the setting up of low-status programs staffed by women. More seriously, coercion cannot change attitudes towards women anymore than towards members of minority groups. "It is difficult," writes Dr. Conway, "to build a more comprehensive curriculum or a livelier intellectual experience for either sex in . . . a climate of politicization and confrontation."[40]

Again the matter of consciousness is involved. Again stress is placed on the need to break with the customary, the taken-for-granted. It appears evident that thoroughgoing compensatory justice for women scholars demands fundamental changes, not simply in attitudes, institutions, and curricula, but in patterns of social life. As has been said, women have been held back by family obligations; they have suffered from the inevitable delays in the development of their careers. It is neither sufficient nor wholly fair to place a kind of compensatory responsibility on the shoulders of the husbands, for all the importance of overcoming sexism and oppression in the home. If women scholars become disadvantaged in the society of scholars because they have chosen to rear children, justice would seem to require that the society of scholars justify the undeserved advantages entailed in being free, white, and male by applying their expertise to the creation of new socialization patterns for the young. Not only ought there to be excellent day-care centers on college campuses, there ought to be imaginative alternatives to the home-bound family life now demanded of the informed intellectual woman who chooses to raise a number of children when she is young. The burden should not be placed solely on the woman, who knows so well that her male classmates are moving up the academic ladder while she is hard put to find the spare moments needed for keeping in touch with her field. The fact that the woman is normally left to make her own arrangements is testimony to how much is taken for granted where opportunity is concerned. It is *because* disadvantages like these are so seldom questioned that numerical quotas have appeared to be necessary. The discouraging reality is that, where there have been quota systems, women have been hired by committees that would never have considered them before.

Preferential hiring, it appears, can be justified on only the most restricted pragmatic grounds: it *has* worked to benefit certain members of disadvantaged groups who otherwise would have been asked to wait for the day of the just meritocracy. Even if, in particular cases, white males cannot claim to have been deprived of employment in consequence, I cannot—on any reasonable philosophical ground—say that the practice is right. From the vantage point of a principle of justice and from the vantage point of a concern for individuality, I find quotas to be indefensible. Yet I know, as Michael Walzer has pointed out, that "they are likely to be resolutely opposed, opposed without guit and worry, only by people who are entirely content with the class structure as it is and with the present distribution of goods and services." He went on:

> For those of us who are not content, anxiety can't be avoided. We know that quotas are wrong, but we also know that the present distribution of wealth makes no moral sense, that the dominance of the income curve plays havoc with legitimate distributive principles, and that quotas are a form of redress no more irrational than the world within which and because of which they are demanded. In an equalitarian society, however, quotas would be unnecessary and inexcusable.[41]

This suggests the dilemma of the philosopher concerned about what happens to individuals when they are submerged in groups, concerned about the maintenance of standards in universities, and concerned about equity and decency. It suggests the dilemma of the philosopher uneasy with prevailing meritocratic values and aware, as Crane Brinton put it almost forty years ago, that the logical conclusion to be drawn from the principle of equality is something other than meritocracy and *laissez faire*. To bring about the kind of social arrangements in which equality would be meaningful requires collective action, as Brinton said. But, as he also said, the believers in this form of equality are "however, rarely logicians."[42]

All we can hope to do, I think, is to work for increased critical reflection on the unfairness taken for granted for so long. Of course there have to be short-range efforts: more involvement of women and blacks in hiring committees, workable accountability schemes, expansion of curricula, and attention to differential rewards. At the same time, however, work must be done to challenge and to criticize the existing consensus where criteria of relevance are concerned. If we take seriously the idea (as we claim to do) that each person should be treated as an end and never as a means, we have also to think about a plurality of values and a diversity of capacities. Contemplating the emergence of a "service society," we have to consider the range of services human beings can provide—and ascribe value to those not yet included in our hierarchies.

Perhaps, above all, we need to think together about what John Dewey called "the Great Community." Dewey knew well the strength of the forces that work against effective inquiry into the taken-for-granted.[43] He knew the importance of communication and participation by persons moved by their associations with others but not obliterated in those associations. Perhaps we have to think again what unites individuals in a community, in any great community. What is common to them all is their equal inviolability, their integrity as human beings. If we are to be fair and to take affirmative actions that are just, individuality must be cherished as justice is pursued. Dewey wrote that Walt Whitman was the seer of the democracy that this implies. And Whitman wrote:

> I swear I begin to see the meaning of these things,
> It is not the earth, it is not America who is so great,
> It is I who am great or to be great, it is You up there, or any one,
> It is to walk rapidly through civilizations, governments, theories,
> Through poems, pageants, shows, to form individuals.
>
> Underneath all, individuals,
> I swear nothing is good to me now that ignores individuals. . . .[44]

No. Nothing is good that ignores individual perspective and opportunity perceived "as a possibility for self-realization" by a particular individual—black, woman, or young white male—entitled to choose, to pursue his or her fulfillment, to strive towards meaningful goals. Nothing is good that ignores the need for critical reflection on the part of each person affected by social policy, reflection on what he or she understands to be his or her situation, not only in the group but in the social system at large. Affirmative action must become emancipatory action, freely undertaken by women and men, working together to reject irrational and unfair limitations and to remake the inequitable world.

References

1. Alfred Schutz, "Phenomenology and the Social Sciences," in *The Problem of Social Reality,* Collected Papers I, ed. Maurice Natanson (The Hague: Martinus Nijhoff, 1967), p. 136.
2. Schutz, "Equality and the Social Meaning Structure," in *Studies in Social Theory,* Collected Papers II, ed. Arvid Brodersen (The Hague: Martinus Nijhoff, 1964), pp. 271-272.
3. Virginia Black, "The Erosion of Legal Principles in the Creation of Legal Policies," *Ethics,* Vol. 84, No. 2, January 1974, pp. 93-115.
4. See Peter L. Berger and Thomas Luckmann, *The Social Construction of Reality* (Garden City, N.Y.: Anchor Books, 1967).
5. R.S. Peters, *Ethics and Education* (Glenview, Ill.: Scott, Foresman, 1967), pp. 87-88.
6. Ibid., p. 51.
7. John Rawls, *A Theory of Justice* (Cambridge: Harvard University Press, 1972), p. 83.
8. Ibid., pp. 75-78, p. 101.
9. Ibid., p. 28
10. Ibid., p. 95
11. Richard Miller, "Rawls and Marxism," *Philosophy and Public Affairs, Vol. 3, No. 2, Winter 1974, pp. 188-189.*
12. Daniel Bell, *The Coming of Post-Industrial Society* (New York: Basic Books, 1973), p. 445.
13. Ibid., p. 450.
14. Ibid., p. 453.
15. *The New York Times,* January 6, 1975, p. 16.
16. Patricia A. Graham, "Women in Academe," *Science,* Vol. 169, September 25, 1970, p. 1284.
17. See Alice Rossi, "Barriers to the Career Choice of Engineering, Medicine, or Science Among American Women," in *Women and the Scientific Professions: The M.I.T. Symposium on Women and the Scientific Professions* (Cambridge: The M.I.T. Press, 1965); Rossi, "Women in Science: Why So Few?" *Science,* Vol. 148, May 28, 1965, p. 1196; Matina Horner, "The Motive to Avoid Success and Changing Aspirations of College Women," in *Readings on the Psychology of Women,* ed. Judith Bardwick (New York: Harper & Row, 1972).
18. See Judith Stacey, Susan Bereaud, and Joan Daniels, eds., *And Jill Came Tumbling After: Sexism in American Education* (New York: Dell, Laurel Books, 1974).
19. William Moore, Jr., and Lonnie H. Wagstaff, *Black Educators in White Colleges* (San Francisco: Jossey-Bass, 1974), pp. 162-165.
20. Kaplan, "Equal Justice in an Unequal World: Equality for the Negro—the Problem of Special Treatment," in Paul M. Dodyk, gen. ed., *Cases and Materials on Law and Poverty* (St. Paul: West Publishing Co., 1969), p. 482 et seq.

21. Ibid.
22. Quoted in John H. Bunzel, "The Politics of Quotas," *Change,* October 1972, p. 25.
23. Jinny M. Goldstein, "Affirmative Action: Equal Employment Rights for Women in Academia," *Teachers College Record,* Vol. 74, No. 3, February 1973, p. 415.
24. Black, *op. cit.,* p. 96.
25. Vernon E. Jordan, Jr., "Blacks and Higher Education—Some Reflections," *Daedalus:* American Higher Education: Toward an Uncertain Future, Vol. II, Winter 1975, p. 161.
26. Sidney Hook, *New York Times,* November 5, 1971, p. 43.
27. Bell, *op. cit.,* p. 418.
28. Peter E. Holmes, quoted by Albert Shanker in "Strong Voices Against Ethnic Hiring," Where We Stand, *The New York Times,* January 12, 1975, p. 9.
29. See Jurgen Habermas, *Knowledge and Human Interests* (Boston: Beacon Press, 1971).
30. Michael Walzer, "In Defense of Equality," *Dissent,* Autumn 1973, p. 400.
31. Robert Simon, "Preferential Hiring: A Reply to Judith Jarvis Thomson," *Philosophy and Public Affairs,* Vol. 3, No. 3, Spring 1974, pp. 317-318.
32. Edmond N. Cahn, *The Sense of Injustice* (New York: New York University Press, 1949), pp. 24-27.
33. See G.W.F. Hegel, "Independence and Dependence of Self-consciousness: Lordship and Bondage," in *The Phenomenology of Mind,* tr. J.B. Baillie (New York: Harper & Row, 1967), pp. 228-240.
34. Dilys Laing, "Veterans," in *By a Woman Writt,* ed. Joan Goulianos (Indianapolis: Bobbs-Merrill, 1973), p. 328.
35. Muriel Rukeyser, "Ann Burlak," Goulianos, ed., *op. cit.,* p. 366.
36. Simon, *op. cit.,* p. 318.
37. Black, *op. cit.,* p. 105.
38. Thomas Nagel, "Equal Treatment and Compensatory Discrimination," *Philosophy and Public Affairs,* Vol. 2, No. 4, Summer 1973, p. 348.
39. Jill K. Conway, "Coeducation and Women's Studies: Two Approaches to the Question of Woman's Place in the Contemporary University," *Daedalus:* American Higher Education: Toward an Uncertain Future, Vol. I, Fall 1974, p. 241.
40. Ibid., p. 245.
41. Walzer, *op. cit.,* p. 408.
42. Crane Brinton, "Equality," in *Encyclopedia of the Social Sciences,* Vol. 3, 1937, pp. 579-580.
43. John Dewey, *The Public and Its Problems* (Chicago: Swallow Press, 1954), p. 170.
44. Walt Whitman, "By Blue Ontario's Shore," *Leaves of Grass* (New York: Aventine Press, 1931), p. 360.

10

The New Freedom and the Moral Life

LBERT CAMUS once wrote a novel called *The Stranger*[1] about
a young man, a French Algerian, given to drifting indifferent-
ly through his life, making no judgments, scarcely making a
single choice. Meursault has a job that means nothing to him. Once,
when offered a new post in Paris, he refused it because he said he had
no ambition, that "one life was as good as another." In many respects,
his is a good life—full of sunlight, weekend swimming, movies, foot-
ball games, nights with young women. When his mother dies, he gives
no evidence of being particularly disturbed. He takes his girl friend
swimming the day after the funeral and even to a comic movie that
night. He is prone to say things like, "I didn't see why not," or "I
didn't care one way or another." When Marie asks him to marry her,
all he says is that he would if she wanted him to, that it means nothing
anyway.

Living in that fashion—an attractive young man, unconstrained,
he probably is neither happy nor unhappy. Before he kills an Arab on
the beach, for no reason apparently, except that the sun was glaring in
the sky—he clearly was a free man, left alone, with no one stopping
anything he wanted to do, and no one judging what he did do. Of
course, after he kills the Arab, he is confronted with society's
judgment—and sentenced to death, not really because he killed an
Arab, but because he does not feel like pretending to the court that he
grieved for his mother or cried at her funeral. He simply refuses to say
the expected things; he strikes his judges as strange, worse than a par-
ricide, one of them says.

When the prison chaplain comes and asks him to repent,
Meursault is outraged and says that he was absolutely right in the way
he lived his life, that nothing meant anything anyway in the wind of
death that blew from his future, levelling out "all the ideas that people

tried to foist on me. . . . What difference could they make to me, the deaths of others, a mother's love—or God—."[2] Nothing made any difference, he now says, looking back. He has lived a life; he was free.

I want to compare Meursault with another of Camus's characters, Dr. Rieux, in *The Plague,* confronting a terrible epidemic in the town of Oran, a sickness for which there is no cure. Most of the townspeople have resigned themselves to hopelessness, denial, and despair; a few, including Dr. Rieux and his friend Tarrou, have formed sanitary squads to fight the plague—believing it is their duty to do whatever can be done. The narrator writes:

> Many fledgling moralists in those days were going about our town proclaiming there was nothing to be done about it and we should bow to the inevitable. And Tarrou, Rieux, and their friends might give one answer or another, but its conclusion was always the same, their certitude that a fight must be put up, in this way or that, and there must be no bowing down. The essential thing was to save the greatest number of people from dying and being doomed to unending separation. And to do this was only one resource: to fight the plague. There was nothing admirable about this attitude; it was merely logical.[3]

Some time later, when asked why he struggles so hard, when there is so little anyone can do, Dr. Rieux says, "It is a matter of common decency." He does not say, "I didn't care one way or the other," although he might have without being thought strange. He and his friends are not compelled to do what they are doing; they are, in many ways, as free—in the sense of being unconstrained—as Meursault. Since most of the townspeople believe nothing can be done, not even public opinion demands the formation of sanitary squads. Moreover, Dr. Rieux knows as much as Meursault does about the indifference of the sky. He understands that there will always be the danger of plague and that joy will always be imperilled, that there are no guarantees. Nevertheless, he and his friends freely choose to exert themselves and fight the plague. We learn something in time of pestilence, says the doctor, "that there are more things to admire in men than to despise."

It is in the contrast between Meursault's attitude and Dr. Rieux's that I find my theme. I associate an unreflective, sometimes benign and drifting life with what I am arbitrarily calling the "new freedom"; I associate a reflective and committed way of acting with what I am calling the "moral life." I want to stress the fact that the Meursault character or those who in some way resemble him is not, are not evil. He does no harm to anyone deliberately. In addition to that, he is a wholly honest young man—so honest that he will not tell the conventional lies even to save his life. He simply says, quite spontaneously, what he thinks; he acts the way he feels. So he is not, in any traditional sense, a bad man—at least before he kills the Arab (a killing, as you know, without intent).

I also want to stress the fact that Dr. Rieux is not following any absolute code of values; he does not, for example, even mention the Hippocratic Oath. As he himself says, he does not see anything admirable about what he does; it is simply logical—as clear as $1 + 1 = 2$. I see him acting consciously on his freedom, creating values as he lives.

In the decade of the '60s, it was much more natural to talk of the "new freedom." Many of the rebellions that took place were rebellions in the name of freedom: freedom from constraints—from bureaucratic pressures that depersonalized (exemplified, it may be recalled, by IBM cards), from manipulations by the government and the so-called power elite. Because of the war in Vietnam and the nature of the Johnson and Nixon administrations, there tended to be an occasional public merging of what was thought of as the new freedom with what was conceived to be the moral life. In other words, to struggle against the "system" often meant to protest inequity and human suffering, to challenge the hypocrisies of the success-orientation, of materialist or calculative attitudes towards the world. All we need to do is to recall such lyrics as those by Joan Baez and Bob Dylan. In their own idioms, they were calling on the young to break with outmoded authorities in order to fight the plague, whether that plague was in Alabama or Vietnam or in suburban living rooms.

Others, of course, were focally concerned with escaping what they called the rat-race, everydayness, or what was mindlessly expected of them; whether in the guise of hippies or not, they responded to the appeals to drop out and to turn on. Some of you may recall the notion of Consciousness III, invented by Charles Reich in his *The Greening of America*[4]—a mode of consciousness that not only rejected hypocrisy and constraint but intended only benevolence, spontaneity, and joy. It seems evident that, in much of the expression of the last decade, demands for personal liberation were linked to diverse articulations of love and care. In many cases, they were only articulations, generalized expressions of good will that did not necessarily lead to action. But now and then, they *did* lead to action—anti-war and civil rights action, notably—a quiet and committed type of action that the disorders at the end of the decade ought not obscure.

What of today? The war is over; there is no visible civil rights movement any longer; Watergate and its attendant evils lie in the past. Like England's angry young men in the 1950s, many young people believe there are "no causes anymore." Cynicism and the conviction of powerlessness have supplanted the idealisms of the last decade. We are told that economic difficulties have made survival and security the primary goals once more. It seems clear, however, that there has been no turning back to the relative stability of earlier times.

For all the preoccupation with "making it," there is a new restlessness, even an extremism in our culture, not limited to the Northeastern cities or to the West Coast. I have in mind the hunger for violence on television and in film (and I do not believe there would be so much violence if it were not what audiences wanted); there is the rising popularity of pornographic movies and the pornographic press; there is the continuing appeal of drug experiences, a certain taken-for-grantedness, in fact, about the value of various drugs. There is the so-called sexual revolution, which has brought with it a new honesty and candor in relationships, but which has also led to peversities and experiments without precedent in our society. It is hardly necessary to remark the divorce rate, the startling changes in sex-roles in many places, or the alterations in family life, any more than it is necessary to note the crime rate, or the restiveness in our prisons, or the questions being raised about deviance, or the challenges to traditional institutions—hospitals, mental institutions, churches, public schools.

I say all this not because I want to lament the decadence of the time, nor to announce that this is Sodom and Gomorrah all over again. I want to identify the range of options available today in personal life, the increasing range of freedom, as the number of constraints lessens and almost anything becomes possible for the individual, anything in the way of sensory excitement, adventure, self-indulgence, or entertainment for anyone so inclined. There are fewer prejudices, and I dare say there is far less guilt when people choose what was once considered unconventional, immoral, unquestionably wrong. Now I do not believe this is to be regretted; the opening of opportunities is never to be regretted. I certainly would not recommend the rebuilding of old fences, the establishment of curfews, the extension of censorship, or the closing of bars. My concern is not with the closing off of possibilities; it is with the ways in which individuals deal with possibilities, the ways in which they act upon the freedoms made available to them, the ways in which they bring values into their worlds.

It seems to me that the new freedom we are witnessing is linked to a terrible alienation, what used to be called anomie. I think that many, many people are moving through their lives as strangers, in the sense that Meursault was a stranger. They are not reflecting; they are not choosing; they are not judging; in some sense, they have nothing to say.

Those who comment on violence in the media, for example, talk about the need for stimulation and excitement, the need to compensate for the blandness of things; it seems evident that it is those who are drifting pleasantly through the world who are the ones who best know that need. The directors of movies like *The Wild Bunch, Taxi Driver*, and even *The Godfather* have justified their work by saying they were attempting to remove the traditional screens from violence and destruction, to show audiences what killing really means, what shooting and stabbing actually do to human flesh. They did not expect, they said, the enthusiastic reactions of their audiences, the pure delight elicited by brutality, the shouts of approval at imaginatively inflicted pain. This type of response must indicate a vacuum in many people's lives. Their very ability to distance suggests a lack of engagement, of consuming or meaningful concern. To look for thrills of the sort aroused in one by scenes of violence is, in some manner, to submit oneself to extrinsic forces. In this case, they are forces that can be relied upon to work manipulatively on the psyche, to send a beholder out of a theatre feeling drained, shuddering, but at least alive.

There is something of the same sort of desperation in what is being called the "new privatism" or the "new narcissism." Many have written about the contemporary preoccupation with self-improvement. Not only is there a new involvement with physical improvement (through jogging, belly-dancing, gymnastics, and the rest); there continues to be widespread investment in sensitivity-training, encounters of various kinds, evangelical experiences, the disciplines of mysticism. There is nothing inherently harmful about any of these. Most such undertakings, however, have to do with the satisfaction of immediate needs; few rest upon actual face-to-face communication among distinctive individuals trying to interpret their intersubjective lives. Frequently, they are responses to discouragement with the social world as it exists. Sometimes (as in the case of marathon running and certain kinds of mysticism), persons devote themselves to self-mastery, even to a kind of sacrifice. But there appears to be less and less likelihood of emotional commitment. Absorbed in self-perfecting, people begin *not* to care or to prefer *not* to be fully involved outside their circles of private space. Often, this is what is experienced as the "new freedom"; it is the freedom (whatever the costume or the challenge) basically of the stranger, the Meursault.

An impersonality accompanies it. In spite of the degree of steely discipline occasionally seen, there is an overriding passivity. My point is not to moralize, nor is it self-righteously to condemn. The long-distance runner, the practitioner of Zen, the nocturnal meditator can still remain a member, still play a part in the human world. The problem arises when they choose their private passions as alternatives to membership, to existence in community. I am suggesting that, on some level, they may be choosing against the moral life.

The moral life is not necessarily the self-denying life nor the virtuous life, doing what others expect of one, or doing what others insist one ought to do. It can best be characterized as a life of reflectiveness and care, a life of the kind of wide-awakeness associated with full attention to life and its requirements.[5] I have an *active* attention in mind to life in its multiple phases, not the kind of passive attention in which one sits and stares—nor the kind of focalized attention that permits one only to see the track ahead of one or the distant light or the clasping hand. In active attention, there is always an effort to carry out a plan in a space where there are others, where responsibility means something other than transcending one's own speed, or one's own everyday.

A person is not simply located in space somewhere; he or she is gearing into a shared world that places tasks before each one who plays a deliberate part. It is only in a domain of human expectations and responses that individuals find themselves moved to make a recognizable mark, to make a difference that others see. And so they trace out certain dimensions of the common space that are relevant to their concerns: music or painting, repairing machines, caring for children, espousing the cause of the African people (or Chile, or Israel, or human rights), working against pollution, or inspecting dams. In the course of acting in the light of what is taken to be relevant, the individual tests himself or herself, tests his or her potency. This does not have to be undertaken by means of employment in the ordinary sense. And it ought in some way to go beyond the realm of privatism, self-improvement, "narcissism" (although it need not wholly exclude self-mastery in the contemporary vein).

Working, or the diverse modes there are of gearing into the world, can signify many things and, indeed, *ought* to signify many things beyond what we associate with "white collar" or "blue collar" jobs.

To have experiences of carrying projects into effect has to do with being adult. It has to do with dignity and the quest for ways of expressing a vision, defining a commitment—achieving a sense of freedom and responsibility.

It seems eminently clear that the freedom of wide-awakeness has to be expressed in intentional action of some kind. The one who drifts, who believes that nothing matters outside of his or her own self-preservation, can hardly be considered to be free. It is, of course, not sufficient to be formally free, to know one is entitled not to be tampered with, to be protected by law. The possibility of freedom has always to be acted upon; it is grounded in our being what we are and not mere imitators of each other, and so it has continually to be achieved. This cannot happen in a vacuum. Situations must exist or be created that will permit the release of individual capacities, that will permit persons to identify themselves. To identify the self is, in a sense, to understand one's preferences; to understand them is to be able to reflect upon them in the light of some standard, some set of values, some norm. The individual who does not choose, who simply drifts, cannot—from this additional vantage point—be considered free. The one who basks in the sun, with little sense of sharing the world with others, is only barely aware of what he or she prefers. He or she cannot but be indifferent, as Camus's Meursault is indifferent, and indifference, as has often been said, is the opposite of morality. One has to be with others actively, reflectively, at least some of the time, in a space one knows is a shared space, and one has to care.

A kind of critical consciousness is also necessary if people are to overcome all the forces that thrust them into indifference and inertia, the forces assocated with a depersonalized society like our own. We have to come to understand that the reality we inhabit is an interpreted one and that we need to be wary about acceding to what is officially defined, interpreted, and named. We are too seldom challenged to think about the ways in which we have come to understand the meanings of bureaucracy, say, or the federal presence, or clocks, or movie lines, or auditoriums, or the roles of women and men. We have too seldom been asked to think about the ways in which we have learned to order the multiplicity around us, or even whether we have ever been given the right to make our own kind of sense. We have agreed (usually without realizing it) to accede to, to accept not only traditional descriptions of clocks and presidents and church bells, but all sorts of patternings, including those that make our life situations seem solidified, even when they are not (as various oppressed peasants have, and abandoned women, and the sons of successful men). Without under-estimating the efficacy of the modes of domination that abound, we must still hold in mind that, if we knew how to identify openings in our lived situations, if we could actualize what we recognize to be our preferences, we would multiply our occasions for choice.

There are characters like the fictional Mary Hartman at one extreme—people who try with more or less success to accommodate to a landscape of goods and services that in some strange way is confused with what is ultimately real. At the other extreme, there are the millions who are excluded or humiliated, those who have internalized visions of themselves as useless and powerless. They see themselves inhabiting a world permanently dominated by the remote and powerful, a world that seems totally resistant to any sort of meaningful change. "What can you do?" they ask in their multiple languages. "This is the way things are." Such persons can be charitable, generous, wholly decent to each other, even as they can be mean and deceitful (like all other human beings). Many of them (surely those who live in the United States) tend to think of themselves as free. Although they —and the Mary Hartmans—are not necessarily living immoral lives, they are not leading moral lives in the sense I have described. They are simply living, following their bent, acting upon impulse (or not acting), or they are waiting out despair. The most urgent problem in education and politics, it seems to me, is to find ways of arousing such persons to active fellowship—and to active engagements with the world.

Literature is full of enactments having to do with such awakenings, with transitions from half-life to action on the world. Let me offer an extreme example of what may be meant by inaction and what may be meant by the demand that some changes be made. This is from a vignette about a man who built a robot named Charles to instruct him in complacency:

> I called him my friend and thought of him as my friend. . . . He sat there, the perfect concombatant. He ate and drank and slept and awoke and did not change the world. Looking at him, I said to myself, "See, it is possible to live in the world and not to change the world." He read the newspapers and watched television and heard in the night screams under windows thank God not ours but down the block a bit, and did nothing. Without Charles, without his example, his exemplary quietude, I run the risk of acting, the risk of risk. I must participate. I must leave the house and walk about.[6]

The moral life may be achieved through active attention and through walking about among other human beings and through the acknowledgment that signifies responsibility. Even as we demand respect for our formal freedoms and protection from encroachments, we need still to look for more. Somehow, persons must be enabled to discover that they are sometimes able to do something other than what they are doing, that they are even able (at many junctures) to direct the course of their own lives. The ability to act in such a fashion depends to a large degree on the sense of personal agency we associate with autonomy; it depends as well on the capacity to break with the notion that the world around is finished and predefined. It ought to be possible to learn how to identify interstices, openings, spaces in which one can move. It ought to be possible, under diverse circumstances, to learn to identify alternatives.

Autonomous people are the ones who manage to be actively attentive to the world around and aware of what they are choosing when they confront situations in which they *can* perceive alternative courses of action. They are likely to be guided by the principles according to which they—and those with whom they are involved—have freely chosen to live. I have in mind principles like regard for fairness, respect for others, concern for human integrity. There are many persons who live this way, persons who do not have to decide on each occasion how they *ought* to behave. This is because they have chosen, at some time and at some level of their beings, to keep their promises, to listen to others' viewpoints, to respond to requests for help, to do their work as decently as they can.

Without the principle he called "common decency," what would have moved Dr. Rieux to decide to organize sanitary squads? Was he not choosing for human decency, as much as for the reduction of suffering? In Andre Malraux's novel, *Man's Fate,* there is Kyo Gisors, a middle-class scholar, who gives up a life of relative comfort to play some part in a revolution—in order to relieve human pain. "His life had a meaning," he thinks at one point, "and he knew what it was: to give to each of these men whom famine . . . was killing off like a slow plague, the sense of his own dignity."[7] He too is responding to the summons of his conscience, even as he is acting in terms of his own preference, his own personal choice.

The situations in which such choices take place are, quite obviously, social ones; indeed, it is unimaginable for a moral decision to be made outside some realm of social life. A moral decision, ordinarily, is taken between right and right or good and good. (Kyo does not have to decide whether or not to deprive a hungry peasant of his food. He has to decide between the good of scholarship and what he believes to be the good of arming the insurgents for a rebellion yet to come.)

The individual, perceiving a situation as one that offers two or more possible courses of action, has to choose the course that appears to be most desirable, better from as many points of view as the individual can summon up in his or her own mind.

Also, the course finally chosen must not be ruled out by the principles by which that person has chosen to live. Should he or she fight in an unjust war or become a war resister? Should he or she help support a family at home or take advantage of a scholarship that permits a year of study in England? Should a frustrated, talented woman abandon her husband and adolescent child in order to commit herself fully to her sculpture? Should a college admissions officer, confronted by a male and female almost equal in qualifications, select the somewhat less qualified female for the law school class because women have been so poorly treated in time past? Should a young movie maker agree to make her or his film more violent or refuse, at the risk of the job, because of her or his aesthetic (or moral) beliefs? All these situations involve more than one person, and the way in which the individual addresses himself or herself to the process of attending, judging, and choosing will be much affected to the degree he or she is with others, the degree to which he or she has experienced the "we-relation" in the world. Again it must be asserted that care and concern are of the first importance, that they are functions of the capacity to be present to other people, and that this is fundamental to the moral life.

Of course there are determinisms, psychic and socio-economic; every situation restricts the individual to a greater or lesser degree. But the wide-awake person is at least free to confer significance upon his or her situation, to identify the alternatives that exist. He or she is free to posit it as a moral situation, since moral situations do not come so labelled, anymore than alternatives are labelled in advance. The capacity to assess a situation, as has been said, to perceive openings, is essential if there is to be moral action. The incapacity to see a situation as anything but opaque, finished, granite-like, leads to passivity, acquiescence, submergence in a pre-interpreted world.

I would return to *The Plague* in conclusion and recall the situation created by the sickness—a situation that (for "fledgling moralists") left no one free to do anything. As the townspeople saw it, moral consideration simply did not exist. Dr. Rieux and Tarrou, however, posited the situation as one in which there were indeed alternatives, possible courses of action involving conceptions of good and right. It was a situation that struck them as profoundly deficient in many ways. Not only was the plague itself wholly impersonal and random in its attack; not only were the citizens acquiescing in that impersonality.

No human voice was making itself heard; no one was intervening, if only to the extent of saying that there was more to admire in men than to despise. So people were dying unattended, as if indeed they were brutes, as if their deaths did not matter.

If Tarrou and Rieux had not found such a situation unbearable, if they had not already chosen to do something about the plague, they would not have conceived conditions as they did. Because they were so intent on stopping the infection, the impersonality itself became an obstacle to them, as it could not have been if they had not cared so deeply. When Tarrou explains why he cares so much, he speaks of the many decent people who consider their peace of mind more important than a human life. He tells how he had decided to speak and act quite clearly, "since this was the only way of setting myself on the right track. That's why I say there are pestilences and there are victims, no more than that. . . . That's why I decided to take, in every predicament, the victim's side, so as to reduce the damage done. . . ."[8] He explains that he is trying to gain peace and that the only path for attaining peace is the path of sympathy. Like Rieux, he is a person whose chosen end-in-view has already illuminated the situation on which he intends to act, with respect to which he has decided to take a stand.

This, for me, is what freedom ought to signify, this release of human capacity, this power to reflect and to choose. If educators, whoever we are, can become challengers to impersonality in this fashion, challengers to suffering and lack of care, if we can take initiative, we can begin to recreate a space in which meanings can emerge for persons as they take the risk of risking and begin choosing the moral life.

References

1. Albert Camus, *The Stranger* (New York: Vintage Books, 1946).
2. Ibid., p. 152.
3. Camus, *The Plague* (New York: Alfred A. Knopf, 1948), p. 122.
4. Charles A. Reich, *The Greening of America* (New York: Random House, 1970), Chapter IX, pp. 217-263.
5. Alfred Schutz, "On Multiple Realities," in *The Problems of Social Reality, Collected Papers I*, ed. Maurice Natanson (The Hague: Martinus Nijhoff, 1967), p. 113.
6. Donald Barthelme, "Subpoena," *Sadness* (New York: Farrar, Straus and Giroux, 1972), p. 116.
7. Andre Malraux, *Man's Fate* (New York: Modern Library, 1936), p. 70.
8. Camus, *The Plague, op. cit.*, p. 230.

ARTISTIC-AESTHETIC
CONSIDERATIONS

II
Towards Wide-Awakeness:
An Argument for the
Arts and Humanities in Education

I N an ironic account of how he "became an author," Soren Kierkegaard describes himself sitting in the Frederiksberg Garden one Sunday afternoon asking himself what he was going to do with his life. Wherever he looked, he thought, practical men were preoccupied with making life easier for people. Those considered the "benefactors of the age" knew how to make things better "by making life easier and easier, some by railways, others by omnibuses and steamboats, others by telegraph, others by easily apprehended compendiums and short recitals of everything worth knowing, and finally the true benefactors of the age . . . (making) spiritual existence systematically easier and easier. . . ." He decided, he says, "with the same humanitarian enthusiasm as the others," to make things harder, "to create difficulties everywhere."[1]

Writing that way in 1846, Kierkegaard was anticipating what certain contemporary thinkers speak of as a "civilizational malaise" reflecting "the inability of a civilization directed to material improvement—higher incomes, better diets, miracles of medicine, triumphs of applied physics and chemistry—to satisfy the human spirit."[2] He saw the individual subsumed under abstractions like "the Public," lost in the anonymity of "the Crowd." Like others responding to the industrial and then the technological age, he was concerned about depersonalization, automatization, and the bland routinization of life.

Originally published in *Teachers College Record*, Fall 1977.

For him, human reality—the *lived* reality—could only be understood as a difficult, indeed a dreadful freedom. To make things harder for people meant awakening them to their freedom. It meant communicating to them in such a way that they would become aware of their "personal mode of existence,"[3] their responsibility as individuals in a changing and problematic world.

Henry David Thoreau was living at Walden Pond in 1846, and, when he wrote about his experience there, he also talked (in the first person) of arousing people from somnolence and ease. *Walden* also has to do with making life harder, with moving individuals to discover what they lived for. Early in the book, Thoreau writes passionately about throwing off sleep. He talks about how few people are awake enough "for a poetic or divine life." And he asserts that "To be awake is to be alive."[4] He speaks personally, eloquently, about what strikes him to be the requirements of the truly moral life. But he never prescribes; he never imposes his own ethical point of view. The *point* of his kind of writing was not simply to describe a particular experiment with living in the woods; it was to move others to elevate their lives by a "conscious endeavor," to arouse others to discover— each in his or her own terms—what it would mean to "live deliberately."

The theme has been developed through the years as technology has expanded, fragmentation has increased, and more and more people have felt themselves impinged upon by forces they have been unable to understand. As time has gone on, various writers and artists have articulated experiences of being conditioned and controlled. Contemporaneous with the advance of scientific and positivistic thinking, therefore, an alternative tradition has taken shape, a tradition generated by perceptions of passivity, acquiescence, and what Thoreau called "quiet desperation." It is what may now be called the humanist tradition, if the human being is understood to be someone always in search of himself or herself, choosing himself or herself in the situations of a problematic life. There are works of art, there are certain works in history, philosophy, and psychology, that were deliberately created to move people to critical awareness, to a sense of moral agency, and to a conscious engagement with the world. As I see it, they ought—under the rubric of the "arts and humanities"—to be central to any curriculum that is constructed today.

My argument, as has been suggested, has to do with wide-awakeness, not with the glowing abstractions—the True, the Beautiful, and the Good. Like Nick Henry in Ernest Hemingway's *Farewell to Arms,* I am embarrassed by, "Abstract words such as glory, honour, courage, or hallow. . . ."⁵ Wide-awakeness has a concreteness; it is related, as the philosopher Alfred Schutz suggests, to being in the world:

> By the term "wide-awakeness" we want to denote a plane of consciousness of highest tension originating in an attitude of full attention to life and its requirements. Only the performing and especially the working self is fully interested in life and, hence, wide-awake. It lives within its acts and its attention is exclusively directed to carrying its project into effect, to executing its plan. This attention is an active, not a passive one. Passive attention is the opposite to full awareness.⁶

This goes beyond ordinary notions of "relevance" where education is concerned. Schutz is pointing out that heightened consciousness and reflectiveness are meaningful only with respect to human projects, human undertakings, not in a withdrawal from the intersubjective world. He is also pointing out that human beings define themselves by means of their projects and that wide-awakeness contributes to the creation of the self. If it is indeed the case, as I believe it is, that involvement with the arts and humanities has the potential for provoking precisely this sort of reflectiveness, we need to devise ways of integrating them into what we teach at all levels of the educational enterprise; we need to do so consciously, with a clear perception of what it means to enable people to pay, from their own distinctive vantage points, "full attention to life."

It is, at least on one level, evident that works of art—*Moby Dick,* for instance, a Hudson River landscape painting, Charles Ives' *Concord Sonata*—must be directly addressed by existing and situated persons, equipped to attend to the qualities of what presents itself to them, to make sense of it in the light of their own lived worlds. Works of art are, visibly and palpably, human achievements, renderings of the ways in which aspects of reality have impinged upon human consciousness. What distinguishes one art form from another (music from poetry, say, the dance from painting) is the *mode* of rendering, the medium used, and the qualities explored. But all art forms must be encountered as achievements that can only be brought to significant life when human beings engage with them imaginatively.

For all the distinctiveness of the arts, there is a characteristic they share with certain kinds of history. I have in mind, as an example, Edward Hallett Carr's conception of history as dialogue. Carr talks about the historian's provisional interpretations of provisionally selected facts and about the subtle changes that take place through the "reciprocal action" of interpretation and the ordering of those facts.

And this reciprocal action also involves reciprocity between present and past, since the historian is part of the present and the facts belong to the past. The historian and the facts of history are necessary to each other. The historian without his facts is rootless and futile; the facts without their historians are dead and meaningless. My first answer therefore to the question, What is history?, is that it is a continuous process of interaction between the historian and his facts, an unending dialogue between the present and the past.[7]

What is striking here is the emphasis on selecting, shaping, and interpreting, the ordering of raw materials according to distinctive norms. The process itself is not unlike the process of art-making. The crucial difference is that the historian is in quest of truth, in some degree verifiable, while the artist strives for coherence, clarity, enlargement, or intensity.

Even more important: in the aesthetic experience, the mundane world or the empirical world must be bracketed out or in some sense distanced, so that the reader, listener, or beholder can enter the aesthetic space in which the work of art exists. Captain Ahab's manic search for the white whale cannot be checked in any history of the whaling industry; its plausibility and impact have little to do with a testable truth. Thomas Cole's painting, "The Ox-Bow," may look in some way like the river, but, if it is not encountered as a drama of color, receding planes, and light, it will not be experienced as a work of art. A historical work—Thucydides' *The Pelopponesian War,* John B. Bury's *The Idea of Progress,* or Richard Hofstadter's *The Age of Reform*—refers beyond itself to events in time past, to the changing situations in humankind's ongoing experience, to whatever are conceived to be the "facts."

Most significant of all, however, is the possibility that these histories, like Carr's own history, can involve their readers in dialogue. Reading any one of them, readers or students cannot but be cognizant of a distinctive individual behind the inquiry. They cannot but gain a sense of a living human being posing questions to the past from his own standpoint and the standpoints of those he chooses to be his fellow-historians, working at different moments in time. Students may well come upon the insight Jacob Burckhardt describes when he speaks of history as "the break with nature caused by the awakening of consciousness."[8] They may begin, from their own vantage points to confer significance on moments in the past, to push back the horizons of the meaningful world, to expand the scope of lived experiences. Maurice Merleau-Ponty, speaking of what this kind of awareness can mean, writes, "My life must have a significance which I do not constitute; there must be strictly speaking an intersubjectivity.... "[9] Engaging with the kind of history I have been describing, individual human beings can locate themselves in an intersubjective reality reaching backwards and forwards in time.

These are the reasons why I would include certain works of history in an arts and humanities program—works that provoke wide-awakeness and an awareness of the quest for meaning, which has so much to do with feeling alive in the world. I would exclude from the program (although not from the total curriculum) mathematicized or computerized history, exemplified by, say, *Time on the Cross.*[10]

I would approach my choices in philosophy, criticism, and psychology in the same fashion: those works that engage people in posing questions with respect to their own projects, their own life situations. William James, John Dewey, George Herbert Mead, George Santayana, Alfred North Whitehead, Jean-Paul Sartre, Maurice Merleau-Ponty: these, among the modern philosophers, are likely to move readers to think about their own thinking, to risk examination of what is presupposed or taken for granted, to clarify what is vague or mystifying or obscure. To "do" philosophy in this fashion is to respond to actual problems and real interests, to the requirements of sense-making in a confusing world. It may also involve identification of lacks and insufficiencies in that world—and some conscious effort to repair those lacks, to choose what *ought* to be. Some of the humanistic or existential psychologies may function similarly as they engage students in dialogue about what it is to be human, to grow, to *be*.

If the humanities are indeed oriented to wide-awakeness, if dialogue and encounter are encouraged at every point, it might be possible to break through the artificial separations that make interdisciplinary study so difficult to achieve. If students (and their teachers as well) are enabled to pose questions relevant to their life plans and their being in the world, they might well seek out answers in free involvement with a range of disciplines. Once this occurs, new perspectives will open up —perspectives on the past, on cumulative meanings, on future possibilities.

The important thing is for these perspectives to be sought consciously and critically and for meanings to be perceived from the vantage points of persons awake to their freedom. The arts are of focal significance in this regard, because perceptive encounters with works of art can bring human beings in touch with themselves. Jean-Paul Sartre writes that literature addresses itself to the reader's freedom:

For, since the one who writes recognizes, by the very fact that he takes the trouble to write, the freedom of his readers, and since the one who reads, by the mere fact of his opening the book, recognizes the freedom of the writer, the work of art, from whichever side you approach it, is an act of confidence in the freedom of men. [11]

I believe this may be said, in essence, about all the arts. Liberating those who come attentively to them, they permit confrontations with the world as individuals are conscious of it, *personally* conscious, apart from "the Crowd."

I would want to see one or another art form taught in all pedagogical contexts, because of the way in which aesthetic experiences provide a ground for the questioning that launches sense-making and the understanding of what it is to exist in a world. If the arts are given such a central place, and if the disciplines that compose the humanities are at the core of the curriculum, all kinds of reaching out are likely. The situated person, conscious of his or her freedom, can move outwards to empirical study, analytic study, or quantitative study of all kinds. Being grounded, he or she will be far less likely to confuse abstraction with concreteness, formalized and schematized reality with what is "real." Made aware of the multiplicity of possible perspectives, made aware of incompleteness and of a human reality to be pursued, the individual may reach "a plane of consciousness of highest tension." Difficulties will be created everywhere, and the arts and humanities will come into their own.

References

1. Soren Kierkegaard, "Concluding Unscientific Postscript to the 'Philosophical Fragments,' " in *A Kierkegaard Anthology,* ed. Robert Bretall (Princeton: Princeton University Press, 1947), p. 194.
2. Robert Heilbroner, *An Inquiry into The Human Prospect* (New York: W.W.Norton, 1974), p. 21.
3. Kierkegaard, *The Point of View for My Work as An Author,* ed. Benjamin Nelson (New York: Harper Torchbooks, 1962), pp. 44-53.
4. Henry David Thoreau, *The Variorum Walden* (New York: Washington Square Press, 1963), pp. 66-67.
5. Ernest Hemingway, *A Farewell to Arms* (London: Jonathan Cape, 1952), p. 186.
6. Alfred Schutz, *The Problem of Social Reality,* in Collected Papers I, ed. Maurice Natanson (The Hague: Martinus Nijhoff, 1967), p. 213.

7. Edward Hallett Carr, *What Is History?* (New York: Alfred A. Knopf, 1967), p. 35.
8. Jakob Burckhardt, *Reflections on History* (London: George Allen & Unwin, 1959), p. 31.
9. Maurice Merleau-Ponty, *Phenomenology of Perception* (London: Routledge & Kegan Paul, 1962), p. 448.
10. Robert William Fogel and Stanley L. Engerman, *Time on the Cross: The Economics of Negro Slavery* (Boston: Little, Brown, 1974).
11. Jean-Paul Sartre, *Literature and Existentialism* (New York: Citadel Press, 1965), p. 63.

12

The Artistic-Aesthetic
and Curriculum

A god can do it. But how shall a man, say,
get to him through the narrow lyre and follow?
His mind's dichotomy. Where two heartways
cross there stands no temple for Apollo.

Song, as you explain it, is not passion,
not striving for some end at last attained;
song is Being. Easy for gods to fashion.
But when shall we be? *And when will he bend*

the earth and stars upon our being? Youth,
it is not that you are in love; although
the voice bursts your mouth open, you must find

how to forget your rash song. That will go.
It is another breath that sings the truth.
A breath round nothing. A gust in the god. A
  wind.

Rainer Maria Rilke
(from *Sonnets to Orpheus)*

I WANT to talk about a different kind of breathing in the realization that many of the songs we have sung in the past have been to no avail. "Song," Rilke wrote in the poem, ". . . is not passion, nor striving for some end at last attained." That may suggest some of the reasons; clearly, there are many more. I am focally concerned with what has happened to our society over the past 30 years, with what Robert Heilbroner calls the "civilizational malaise"[1] that now afflicts us with oppressiveness and manipulation, with the lying

---

Originally published in *Curriculum Inquiry.* Volume 6, Number 4, 1977.

that goes on in public,[2] with the institutionalization of "benign neglect." All this leads me to a preoccupation with ways of moving young people to self-reflectiveness and critical awareness. Perhaps it is a preoccupation with rebellion in Albert Camus's sense. He said that, "Rebellion, in man, is the refusal to be treated as an object and to be reduced to simple historical terms. It is the affirmation of a nature common to all men, which eludes the world of power."[3] And then he said that rebellion in its purest form can be found in the activity of art, because artistic creation "rejects the world on account of what it lacks and in the name of what it sometimes is."[4]

My intention here is to focus on the part the artistic-aesthetic might play in contemporary curriculum; it is an intention informed by a concern much like Camus's—a concern for refusals and recreations, for the reconstruction of the world. My desire to do this does not simply stem from belief in the intrinsic value of the arts, in the good of fulfillments and consummations. It derives as well from a sense of the anaesthetic character of so many institutions in our culture, including schools. It derives from a sense of social structures and explanatory systems pressing down on human beings and rendering them passive: gazers, not see-ers; hearers, not listeners. Questions about the arts and perceptive encounters with the arts at least have the potential, it seems to me, of arousing persons to what Alfred Schutz called "wide-awakness," defined as "a plane of consciousness of highest tension originating in an attitude of full attention to life and its requirements."[5] The very asking of such questions, the very exploration of ways of fostering such encounters (and, indeed, the investigation of what such encounters *are*) may well open new perspectives on what it is to learn and what it is to see. One-dimensional viewing may be surpassed; so may notions of the self-evidence, the *given*-ness of things. Like Maurice Merleau-Ponty, I am concerned with finding a mode of thinking, a mode of sense-making that "is as painstaking as the works of Balzac, Proust, Valèry, or Cezanne—by reason of the same kind of attentiveness and wonder, the same demand for awareness, the same will to seize the meaning of the world or of history as that meaning comes into being."[6] Curriculum, to me, ought to be a means of providing opportunities for the seizing of a range of meanings by persons open to the world, especially today.

My feeling of urgency about this comes from a number of assumptions I make, all having to do with the character and impact of what is called "the advanced industrial society."[7] One is that our schools, although always prone to serve the interests of whatever social and economic institutions have been dominant, stand in a somewhat different relation to the culture than they did in time past. This is partly because of the many competing modes of socialization: television, rock music, peer group life, training programs, and experiences on the streets, in clinics, welfare offices, agencies, and the rest. It is partly because of changing attitudes towards the schools and what they are expected to achieve in the lives of children. Conservative and radical critiques have altered expectations, as they have eroded confidence in the efficacy of schools.

The so-called "marginality"[8] of public education is taken for granted in diverse ideational contexts; as support declines, the function of the schools is more and more narrowly conceived. For different reasons, revisionist critics[9] and establishment report writers have called upon schools to focus mainly upon skill-teaching, on the "basics," perhaps, on "competencies," and to leave other kinds of learning to the work-places, the informal networks, the world outside the walls. One consequence of this may be that, as attention concentrates on the technical and the behavioral, the so-called "hidden curriculum" will become all the more potent, because its component precepts and values will be more effectively excluded from what is taken to be acceptable classroom talk. I am not absolutely sure what the primary interests in society are as they now affect that hidden curriculum, but I am fairly sure they have to do with what Daniel Bell calls "functional rationality"[10] and with the extension of technocratic controls. I am fairly sure that the "regulative mode" Bell describes as "economizing"[11] sustains and perhaps justifies the unequal distribution of knowledge, as I am convinced that the response to Robert Nozick's recommendation of a "minimal state" based on what is called "entitlement"[12] embodies a desire to perpetuate (and to legitimate) existing inequalities. I am struck by the liberal rejection of John Rawls's conception of justice and especially by the bland setting aside of the view that "a confident sense of their own worth" ought to be sought for the "least favored."[13]

It appears evident that feelings of powerlessness and hopelessness are increasing among the excluded and the poor; it seems equally evident that *ennui,* the "boredom and vacuity" that have haunted so much of modern experience,[14] afflicts more and more of the privileged young. I believe that these are the moods evoked by the messages of present-day society, moods that can only lead to further apathy, inaction, and despair. Largely because of the influence of technocratic or "efficiency" approaches on the schools, messages of this sort (often embedded, of course, in the "positive images" so insistently purveyed by the media) are not being articulated, confronted, or subjected to critique. They are far more complex, far more mystifying, far more manipulative than the statements about social ills that motivated critical thinking in the past. The consequence of uncritical absorption of such messages seems to me to be acquiescence of withdrawal, a submission to official renderings of what is right and what is real. What Paulo Freire called a "culture of silence"[15] is in some sense transmitted in the schools—perhaps through neglect, perhaps through design. And this is what I think we have to look at; this is what I think "a different kind of breathing" might transform.

John Dewey wrote that the uniqueness of aesthetic experience is "a challenge to that systematic thought called philosophy";[16] and I would choose to think of it as a challenge to many kinds of linear, positive thinking, as well as to the taken-for-grantedness of much of what is taught. Dewey called aesthetic experience, you will recall, "experience in its integrity . . . experience freed from the forces that impede and confuse its development as experience."[17] He was, of course, fundamentally interested in the ways in which works of art concentrated and enlarged immediate experiences, in the ways in which they moved people to an imaginative ordering and reordering of meanings, to the effecting of connections, to the achieving of continuities. He spoke in various ways of the "gap between the here and now of direct interactions whose funded result constitutes the meanings with which we grasp and understand what is now occurring." And he went on: "Because of this gap, all conscious perception involves a risk; it is a venture into the unknown, for as it assimilates the present to the past it also brings about some reconstruction of that past."[18]

Because of the importance of ordering and reconstructing, Dewey thought of the aesthetic experience as paradigmatic; not surprisingly, many theorists of curriculum have turned to the artistic-aesthetic when they wished to incorporate notions of organic development, coherence, and consummations. They have turned to the artistic-aesthetic when they have wished to enrich their conceptions of cognition by pointing to what Dewey described as *felt* qualitativeness, the "underlying unity of qualitativeness (which) regulates pertinence or relevancy and force of every distinction and relation. . . ."[19] There is no question that this remains important, especially for those centrally concerned about breaking with the mechanical, the sporadic, the routine, and those concerned with challenging splits between ends and means.

We need to go further today, I believe. The uniqueness of the artistic-aesthetic ought to be reaffirmed, as the problematic of art ought to be recognized and explored. Consider Jean-Paul Sartre, for instance. He has often talked about the changing nature of reality and about the dangers of fixity. In one of his prefatory essays, he has written:

> It is the artist who must break the already crystallized habits which make us see in the *present* tense those institutions and customs which are already out of date. To provide a true image of our time, he must consider it from the pinnacle of the future which it is creating, since it is tomorrow which will decide today's truth. . . . I have always thought that nothing was sillier than those theories which try to determine the mental level of a person or of a group. There is no such level; to be "his age" for a child, is to be simultaneously below and above that age. The same is true of our habits of intellect and feeling. "Our senses have an age of development which does not come from the immediate environment but from the moment of civilization," Matisse wrote. Yes, and reciprocally, they go beyond this moment and perceive confusedly a crowd of objects which will be seen tomorrow; they discern another world in this one. But this is not the result of some sort of prophetic gift: the contradictions and conflicts of the era stimulate them to the point of bestowing upon them a sort of double vision. Thus is it true that a work of art is at the same time an individual achievement and a social fact.[20]

There are notable differences between this point of view and Dewey's, for all the fact that both Sartre and Dewey have treated the problem of fixity. For one thing, Sartre emphasizes the unique function of the artist and the work of art, a function that cannot be subsumed under whatever is understood to be the aesthetic experience. For another, in contrast to Dewey's emphasis on the present and the reconstruction of the past in the light of the present, Sartre's stress is on the reconstruction of the present in the light of future possibility. Dewey, it is true, talked of ideals being framed "out of the possibilities of existing conditions" and of those ideals gaining content "as they operate in remaking conditions"[21] but, as is well known, his focus was on process, on continuing alterations of tension and resolution, on open-ended growth. The going beyond, the intimations suggested in Sartre's writing have to do with the identification of lacks in present situations, with the struggle to surpass, with the transformation of the world.

It may be that one point of view need not negate the other; in any case, my present point has to do with the relevance of a conception of futuring for a viewing of the artistic-aesthetic in relation to curriculum. Futuring relates, for me, to the critical consciousness I would like to stimulate, as it does to the attentiveness and "the will to seize the meaning of the world" of which Merleau-Ponty spoke. This is because the "double vision" evoked in artists by their awareness of contradictions, the *possibilizing* they become capable of, give their works the power to disclose present insufficiencies to the consciousness of those they address. In another place, Sartre has written that people can never conceive the failures and lacks of their historical situation if they are immersed in it. They can only acknowledge the harshness of their situation, he said, "on the basis of what is not." And then: "It is on the day that we can conceive of a different state of affairs that a new light falls on our troubles and our suffering and that we *decide* that these are unbearable."[22] I want to argue that encounters with the arts can lessen the immersion we see around us today and that they may do so by enabling people to break through the horizons of the ordinary, of the taken-for-granted, to visions of the possible, of "what is not."

I am not suggesting that the fostering of aesthetic experiences is the single way or even the primary way of opening critical perspectives. My conception of the relation of aesthetic meanings to the diverse and integrated meanings that make up each human being's life-world stems in part from Alfred Schutz's view of "multiple realities." Schutz wrote that, "It is the meaning of our experiences . . . which constitutes reality"[23] and went on to discuss the various provinces of meaning he associated with different sets of experiences. These provinces, these "worlds," are distinguished from each other by the cognitive style or the mode of attention peculiar to each one. "All these worlds—the world of dreams, of imageries and phantasms, especially the world of art, the world of religious experience, the world of scientific contemplation, the play world of the child . . . are finite provinces of meaning. . . . The passing from one to the other can only be performed by a 'leap', as Kierkegaard calls it, which manifests itself in the subjective experience of a shock." The shock, he explained, "is nothing else than a radical modification in the tension of our consciousness, founded in a different *attention a la vie.*"[24] These shocks, these shifts of attention, make it possible to see from different standpoints; they stimulate the "wide-awakeness" so essential to critical awareness, most particularly when they involve a move to the imaginary—away from the mundane.

The curriculum, as I see it, may be regarded as a number of provinces of meaning, each one associated with the kinds of experiences available to young people of different ages, with different biographies, and different locations in the social world. Our concern in teaching, it seems to me, is to enable our students to interpret these experiences, to acquaint them with and free them to reflect upon the range of cognitive styles. Again, the world of art can be considered to be one of the worlds, one of the provinces of meaning, with which the young become engaged.

How are we to understand the uniqueness of this finite province? How are we to understand the nature of aesthetic involvement? It is undoubtedly clear that my philosophical orientation is existential phenomenological, that my views of art and the aesthetic experience are much affected by my understanding of the existing person in his or her relation to social reality. Nevertheless, there are crucial questions to be raised, questions for which theories of art can serve as pointers; I have in mind traditional theories as well as phenomenological views. If these questions are not confronted, too much may be taken for granted about such matters as form and content, sensuousness, emotivity, and import, not to speak of what Joyce's Stephen Dedalus calls "wholeness, harmony, and radiance,"[25] or what Susanne Langer describes as "virtual realities."[26] If all these things are taken for granted, debate ceases; reflectiveness becomes unlikely; the necessary "shock" is dulled.

Morris Weitz, speaking from quite another philosophic vantage point, seems to me to be saying something relevant in this regard when he remarks that, even though theories of art fail when it comes to defining art, aesthetic theory cannot be called worthless:

> Indeed, it becomes as central as anything in aesthetics, in our understanding of art, for it teaches us what to look for and how to look at it in art. What is central and must be articulated in all the theories are their debates over the reasons for excellence in art—debates over emotional depth, natural beauty, exactitude, freshness of treatment, and so on, as criteria of evaluation—the whole of which converges on the perennial problem of what makes a work of art good. To understand the role of aesthetic theory is not to conceive it as definition, logically doomed to failure, but to read it as summaries of seriously made recommendations to attend in certain ways to certain features of art.[27]

I appreciate the insistence that "art" be treated as an open concept, and, although I do not share Weitz's commitment to conceptual analysis, I respond to his emphasis on the "expansive, adventurous character of art."[28] Because I would relate his various proposals to processes of self-understanding on the part of individuals actually experiencing art, I see his stress on the need to *attend* as leading into an ongoing hermeneutic (a term he would never use). His approach helps me hold in mind problems having to do with the relation between structures and existing individuals living in historical time. It helps me hold in mind the place of critical choosing when it comes to generating the meanings in particular works of art and discovering the light thrown by such meanings on existence, and on what human beings identify as their "world." I am suggesting that, if we want the arts to help in disclosures and to promote critical awareness, if we want students to experience the "radical modification in the tension of consciousness" that enables them to see what they would not otherwise see, we surely need (as we make a wide range of art forms available) to keep the questions open and alive.

Aesthetics, after all, involves an exploration of the questions arising when people become self-reflective about their engagements with art forms. They may wonder about the pleasure and pain certain engagements arouse, about their perceptions of beauty, horror, harmony, about the peculiar queries that rise up in them because of things read or seen. The burning questions, the significant questions probably arise after privileged moments of encounter with works of art. The *content* of such questions may well be derived from theory.

Morris Abrams' categorization of the theories that have been devised[29] is provisional; it is a useful one, because he treats them as overlapping perspectives, each one revealing dimensions of the artistic-aesthetic rather than defining it for all time. The four poles of his schema are: universe, artist, work of art, and audience. The classical theory draws attention to the relation between the work and the universe. Invented by Aristotle,[30] this mimetic theory explains a work of art as an imitation, a rendering of the essence of some universal phenomenon. *Oedipus Rex,* Aristotle explained, was a great work because it presented the *form* of a human plight. He did not mean that the tragedy was a realistic version of something that had actually happened to the "representative man." The play, by presenting the misfortunes Oedipus brought upon himself in his calculativeness and pride, revealed something essential about the human condition. It aroused "pity and terror," then, among those who shared in that condition.[31] They found pleasure in it, because they learned something fundamental; people find pleasure in learning, as they do in catharsis, or so Aristotle believed.

Shakespeare's *Hamlet* functions in the same way; it also holds within it a version of the mimetic idea. Not only does Hamlet speak of a play holding "a mirror up to nature, to show virtue her own feature, scorn her own image, and the very age and body of the time his form and pressure,"[32] he instructs Horatio at the end to draw his breath in pain—and "tell my story," a story that can only be the form of the human story, giving Horatio "cause to speak."

Why does that move us? When Hamlet speaks, earlier, about the "brave, o'erhanging firmament" appearing nothing to him "but a foul and pestilent congregation of vapors" and about man ("How noble in reason! how infinite in faculties!") appearing nothing to him but the "quintessence of dust,"[33] how do we explain the feeling of import, of disillusionment we derive? In *King Lear,* Gloucester cries out: "As flies to wanton boys, are we to the gods;/They kill us for their sport."[34] What accounts for the feeling of startled recognition many report? After confronting da Vinci's *The Last Supper,* a Michelangelo *Pieta,* Beethoven's Ninth, or *Moby Dick,* we may find ourselves pondering the vast sadness we experience, or the awe, or the exaltation. Is the sense of import attributable to coming in touch with something "out there" in the cosmos? Or have we been made abruptly conscious of something fundamental to the human condition under the sky? To what degree does greatness in art depend upon the self-transcedence certain forms make possible? What of forms that disclose wastelands to us, emptiness? What of the derelict in *Waiting for Godot,* confiding to his friend, "There's no lack of void."?[35]

Expressivist theories, developed in response to the lyrical preoc-cupations of the Romantic period, hold pointers to modes of thinking about art works as the utterances of individual artists. Wordsworth's "Tintern Abbey," Keats's "Ode to the West Wind," Constable's paint-ings of the Stour Valley, or Liszt's piano concertos are talked about as expressions of feeling imaginatively transmuted into form. Art, Col-eridge once said, originated in the primitive utterances of human pas-sion, not in a desire to imitate great representative forms. Word-sworth, defining poetry as "emotion recollected in tranquillity,"[36] shaped the stuff of his memories and perceptions as he tried to recap-ture "the growth of a poet's mind."[37] Turner, Berlioz, and Victor Hugo spoke on occasion of their works as embodiments of material related to their inner lives, communicated by means of an organization of sensual elements: sounds, colors, contours, waving lines. "We com-monly do not remember that it is, after all, always the first person that is speaking," wrote Thoreau. "I should not talk so much about myself, if there were any body else whom I knew as well."[38] "It is time to explain myself," sang Whitman, "—let us stand up."[39] In a different mood, with a heightened sense of tension about the "I," Baudelaire addressed himself to his reader, trying to arouse that reader to an awareness of his own "folly and error, avarice and vice." At the end, there is the following:

> Boredom! He smokes his hookah, while he dreams of gibbets, weeping tears he cannot smother. You know this dainty monster, too, it seems —Hypocrite reader!—You!—My twin!—My brother![40]

Suddenly we are accomplices in an ironic division of the self; we, too, have to break through inauthenticity, bad faith. Dostoyevsky, not much later, exposed some of the anguish of such an effort when he created the *persona* of the "underground man" wrestling with paradox and doubt:

> I'll explain it to you: I derived pleasure precisely from the blinding realization of my own degradation; because I felt I was already up against the wall; that it was horrible but couldn't be otherwise; that there was no way out and it was no longer possible to make myself into a different person; that even if there were still enough time and faith left to become different, I wouldn't want to change myself; and that, even if I wanted to, I still wouldn't have done anything about it, because, actually, there wasn't anything to change into.[41]

In our own time, most people seem to think of art as expressive of feelings, nightmares,[42] forbidden fantasies, lust. They think of art forms as communicating a type of non-conceptual awareness, not always "civilized," but tapping the realm of what Susanne Langer describes as "sentiency,"[43] a subjective domain propositions cannot express. Yet they also realize, sometimes vaguely, that expressiveness can only occur when events or objects are patterned in some distinctive fashion, when form and content are no longer separated, when language and events (in the case of literature) interpenetrate, when color creates contour in painting, when somehow there is a need for prehension of an embodiment rather than a need to go behind it or beyond. So the work itself is *intended* by the consciousness of a living being in search of his or her own expression, his or her own being, and new questions rise.

Mysteriously, persons come to perceive differences between a created form and a represented one, between a photograph of Salisbury Cathedral and a Constable painting of the same cathedral against the clouds, between a newspaper picture of a distraught woman and a Munch rendering of a woman in distress, between a historical account of the Shanghai Revolution in 1927 and André Malraux's *Man's Fate*. But how can we *know* what Munch is expressing, what Mahler is saying in his *Song of the Earth,* what private perceptions Martha Graham is embodying in her *Lamentations?* How can we identify what is being communicated, the intention or the anguish or even the delight that gave rise to the making of the form? How can we judge a work we take to be expressive of a person's innerness? By its "truth," its sincerity, its coherence with the artist's corpus of work? How do we distinguish such a work from one that asserts a kind of self-sufficiency: a Minimalist painting or a piece of serial music or an abstract ballet?

Many makers and interpreters of contemporary art forms still focus on their self-sufficiency; they treat works of art as "significant forms,"[44] interesting, even fascinating for their own sake. Viewed through such a perspective, works of art inhabit a domain distinct from that of ordinary life. Art itself imposes a kind of aesthetic framework that removes the life of the poem or the sonata or the sculpture from the common-sense world. Because it does, those who listen or behold or read are required to attend to the qualities of the work in question, to attend to it on its own terms. The aesthetic function is considered to be the dominant one, not some cognitive purpose or moral intention or revelation of feeling, perception, or point of view. Some would insist that all works of art, no matter what is claimed about their representativeness or expressiveness, ought to be encountered in this way. They assert that Edward Albee's *Who's Afraid of Virginia Woolf?* ought to be granted the same autonomy as his *Seascape,* that *Notes from Underground* creates as independent and as "unreal" a world as *A Portrait of the Artist as a Young Man* or William Butler Yeats's "Byzantium." Encountering any one of these, we are asked to set aside what we know of the artist's biography, even what we know of his cultural moment, because these are external to the work and distract from the detached "noticing" required if appreciation is to occur. But, if a work of art has been made for someone to *have* it as an intentional object, can the experience with it be entirely hermetic? What would it mean to perceive a work for itself alone? How much of life-history can be bracketed out in the apprehension of a work of art? "Poetry makes nothing happen. . . ." wrote Auden;[45] "A poem should not mean, but be," wrote Archibald MacLeish.[46] Can such comments be generalized? What do they signify for our appreciation of art forms?

There is, finally, the kind of theory that focuses upon the response to a work of art in order to account for it, or to account for the importance of the aesthetic mode in human life. Like the other theories, this one cannot overlook the other aspects of the artistic-aesthetic; since it would be as meaningless to talk about aesthetic involvement without considering an event or object that commands such involvement, as it would be to talk about such involvement without presuming the existence of an intended world. What is the role of perception, for instance, in the bringing into being of a work of art? Of cognition? Of detached contemplation? What bearing does the biography of the beholder have on his or her involvement with a work? Is any work of art susceptible to instant apprehension, or does it have to be gradually achieved? Does an encounter with a work involve, as Schutz suggested, a sharing of another's "flux of experiences in inner time . . . living through a vivid present in common. . .a mutual tuning-in relationship. . .?"[47] Or, as it does for Henry James' Isabel Archer, does it promise an opportunity "to feel the continuity between the movement of (one's) own soul and the agitations of the world"?[48] Or should we follow E.M. Forster's Margaret Schlegel, who objects so vehemently to labelling music with meanings, who demands that music be treated simply as music—and every other art form in terms of what it is?[49]

I do not propose such questioning in an eclectic state of mind, in the belief that one particular perspective must be chosen and one alone. Again, these theories suggest ways of attending; no one of them explains or defines (in a manner that would apply to all artistic phenomena everywhere) the *essence* of art. Nor do I believe that precisely the kinds of questions I have asked should be asked in every classroom, in the hope that—if they are asked—young people will become more aware of how art means and what it signifies in human life. I do think that curriculum theorists and teachers, however, ought to frame such questions for themselves and that the sense of open questions ought to pervade the teaching of art. The alternative, as I see it, is to reify the very notion of art, to confuse it with provinces of meaning that do not refer in the same way to *lived* experience. History, for instance, or the sciences depend a great deal on principles of explanation; to enter into their provinces demands a mastery of certain protocols, sometimes certain techniques, certain norms of inquiry. It is true that, in order to penetrate and to realize a work of art, individuals must be equipped with a degree of cognitive understanding: they ought

to have some acquaintance with figurative language in the case of literature, with the distinctively dynamic images created in dance, with
tonal structures and sound relations in music, with plastic and pictorial values in painting. It is possible, however, to understand a
metaphor or oxymoron or paradox so well that one can write scholarly
treatises on figures and symbols—and to be incapable of aesthetic involvement. Perceptual and cognitive awareness, therefore, is vitally
important; it opens the way to apprehension. But it is a necessary and
not a sufficient condition for a full engagement with the arts, while it
might well be both necessary and sufficient for mastery of one of the
social sciences.

Aesthetic experiences, as I have suggested, involve us as existing
beings in pursuit of meanings. They involve us as historical beings
born into social reality. They must, therefore, be *lived* within the contexts of our own self-understanding, within the context of what we
have constituted as our world. Richard E. Palmer, in his
"hermeneutical manifesto," has written:

> Art, then, is ultimately not a matter of knowing through sense
> perceptions but of understanding. When one encounters a great work
> of art, he finds the horizons of his own world, his way of seeing his
> world, his self-understanding, broadened; he sees "in a different
> light," sometimes for the first time, but always in a more "ex-
> perienced" way.[50]

Palmer makes clear that the world we enter when encountering a
work of art cannot be, no matter how far removed in time and space,
divorced from our own. Mimetic theory, it seems to me, makes it possible to focus on the question of the world and on the question of *our*
world's—each person's world—horizons; since our ability to enter the
universe of *Hamlet,* say, is partially a function of our perception of
those horizons, partially of our ability to break through them, to transcend. And having transcended, have penetrated what is not, we see
from another standpoint. We see critically, through new eyes.
Granted, Shakespeare does not reveal our reality to us from the perspective of our own future, but he does disclose, through his own
"double vision," the corruption of a state in an imaginary world con-
tiguous to our own. This in itself, coupled with the action of the play,
the *praxis* that transforms, may enable us to experience what Sartre
called "a true image of our time" as we intend it—at the very least to
see.

The questions evoked by expressivist theory may become questions
that go quite beyond the individual creation. Gyorgy Lukacs has writ-

ten that, "The creative personality that figures in the emergence of the work of art is not simply or immediately identical with its everyday identity." And then:

> ... the artist's creating demands from him a generalizing on himself, a movement upward from his particular singularity to aesthetic uniqueness. We see now that the effectiveness of important works, at their most striking—when the formed content is alien in spatio-temporal terms, or in terms of nationality or class—conveys a broadening and deepening, a transcending of the unmediated everyday individuality. And above all, in this enrichment of the "I," stands the felicitous experience which genuinely great art provides.[51]

Lukacs also made the point that the individual engaging with a work, enjoying it, moving into it, discovers realities that would otherwise have been inaccessible, new conceptions of man and his possibilities. He emphasized as well (and this is of crucial importance to me) the fact that the social character of human personality must never be forgotten as we talk about the enrichment of individuality.

This means that an artist—be he or she Shakespeare, Sylvia Plath, Donald Barthelme, Harold Pinter, Virginia Woolf, Cezanne, de Kooning, Martha Graham—is always an artist-in-society; what he or she is presenting is presented against the social meaning system of the group to which he or she belongs. Moreover, many of the meanings in the individual's existential reality (perhaps most of them) have had a social origin. This does not necessarily mean that the artist must be, whatever his or her intention, expressing a "world view." It does not even mean that the meanings in the background form a coherent whole. But even such an ostensibly autonomous world as the one created by Virginia Woolf in *To the Lighthouse* arises against a background of interpreted experiences—domestic experiences in the Hebrides, academic experiences, artistic experiences—all of which are functions of constructed social reality. This, too, suggests ways in which art can work to stimulate questions about the social world, with its lacks, its deficiencies, its possibilities. As individuals experience the work through and by means of their own lived worlds, the realities they discover may well provide new vantage points on the intersubjective world, the world they share with others; the "enrichment of the 'I' " may become an overcoming of silence and a quest for tomorrow, for what is not yet.

Again, this is only possible if individuals are enabled to understand that it is through the imaginary mode of awareness that they can break with the taken-for-granted, with the ordinary and the mundane. The questions raised by those concerned with the work of art in its autonomy may involve us with the recognition that the natural world (and the natural standpoint) must be bracketed out if we are to enter the province of meaning we associate with the arts. There must be a choice, a choice that ordinary discourse makes somehow suspect. There must be a choice to set aside what is ordinarily believed, what is routine and everyday. Moving into the microcosm, let us say, of *Moby Dick* or into the reality created by Rodin's sculptured hands, we bring them into being for ourselves and, in doing so, open realms of possibility to our imagination. Moving back, into another province of meaning, experiencing the "shock"we ought to—and students ought to—undergo, we may achieve the reconstruction of experience Dewey spoke of; we may find ourselves in a critical stance, ready to surpass what *is*.

The test, finally, is in the aesthetic experiences we can make possible, the privileged moments through which we can enable our students to live. There must be attending; there must be noticing; at once, there must be a reflective turning back to the stream of consciousness —the stream that contains our perceptions, our reflections, yes, and our ideas. Clearly, this end-in-view cannot be predetermined, anymore than the imaginative mode of awareness can be predefined. I am arguing for self-reflectiveness, however, and new disclosures, as I am arguing for critical reflection at a moment of *stasis* and crystallized habits. If the uniqueness of the artistic-aesthetic can be reaffirmed, if we can consider futuring as we combat immersion, old either/ors may disappear. We may make possible a pluralism of visions, a multiplicity of realities. We may enable those we teach to rebel.

References

1. Robert Heilbroner, *An Inquiry into the Human Prospect* (New York: W.W. Norton, 1974), p. 21.
2. Hannah Arendt, "Lying in Politics," in *Crises of the Republic* (New York: Harcourt Brace Jovanovich, 1972), pp. 3-47.
3. Albert Camus, *The Rebel* (New York: Alfred A. Knopf, 1954), p. 219.
4. Ibid., p. 222.
5. Alfred Schutz, "On Multiple Realities," in *The Problem of Social Reality* Collected Papers I, ed. Maurice Natanson (The Hague: Martinus Nijhoff, 1967), p. 213.

6. Maurice Merleau-Ponty, *Phenomenology of Perception* (London: Routledge & Kegan Paul, 1967), p. xxi.
7. See Daniel Bell, *The Coming of Post-Industrial Society* ((New York: Basic Books, 1973) and Jurgen Habermas, *Toward a Rational Society* (Boston, Beacon Press, 1971).
8. See Christopher Jencks et al., *Inequality* (New York: Basic Books, 1972.)
9. Michael B. Katz, *Class, Bureaucracy, and Schools* (New York; Praeger Publishers, 1971).
10. Bell, *op. cit.,* pp. 214-215.
11. Bell, *The Cultural Contradictions of Capitalism* (New York: Basic Books, 1976), p. 11.
12. Robert Nozick, *Anarchy, State, and Utopia* (New York: Basic Books, 1974), pp. 149-182.
13. John Rawls, *A Theory of Justice* (Cambridge: Harvard University Press, 1971), p. 107.
14. George Steiner, "The Great Ennui," in *In Bluebeard's Castle* (New Haven: Yale University Press, 1971), pp. 6 ff.
15. Paulo Freire, *Cultural Action for Freedom* (Baltimore: Penguin Books, 1972).
16. John Dewey, *Art as Experience* (New York: Minton, Balch & Co., 1934) p. 274.
17. Ibid.
18. Ibid., p. 172.
19. Dewey, "Qualitative Thought," in *Philosophy and Civilization* (New York: Minton, Balch & Co., 1931), p. 99.
20. Jean-Paul Sartre, "The Artist and His Conscience," Preface to *L'Artiste et sa Conscience,* by Rene Leibowitz. Reprinted in *Marxism and Art,* eds. Berel Lang and Forrest Williams (New York: David McKay, 1972), p. 222.
21. Dewey, *Individualism Old and New* (New York: Capricorn Books, 1962), p. 169.
22. Sartre, *Being and Nothingness* (New York: Citadel Press, 1969), p. 411.
23. Schutz, "On Multiple Realities," *op. cit.,* p. 210.
24. Ibid., p. 232.
25. James Joyce, *A Portrait of the Artist as a Young Man* (New York: Viking Press, 1957), p. 213.
26. Susanne Langer, *Problems of Art* (New York: Charles Scribner's Sons, 1957), pp. 6-7.
27. Morris Weitz, "The Role of Theory in Aesthetics," in *Problems in Aesthetics,* ed. Morris Weitz (New York: Macmillan, 1959), p. 155.
28. Ibid, p. 152.
29. Morris H. Abrams, *The Mirror and the Lamp* (New York: W.W. Norton, 1958), pp. 3-8.
30. Aristotle, *Poetics,* in *A Theory of Poetry and Fine Art,* ed. C.H. Butcher (New York: Dover Books, 1951), XIV 1453b, p. 49.
31. Ibid., IX 1452a, p. 39.
32. William Shakespeare, *The Tragedy of Hamlet Prince of Denmark* (New Haven: Yale University Press, 1954), Act III, Sc. 2, p. 87.

33. Ibid., Act. II, Sc. 2, p. 65.
34. Shakespeare, *The Tragedy of King Lear* (New Haven: Yale University Press, 1956), Act IV, Sc. 1, p. 103.
35. Samuel Beckett, *Waiting for Godot* (New York: Grove Press, 1954), p. 42.
36. William Wordsworth, "Preface to the Lyrical Ballads," in *The Prelude: Selected Poems and Sonnets,* ed. Carlos Baker (New York: Holt, Rinehart and Winston, 1962), p. 25.
37. Wordsworth, "The Prelude," *op. cit.,* p. 203.
38. Henry David Thoreau, *Walden,* ed. Walter Harding (New York: Washington Square Press, 1963), p. 1.
39. Walt Whitman, "Song of Myself," in *Leaves of Grass* (New York: Auentine Press, 1931).
40. Charles Baudelaire, "To the Reader," in *Flowers of Evil* (New York: New Directions Press, 1955), p. 5.
41. Fyodor Dostoevsky, *Notes from Underground* (New York: Signet Books, 1961), p. 94.
42. See, e.g., Richard Kostelanetz, "Introduction: On the New Arts in America," in *The New American Arts,* ed. Richard Kostelanetz (New York: Collier Books, 1969), pp. 11-30.
43. Langer, *op. cit.,* pp. 45-46.
44. Clive Bell, *Art* (New York: Charles Scribner's Sons, 1914).
45. W. H. Auden, "In Memory of W.B. Yeats," in. *Selected Poetry of W.H. Auden* (New York: Vintage Books, 1971), p. 53.
46. Archibald MacLeish, "Ars Poetica," in *Modern American Poetry,* ed. Louis Untermeyer (New York: Harcourt, Brace, and Company, 1932), p. 657.
47. Alfred Schutz, "Making Music Together," in *Studies in Social Theory* Collected Papers II, ed. Arvid Brodersen (The Hague: Martinus Nijhoff, 1964), p. 173.
48. Henry James, *The Portrait of a Lady* (New York: Dell Books, 1961), p. 40.
49. E. M. Forster, *Howard's End* (New York: Vintage Books, 1956), p. 39.
50. Richard E. Palmer, *Hermeneutics* (Evanston: Northwestern University Press, 1969), p. 239.
51. Gyorgy Lukacs, "Art as Self-Consciousness in Man's Development," reprinted in *Marxism and Art, op. cit.,* p. 234.

13
Imagination and Aesthetic Literacy

IN Virginia Woolf's *Moments of Being,* there are passages in which non-being is described, moments when everything seems "embedded in a kind of nondescript cotton wool."[1] The point is made that "a great part of every day is not lived consciously": nothing makes any impression; the world seems bland, muffled, and vague. Now and then, however, there are exceptional moments, moments of response to "shocks of awareness." One abruptly perceives willow trees, "all plumy and soft green and purple against the blue" or one sees a connection between an apple tree and someone's suicide, between a children's quarrel and the darkness of the earth. At such times, one may be moved to "put the severed parts together," to impose some order or some meaning on it all. Virginia Woolf believed that the "shock-receiving capacity" made her a writer; the shock, the blow, seemed to her a token of some real thing behind experiences; "and I make it real by putting it into words." [2]

Surely similar thoughts might be expressed by artists who work with materials other than words. Painters, for instance, make their perceptions real by embodying them in images. This must be what Paul Cezanne meant when he said he thought "in painting,"[3] when he spoke of his struggle to make light and space speak to those with the capacity to heed. I would like to hear such things said by all those we enable to engage—openly and perceptively—with the several arts, as they try (each from his or her own vantage point) to put "severed parts" together and unify their own lived worlds.

My concern is to enable diverse persons to break through the cotton wool of daily life and to live more consciously. It seems to me that engagement with the arts makes possible moments of being—the ex-

Originally published in *Art Education,* October 1977.

ceptional moments of which Virginia Woolf spoke. By that I mean that those who can attend to and absorb themselves in particular works of art are more likely to effect connections in their own experience than those who cannot. They are more likely to perceive the shapes of things as they are conscious of them, to pay heed to qualities and appearances ordinarily obscured by the conventional and routine. I believe that teachers can release people for this kind of seeing if we ourselves are able to recover—and help our students to discover—the imaginative mode of awareness that makes paintings available, and poetry, and sculpture, and theatre, and film. This is the point, I think, of the creative activities we foster in our classrooms and of the creative encounters we try to nurture with works of art. If we do not do our work intentionally, if we do not have a clear sense of what aesthetic perceptions and aesthetic objects signify, we are likely to deprive our students of possibilities. We may leave them buried in cotton wool, in fact, and passive under the hammer blows of the fragmented, objective world.

Provided with opportunities to speak about it, young people often express a desire to overcome their own passivity, their own *ennui*. They make groping efforts to bridge between their subjectivities and that which exists apart from them, to find ways of identifying with a reality that afflicts them like an alien presence. Wallace Stevens described some of this in a poem entitled "The Motive for Metaphor." In the course of the poem, he said:

> The motive for metaphor, shrinking from
> The weight of primary noon,
> The A B C of being,
> The ruddy temper, the hammer
> Of red and blue, the hard sound—
> Steel against intimation—the sharp flash,
> The vital, arrogant, fatal, dominant X.[4]

The "weight of primary noon," the "A B C," the "dominant X" seem to refer to a reality translated into abstractions and discrete, metallic parts. It is a wholly objective, depersonalized reality, requiring some human transformation if it is to become personally meaningful. What Wordsworth once called "a dark, invisible workmanship" is needed to reconcile the "discordant elements"[5]—in this case, the crude colors, the thud of steel, the flash, the X. It is the kind of imaginative workmanship that perceives correspondences, that discerns analogies, that brings "severed parts together." What is distinctive about the realm of the artistic-aesthetic, of course, is that—

within that realm—the bringing together is achieved by means of expression in a particular medium: paint, language, the body-in-motion, musical sound, clay, film.

This, it seems to me, is the insight we want to make available to students when we provide opportunities for them to become acquainted with textures, say, with line in its multiple variety, with color, area, and space. To explore a medium, to work with it, to try to express something seen or felt or heard is to come to understand, on some level, that visions are made real when they are transformed into perceptual realities and given intelligible form. This does not mean that young people's explorations must culminate in fully realized embodiments or even in objects with intelligible form. What is important is the effort to define a vision and to work on giving it expression. An understanding of the struggle, a sense of having been inside it even for a moment, cannot but feed into an awareness of the privileged realities artists create. To know how to attend to such realities is to open oneself to altogether new visions, to unsuspected experiential possibilities. It is to become personally engaged in looking, from an altered standpoint, on the materials of one's own lived life, and in imaginatively transmuting (from the fresh standpoint) the fragments of the presented world.

For Wallace Stevens, imagination is an aspect of the conflict between the human being and what he called "organized society." In a book of essays called *The Necessary Angel,* he wrote, with regard to the imagination:

> It is part of our security. It enables us to live our own lives. We have it because we do not have enough without it. This may not be true as to each one of us, for certainly there are those for whom reality and reason are enough. It is true enough of the race.[6]

If we think of what Stevens called "organized society" in contemporary terms, we cannot but envision something like what Erich Kahler described as:

> the various forms of collectivization—scientification, specialization, functionalization, standardization, anonymization, commercialization —all of them orignally springing from rationalization and technicalization and all of them splitting the individual, dividing him into a collective, functioning part, and an individual human part. The collective part keeps extending while the individual part shrinks.[7]

Obviously, Kahler was not proposing a kind of either/or. He was not saying that one can only be an individual by separating oneself

from the society. He was suggesting that a collective made up of func-
tionaries, automata, other-directed and passive people, cannot be conceived of as a human community. Only when the split he spoke of is
overcome, only when "the individual, human part" is fully involved in
membership, will we see an emergence of what John Dewey once
called a "great community." And it is not accidental that, when Dewey spoke of such a community, he also spoke of art—whose function,
he said, "has always been to break through the crust of conven-
tionalized and routine consciousness."[8]

If our present situation is as Kahler described, "the motive for
metaphor" may well inform a suppressed desire to be, to find one's
own vision, to break with the collective and the crowd. Were we to
succeed in making the artistic-aesthetic central to the educational undertaking, we would be committing ourselves to the expansion of the
"individual, human part" of those we teach. We would be committing
ourselves to new modes of personal integration, new patterns of
wholeness, as we learned to nurture the imaginative mode of awareness, the power to shape and to see.

It is important, when we consider integrations and wholeness, to
break with such notions as those that split the cognitive from the emotional, the rational from the affective capacities. Too often, when we
treat the artistic-aesthetic as a necessary alternative to the abstract and
the technological, we focus our attention on the non-cognitive, the
emotive, the purely expressive; we treat the cognitive as an aspect of an
alien domain. Now it may well be that the perceptual, creative part of
the brain (what Robert Ornstein calls the "right hemisphere"[9]) suffers
neglect in our culture, particularly if "the collective part keeps extending" in Kahler's terms. But it does not follow that the perceptual,
creative part should now be favored at the expense of other human
capacities.

It is worth noting that, when Maurice Ravel was disabled by a
stroke, he did not appear to lose his artistic sensibility, because the
right hemisphere of his brain was not involved. But, because the left
hemisphere was damaged, Ravel was no longer able to recognize musical notation and, in consequence, could no longer create. Similar discoveries have been made with respect to literary artists afflicted by
aphasia, writers who gave every sign of having retained their creativity
nonetheless. Their aphasia, however, prevented them from recognizing
grammatical sentences and literary techniques; they were therefore unable to express themselves.[10]

My point is that our desire to combat the positivistic, highly rationalized components of our culture ought not to temp us into the kind of one-dimensionality that might keep us from recalling the inseparability of cognition and sensibility—in the aesthetic as well as other domains. For one thing, we would be likely to falsify the processes of art-making, the very processes in which we want our students to engage. For another, we would be likely to overlook or set aside precisely those awarenesses and sensitivities that make aesthetic experiences possible for human beings.

Henry David Aiken, like many other scholars of the arts, has written that the basis of an aesthetic experience is always to be found in the thing perceived, in the particular work itself.[11] Recall, for an instant, such works of art as Rembrandt's *The Anatomy Lesson,* Shakespeare's *Romeo and Juliet,* Melville's "Billy Budd," Cezanne's *The Cardplayers,* Virginia Woolf's *To the Lighthouse,* Bergman's *Face to Face.* Whatever emotional response any one of these arouses is—or ought to be—a response to a perceived situation, not a mere upsurge of delight, wonder, excitement, or awe.

Consider *Romeo and Juliet.* Without some degree of understanding that its expressiveness arises, "at lease in part, from the fact that it provides a dramatic representation of an action of which the evoked emotion is the expressive counterpart,"[12] we would not be able to realize the play's expressive values—the poetic imagery and the wordplay, the light on the balcony and the flash of swords, the murmur of crowds, the glow of velvet, the girl's pale face in the shadowed tomb. We have to be, in some sense, passionately detached; we have to be aware somehow of the stance required if we are to perceive the play as a work of art. There must be some ability to uncouple the work from the everyday world—the world of utility and empirical fact, the world where dynastic feuds are quite unthinkable, where adolescent love affairs rarely, if at all, undo the state. We need, in other words, the capacity to distance, to detach the experience from practical interests and ordinary happenings, to locate it in aesthetic space. To be capable of aesthetic perception, Dewey once said, is to find one's "desires fulfilled in the perception itself,"[13] not to want it for the sake of something else.

Without some conscious realization of all this, newcomers brought to witness the play might well confuse the events occurring with an actual event, an actual love affair. More probably, they might see the play as a historical documentation of the lives of two young people in a real Verona back in Renaissance times. In either case, the onlookers might be moved to tears, but the emotions they experienced would have no ground. As Aiken has said, they would be accidental and private, a "subjective coloring" with no aesthetic relevance to the play. And I am fairly sure that such vague and groundless tearfulness as I have described is far less likely to bring a "shock of awareness" than would a slowly developing imaginative response to the drama perceived as such.

The same thing might well happen if individuals were unable to perceive *The Anatomy Lesson* as a created work—if they could not respond to it as a painting as such. Horror or awe might be summoned up at the sight of it because of what the painting appeared to represent. It might strike observers simply as a record of Dr. Tulp's teaching; they might be horror-struck by the thought of the real cadaver or awed by the attentive faces of the doctors or medical students who (the spectators might think) actually existed in history. Again, these emotions would not have been evoked by the qualities or expressive values in the painting. The painting would have become a transparency, a window on the medical past. The emotions summoned up would have had little or nothing to do with Rembrandt's work; they would be thin, self-indulgent, and purely personal.

I am saying that the sensibility we hope to nurture where the arts are concerned cannot be divorced from conceptual awareness. There is what some of us call a minimal "aesthetic literacy" which can be taught at least from the moment a child is old enough to understand that a painting or a play or a cartoon is a created thing, deliberately made by a living human being. I would stress the fact, however, that the teaching is likely to be weak and ineffectual, perhaps wordy and overly abstract, if the teacher is not clear about perceptual realities and aesthetic space—and, even more important, capable of the excited and passionate absorption attentive perceiving makes possible. Only such a teacher can take the risks required in opening young people to works of art. Only such a teacher can decide how much—and how little—information must be given to make attending possible, precisely how to communicate what young people need to know in order to single out pictorial space, color, line, or contour, say, as elements to be perceived, to be attended to as ground.

There must be a readiness; there must be some realization that an aesthetic object—*Romeo and Juliet,* "Billy Budd," Cezanne's *The Cardplayers*—is something that has to be achieved, brought into being by the one who perceives, who reads, who attends. Many people simply do not understand that mere printed words, musical notes, brushstrokes on canvas cannot be regarded as works of art. They do not realize that works of art only come into existence when a certain kind of heeding, noticing, or attending takes place; they do not realize that living persons, through and by means of an encounter with a work, constitutes it (if they are wide-awake and attentive enough) as a work of art.

Take Cezanne's *The Cardplayers*. Even the expressiveness of a work like this has somehow to be perceived as such. Cezanne was not, after all, presenting a photographic image of the faces and bodies of two men, nor was he especially concerned with creating an illusion of space and angularity. Encountering his work, we have in some manner to be aware that we are in the presence of an orderly arrangement of forms modelled in paint, of a strange solidity and depth contending with the flatness of the canvas. The expressiveness is in the jutting planes, the hands, the table, not in something beyond the picture—in the social situation of the town in Provence, the morality of the cardplayers, or the subjectivity of the beholder, looking on. Maurice Merleau-Ponty has written that, "The meaning Cezanne gave to objects and faces in his paintings presented itself to him in the world as it appeared to him. Cezanne simply released this meaning: it was the objects and the faces themselves as he saw them which demanded to be painted, and Cezanne simply expressed what they *wanted* to say."[14]

The clear implication is that the only way to seize the meaning of paintings—to permit them to grow in our own experience—is to attend to their attributes and qualities, attributes and qualities that exist in aesthetic space in a particular perception of them. In other words, those able to transmute the brushstrokes on the canvas into an aesthetic object are those who know how to attend to colors, masses, shadings in compresence, in relationship, those who know how to fuse color, volume, and plane into coherent and harmonious wholes. Once all this is achieved, the beholders (perceiving Cezanne's forms against their own backgrounds of seeing and feeling, their own biographies) grasp Cezanne's vision as a vision for them, feel no break between their perceiving and what is there to be perceived, and, at that point, they respond to—or perhaps resonate to—what the objects and faces *"wanted* to say."

What does all this attending and noticing have to do with "moments of being," with heightened consciousness? What does a perception of a painting *as* a painting have to do with bringing order into the world? If the pleasure made possible by engagement with works of art derives mainly from an apprehension of their qualities, how does this expand the "individual, human part" and make the individual feel more at home in the world? And how does all this connect with what teachers do in art education classrooms, with the explorations that take place there, with expressive undertakings, with what we call "child art"?

The point has been made that a work of art can never be brought into being unless a living person encounters it in person and in the light of his or her reality. This means that a painting, play, film, or piece of music must be grasped by some individual consciousness, grasped imaginatively, if it is to function as art. There is no way of bringing about an aesthetic experience in another by describing or summarizing or interpreting a work that person does not know. A direct encounter is required. Time must be taken, so that the work of art has some opportunity to inhabit the individual's consciousness.[15] As it does so, the qualities and forms perceived as properties of the work gradually take shape in experience. At that juncture, the beholder (or reader or listener) is enabled to perceive things never before perceived in the surrounding world. But again, as has been suggested before, he or she must know how to "read" the work of art in question, how to select, how to attend, how to decode. As George Steiner has recently written, "If one is color blind or myopic, the landscape of one's perceptions is modified accordingly. But normal vision also derives from education and choice."[16] And, indeed, it is education and choice that we are talking about: the modes of education that will enable people to choose themselves as open to works of art.

"The eye is never naked," Steiner wrote. Our seeing is affected by our culture, our experiences, and certainly by what we have learned. The consequences for our understanding of the visual arts have been radical. Steiner went on:

> There is a literal sense in which major artists change what we see and the ways in which we see it. Rembrandt altered the Western perception of shadow spaces and the weight of darkness. Since van Gogh, we notice the twist of flame in a poplar. No one before Picasso had seen the now obvious similitude between the pointed saddle and handlebars of a bicycle and the visage of a bull. Viaducts have not stood still since Paul Klee put shoes on their pillared feet.[17]

Describing similitude between flame and poplar, handlebars and the head of a bull, these words bring back the notion of metaphor, the idea of "putting severed parts together," the processes so fundamental to ordering and humanizing the world. We are asked to think about what happens to our perceived reality after we have learned to attend to a work in its integrity, to notice and decode.

There is a movement back and forth between what one writer calls the "worldhood" of the beholder and the "world" of the work of art. Appreciating a work in its *thereness,* the beholder then incarnates it in his or her own consciousness, lends it some of his or her own life. Melvin Rader, in an article on "The Imaginative Mode of Awareness," described the same movement, the same tension, when commenting on the "attentional" and "elaborative" phases of imaginative awareness. The attentional phase is the one I have been discussing, the way of perceiving that allows us "to grasp the object in its full qualitative richness and imaginative fecundity," to use Rader's words. The elaborative phase is a more active one; it "transforms the object by imaginative vision." Focussing our attention, we "feel things as things, qualities as qualities, as interesting and satisfying in direct experience." Then, wrote Rader:

> We linger; we savor and enjoy. We then elaborate the experience on the basis created by this tranquillizing and focussing of attention. The elaboration is a moody and imaginative mode of vision for the enrichment of the intrinsic perceptual value of the object.[18]

As he said in another place, "The dystole of contemplation precedes the diastole of full-bodied aesthetic enrichment." It is this enrichment that provides our "moments of being," that allows us to transform our worlds.

How does this relate to what we ordinarily mean by art education? I would like to believe that the concerns of art educators are akin to those I have described: to enhance qualitative awareness, to release imagination, and to free people to see, shape, and transform. I would hope for the kinds of curricula that permit an easy and articulated transaction between making and attending, that will eradicate either/ors. For me, there is a continuity between creative work, art appreication, and aesthetic literacy; I would not like to see one phase subordinated to another. There is widespread agreement that creative activity is a continuation of childhood play; there is a need to encourage play, especially dramatic play, and to encourage children to externalize through various kinds of action their own imaginings. "Play," wrote Ruben Alves, ". . .creates an order out of imagination and therefore out of freedom. As with magic, here imagination assumes flesh—takes the impossible and treats it as if it were possible." And later:

> In play children do not allow the rules of the so-called real world to control their activity. They set apart space and time, and organize it according to the requirements of their heart. Thus we see arise a social reality, a community, which right in the middle of the adult world stands as a protest against it. Its very existence implies the refusal of children to be organized by our reality. Deeply, unconsciously, children are saying along with the magician, "What is, cannot be true!" And they set out to build a world according to their search for joy. They operate on the assumption of the omnipotence of imagination, and therefore of man's will to create a world which will produce happiness. They are a living indictment of the domestication of our imagination, spellbound by the assumption that action is only justified by its external product.[19]

This is another expression of the "motive for metaphor." It is also an essential foundation for later experiences with works of art. This is why I would wish to see explorations of media— paint, clay, language, sounds—taking place under the rubric of play.

Imaginative play and imaginative explorations of media may well be linked to qualitative adventures—the kinds of experiences that enable young people to attend on occasion to the appearances of things. I have in mind natural things as well as man-made objects and works of art. There are blades of grass, rocky hillsides, sunflowers, blue jeans, awls, chisels, rubbed tabletops; there are lights, sounds, movements, nuances of color, reflections, vibrations, spaces—open and closed. Much of our involvement with things, necessarily, is instrumental. We *use* them to accomplish ends-in-view, and we understand them in terms of their use. Jeans are to wear; tabletops are to eat on; awls and chisels are simply tools. Many things or events (including blades of grass, the branches of trees, people walking dogs, children holding hands, trucks clattering by) exist on the periphery of consciousness. We brush against them, move through them, or pay them no heed. And there are phenomena that serve us as signs, signals, pointers, and clues. They require interpretation or explanation; they refer beyond themselves. A menacing cloud on the horizon may be like that; so may a description of the oil crisis, a voice behind a classroom door, a rattle in a motorcycle motor, or the philosopny of Immanuel Kant.

Work has to be done; problems have to be solved; but there remain the appearances of things—which few people know how to see. Sunflowers and blue jeans and even chisels, however, can be disconnected from their ordinary contexts and looked at in a new way, as if they first surged up in the world. People can be asked to note the glow of the petal of the sunflower in the half-light or the black center's stare; they can be asked to contemplate the peculiar blue of someone's jeans and to match it against the afternoon sky. They can even be invited to examine the skeletal shape of the chisel and to watch its glint against a piece of wood. More appropriately, they can be asked to articulate some of the marvelous experiences they have had by chance: the sight of a crocus on a rainy day, the choreography of a basketball game, the halo around a woman's hair in lamplight, the soft purr of voices on the street at night. Such impressions, such visions, often find expression in and through the media teachers offer. But I want to stress the equal importance of articulating what it signifies when a flower or a smoky haze becomes suddenly visible, when a person finds himself or herself seeing a kind of aura around an ordinary object, when some part of the world is renewed.

It seems to me that young people, against the background of such experiences, are in a position to understand that works of art are privileged objects, created for the kind of perceiving just described. An aesthetic experience is, as some have said, an extraordinary perceptual event. It takes place in a province of meaning too often closed to young people in our schools. Yet it is clear enough that all children, even very young ones, are capable of responding to works of art. There is, in fact, a growing realization that early experiences with art are in an important sense foundational to the later development of aesthetic experience.[20] Even the misconceptions children have may be, as Howard Gardner and his associates suggest, necessary stages in the development of aesthetic sensitivity. Those that are destructive should be corrected. "One cannot, for instance, be sensitive to style if all one sees is subject matter. One cannot appreciate abstract works if one insists on fidelity to the 'real world'. . . . And if steps are not taken during childhood to expose. . .false notions, to bring about a more veridical and humanistic view of the arts, the adolescent or adult may have become so alienated from the arts that, as in much of our society today, the whole domain seems as distant as a star."[21]

Teachers must take risks if they are to enable students to open themselves to art forms, to overcome false notions, and to take a "humanistic view." Moreover, teachers must themselves be sensitive to the qualities of things as they must know personally what it means to be receptive to the arts. Only teachers like these can move the young to notice more, to attend more carefully, to express their visions, to choose themselves. Much depends upon how teachers choose *them* selves—whether they authentically delight in certain art experiences, whether they are informed enough to articulate what there is about the arts that expands human possibilities.

Art education, like aesthetic education, can create domains where there are new possibilities of vision and awareness. Art educators can help awareness feed into an expanding life of meaning, can make increasingly available moments of clarity, moments of joy. We have to work together for new continuities, new openings, as we move towards our own moments of being, our own shocks of awareness. There is cotton wool all around—and there are living beings waiting, hoping to break through. Virginia Woolf spoke of an instinctive notion she used to have—"the sensation that we are sealed vessels afloat on what it is convenient to call reality; and at some moments, the sealing matter cracks; in floods reality . . ."[22] Near the end of *A Room of One's Own,* she called upon her readers or her listeners to live "in the presence of reality, an invigorating life, it would appear, whether one can impart it or not."[23] I am convinced that we teachers can make this possible through the work we do, as we move more and more persons into the imaginative mode of awareness, as we free them to make their visions real.

References

1. Virginia Woolf, "A Sketch of the Past," in *Moments of Being: Unpublished Autobiographical Writings,* ed. Jeanne Schulkind (New York: Harcourt Brace Jovanovich, 1976), p. 70.
2. Ibid., p. 72.
3. Maurice Merleau-Ponty, "Cezanne's Doubt," in *Sense and Non-Sense* (Evanston: Northwestern University Press, 1964), p. 17.
4. Wallace Stevens, "The Motive for Metaphor," *Poems* (New York: Vintage Books, 1959), p. 109.
5. William Wordsworth, "The Prelude," in *The Prelude: Selected Poems and Sonnets,* ed. Carlos Baker (New York: Holt, Rinehart and Winston, 1962), p. 213.
6. Stevens, "Imagination as Value," in *The Necessary Angel* (New York: Vintage Books, 1965), p. 150.
7. Erich Kahler, *The Tower and the Abyss* (New York: George Braziller, 1957), p. 45.
8. John Dewey, *The Public and Its Problems* (Chicago: Swallow Press, 1954), p. 183.

9. Robert E. Ornstein, *The Psychology of Consciousness* (New York: Viking Press, 1973).
10. Joseph E. Bogen, "The Other Side of the Brain: An Appositional Mind," in *The Nature of Human Consciousness: A Book of Readings,* ed. Robert E. Ornstein (New York: Viking Press, 1974), p. 106.
11. Henry David Aiken, "Some Notes Concerning the Aesthetic and the Cognitive," in *Aesthetics Today,* ed. Morris Philipson (New York: Meridian Books, 1961), p. 271.
12. Ibid., p. 270.
13. Dewey, *Art as Experience* (New York: Minton, Balch & Company, 1934), p. 254.
14. Merleau-Ponty, *op. cit.,* p. 21.
15. Diane Collinson, "Aesthetic Education," in *New Essays in the Philosophy of Education,* ed. Glenn Langford and D. J. O'Connor (London: Routledge & Kegan Paul, 1973), p. 199.
16. George Steiner, "The Kingdom of Appearances," *The New Yorker,* April 4, 1977, p. 132.
17. Ibid.
18. Melvin Rader, "The Imaginative Mode of Awareness," *The Journal of Aesthetics and Art Criticism,* Winter 1974, p. 136.
19. Ruben Alves, *Tomorrow's Child* (New York: Harper & Row, 1972), p. 94.
20. Michael J. Parsons, "A Suggestion Concerning the Development of Aesthetic Experience in Children," *The Journal of Aesthetics and Art Criticism,* Spring 1976, pp. 305-314.
21. Howard Gardner, Ellen Winner, and Mary Kircher, "Children's Conceptions of the Arts," *The Journal of Aesthetic Education,* July 1975, p. 76.
22. Woolf, *op. cit.,* p. 122.
23. Woolf, *A Room of One's Own* (New York: Harcourt, Brace & World, 1957), p. 114.

14

Significant Landscapes: An Approach to the Arts in Interrelationship

Rationalists, wearing square hats,
   Think in square rooms,
   Looking at the floor,
   Looking at the ceiling.
They confine themselves
   To right-angled triangles.
   If they tried rhomboids,
   Cones, waving lines, ellipses—
      As, for example, the ellipse of the half-moon—
   Rationalists would wear sombreros.

THIS is from Wallace Stevens' poem, "Six Significant Landscapes."[1] Although I do not consider the aesthetic to exist in a non-rational domain, I choose those lines because I believe that one of the distinguishing marks of art, music, and dance is a concern with rhomboids, cones, waving lines, ellipses—including the ellipse of the half-moon. A waving line is one kind of phenomenon in a painting, of course, another in a sonata, and still another in a dance. The half-moon finds diverse embodiments in the diverse art forms, but there is something that holds them together and justifies their being interrelated in some way. All are concerned with delineations of the possible. All break with the mundane and the stereotyped. All, if authentically encountered by a living being, make possible a recovery of self.

This seems to me to be important. So many of us today confine ourselves to right angles. We function in the narrowest of specialties; we lead one-dimensional lives. We accommodate ourselves so easily to

198

the demands of the technological society—to time schedules, charts, programs, techniques—that we lose touch with our streams of consciousness, our inner time. We become numb to our own bodily rhythms and sensations; we become incapable of seeing the visible surfaces of the world as they disclose themselves to human eyes. We become, as it were, submerged in reality, or we become members of what Soren Kierkegaard called "the Crowd."[2] An individual who is part of a crowd becomes anonymous; the sense of responsibility is weakened; autonomy erodes. In such a state, we are hardly likely to engage in the kinds of perceptual and cognitive activities needed for ordering experience and making sense of the world. We are unlikely to frame the significant questions that move human beings to go in search of meaning, to pursue themselves, to learn.

Because participation in and informed encounters with the arts are only possible for those who are present as persons with distinctive biographies and an awareness of their own life-worlds, it follows that the process of educating people for engagement with the arts is in part a process of liberating them for the wearing of sombreros, for seeing beyond the actual, and for pursuing themselves. Education in the arts also involves, of course, enabling people to learn how to confront and comprehend aesthetic objects, which must be *transformed* into works of art. But this does not exclude being there in person, being present to ourselves in the encounters. To engage authentically with a painting, a ballet, a musical work, we must—by dint of imaginative activity—be released into our own streams of consciousness, our own inner time. We must cultivate an awareness of our awareness, even as we work to realize an object as a work of art.

John Dewey wrote:

> Art throws off the covers that hide the expressiveness of experienced things; it quickens us from the slackness of routine and enables us to forget ourselves by finding ourselves in the delight of experiencing the world about us in its varied qualities and forms. It intercepts every shade of expressiveness found in objects and orders them in a new experience of life.[3]

To find ourselves "in the delight of experiencing" requires a transaction with the world, an ongoing transaction with "qualities and forms." This kind of transaction may be thought of in terms of acts of consciousness, meaning a series of moments in which we *grasp* what is given, in which we thrust into the world. To be aware of such moments is to be sensitive to the ways in which we originate them; it is to be conscious of the fact that we are the motivators of what is happening, that we are subjects responsible to and for ourselves.

This means, again, being in touch with our inner time, which is time inwardly lived as compared with time measured by the clock. An illustration of it is to be found in an essay by Alfred Schutz called "Making Music Together," where the point is made that an attentive listener to a work of music must reproduce in his own inner time the flow of tones composing the musical work. When this happens, the listener becomes united with the composer in a time dimension like the "vivid present shared by the partners in a genuine face-to-face relation . . ."[4] This does not only make possible a new experience of sound. Listeners reperforming the work within their own stream of consciousness are enabled to uncover aspects of themselves they never suspected, even as they achieve a communion with an artist and (by means of that communion) discover new expressive qualities in his world. There is a sense in which what Schutz describes is paradigmatic for the kinds of experiences aesthetic engagements make possible; it may be in the nurturing of such experiences that the representatives of the different art forms with which we are concerned find their most fundamental common cause.

I want to stress the fact, however, that the work of art achieved or reperformed by a viewer or a listener cannot be wholly predefined. Nothing teachers do can be counted upon to institute awareness of or experience with a work in a particular individual; there can never be assurance or guarantee. Tacit awarenesses are involved: there is always a surpassing of what the instructor says, even of what the instructor knows. Partly for this reason, teaching in the fields of art can never be reduced to a set of predetermined competencies. Nor can the encounters or experiences we hope to make possible be finally defined in terms of specified behaviors. There is always a dimension of the problematic; there is always a mode of questioning below the surfaces, in the silences. Whether the work is a poem, a watercolor, or a symphony, questions arise that touch on the fundamental themes of a person's life, on what she or he is seeking for, on all that she or he has learned.

Take, for example, a picture as familiar as *Guernica*. People are all too prone to see it as a rendering of an actual bombing or a protest against the Spanish Civil War. If they do, however, they are doing the painting a disservice; at once, they are depriving it of its mystery. Actually, it must be encountered in terms of the images presented, the shapes, the whites and blacks. Pain is imaged in the mouth of the screaming woman, in the open palm of the man.[5] Violence is communicated through the stark plunging of the lines, the abrasive thrust of forms. Even as beholders respond as they should, against their own background consciousness of paintings previously beheld, they cannot but find themselves questioning, perhaps even rebelling against, destruction and tragedy. They cannot but find themselves overwhelmed by the endless history of pain and man's inhumanity to man, somehow present here in Cubist space.

But it is not simply paintings with subjects like *Guernica* that arouse such questioning. We might take a painting like one of Cezanne's landscapes, say *Mt. St. Victoire.* Merleau-Ponty has written about the way in which Cezanne would sketch the geology of a scene in charcoal, then paint all parts of his painting at the same time.

> The picture took on fullness and density; it grew in structure and balance; it came to maturity all at once. "The landscape thinks itself in me," he said, "and I am its consciousness." Nothing could be farther from naturalism than this intuitive science. Art is not imitation, nor is it something manufactured according to the wishes of instinct or good taste. It is a process of expressing. . . .Cezanne, in his own words, "wrote in painting what had never yet been painted, and turned it into painting once and for all."[6]

Merleau-Ponty remarked on the feeling of strangeness this occasioned, the emotion evoked by what is encountered as "the continual rebirth of existence." Here, too, having attended to colors, appearances, and emerging structures, we are left with questions touching on the foundations of our lives, on the ways in which we exist in the world.

Somewhat the same things can be said about certain musical works, which are so frequently thought of in terms of their emotional and intuitive appear. We are expected to attend above all to their expressive sounds; we are to assume that thought and form are one. Yet Leonard B. Meyer has spoken of the "ultimate uncertainties" of which music makes us inexorably aware. This awareness is attributed to a necessary interaction between formal relationships and the associative aspect of music (which cannot, according to Meyer, be excluded or bracketed out), an interaction that "gives rise to a profound wonderment—tender, yet awful—at the mystery of existence."[7] Gabriel Marcel has said that the very emotion evoked by a work of music brings us back to a consciousness of our existence; emotion, he wrote, "is actually the discovery of the fact that 'this concerns me after all.' "[8]

Whether or not we believe that experiences with the visual and musical arts lead inevitably to questioning, we may at least take seriously the idea that they do confront us with ourselves. Along with such confrontation comes a recognition of tension between the self recovered in this fashion and the self of the public and the everyday world. This tension is partially due to the fact that works of art always involve an imaginative transformation of the given. Also, the possibilities they delineate are always open; they cannot be realized in the public, intersubjective world. Unlike empirical problems and possibilities, they cannot be solved or resolved; there is always something more.

Moby Dick, for example, can never be finally encompassed; its meanings can never be constituted for all time. For one thing, the symbols point so far beyond themselves that the referents of doubloon, harpoon, tryworks, Ishmael, and the white whale can never be finally identified. For another, every human consciousness, addressing itself to the novel in a particular moment of history, is bound to disclose something new, to transcend what has already been perceived. So it is with the ballet, *Swan Lake;* so it is with Beethoven's Ninth Symphony; so it is with Turner's *Burning of the Houses of Parliament,* Francis Bacon's *Triptych—Studies of the Human Body,* or Michelangelo's *Pieta.*

I am suggesting that the transcendences and tensions occasioned by authentic aesthetic encounters are similar, that the questions fundamental to the constitution of art works are akin. The integrations that take place, however, must take place within the individual beholder or listener or reader, as individuals pursue their own sensemaking and their own coherence. Merleau-Ponty has talked of the ways in which we continually witness the miracles of related experiences and has written that, "Nobody knows better than we do how this miracle is worked, for we are ourselves this network of relationships."[9] He meant that each living individual, existing in a multiplicity of realities, seeks at some level to integrate them, to overcome incompleteness and unify his or her own world.

There are exemplars of this process in many works of literature; I shall point to two of the most familiar to clarify what I have in mind. In James Joyce's *A Portrait of the Artist as a Young Man,* Stephen Dedalus struggles, through seeing and naming, to create order out of a life composed of disparate parts: Jesuitry, Irish nationalism, the squalor of Dublin, ships on the river, an alcoholic father, an indifferent God, and the enticements of art. When he finally breaks with the sentries of his past and exorcises the forces that have determined him, he has succeeded in transcending the fragmentations and the conflicts. He has achieved the kind of meaning that enables him to talk of encountering the reality of experience and forging "the uncreated conscience of my race." He has become what Merleau-Ponty described as a "network of relationships"; he is no longer entangled in a network others have made.

Much the same thing happens in Ralph Ellison's *Invisible Man,* which begins and ends with the narrator hibernating underground after shattering experiences in a world that has refused him. His object is to weave a coherent fabric out of all that has happened; he does so by going a long way back in time. "All my life I had been looking for something," he says, "and everywhere I turned someone tried to tell me what it was. I accepted their answers too, though they were often in contradiction and even self-contradictory. I was naive. I was looking for myself and asking everyone except myself questions which I, and only I, could answer." And finally, after the journey into himself and his past, he says: "In going underground, I whipped it all except the mind, the mind. And the mind that has conceived a plan of living must never lose sight of the chaos against which that pattern was conceived."

This forging of orders, this creation of plans of living: these are the kinds of integrations made possible by reflective encounters with the arts. They are the crucial ones, it seems to me, more important than any other principle of integration among the arts, each form of which is in some manner dintinct.

It seems evident that each art form works in a distinctive fashion to make such experiences possible. It seems evident that each is grounded in a particular tradition, in a context, even when the kinds of landscapes being disclosed are alike in definable ways. I do not believe, in other words, that painting, music, and dance can be—or should be—merged or integrated (except by the few who are Wagners or Stravinskys or Diaghilevs or Merce Cunninghams). Nor do I believe that parallelisms should be too easily assumed. Poetry has sometimes drawn its inspiration from paintings, sculpture, or music, it is true. Paintings have often become themes for poetry, as poems have been made part of musical works. Iconologists, studying the symbolic meanings in paintings, have often identified relationships between the meanings that have emerged and works of literature. The arts have occasionally tried to borrow effects from one another as well. Literature has tried to achieve the effects of music. Proust and Flaubert, rendering the flow of time and phenomena, were able to communicate something resembling what Impressionist painters were capturing when they rendered their equivalents of the shimmering and fluid world.

But, like the literary theorists Wellek and Warren,[10] I cannot conclude that musicality in poetry is the same as melody in music. Verlaine, Wellek and Warren point out, tried to achieve musical effects through a suppression of the meaning structures in his poetry and by means of an arrangement of phonetic patterns, but the blurred outlines and the lack of logical structure did not result in anything literally musical, although it did result in exquisite verse. An example follows, a poem entitled "Art Poetique," which begins by calling music paramount:

> De la musique avant toute chose,
> Et pour cela prefere l'Impair
> Plus vague et plus soluble dans l'air,
> Sans rien en lui qui pese ou qui pose.

No matter what the tone of voice in which the poem is read aloud, no matter how mellifluous the words may sound, the poem is not a musical work.

The moods induced by a Mozart minuet and a Watteau landscape may seem similar when reflected upon, but the gaiety induced by the minuet is not the same gaiety experienced in the presence of the painting. The gaiety—or the joy, or pleasure—aroused is not gaiety or joy or pleasure *in abstracto;* it cannot be equated with the emotion evoked by extra-aesthetic means. Whatever the feeling, it is specifically a function of the pattern of musical sounds or the pattern of colors and forms. It cannot be separated out; it cannot even be conceptualized about from a particular work. The crucial point is that every artist conceived his or her expression in terms of a definite medium and in the light of a distinguishable tradition. No effort to discover similarity or parallelism must obscure that reality. J. W. N. Sullivan goes so far as to say that a musical composition—say, the *Eroica*—is never *about* the program developed for it (the death of Napoleon, for example).[11] I believe that it is almost always futile to look either for similarities in intention or in structure or in "message" when we look for interrelationships. "Line" means differently in music, poetry, and painting. So do "rhythm" and "harmony."

Still, there are interrelationships to be found. They are the kind that ought to open up new possibilities for aesthetic encounters and for teaching the arts. The principles governing these, I suggest, derive in part from a notion of performance or studio work. They may also be derived from a conception of cultural history or the history of styles. Consider, for instance, the importance of the expressionist and formalist elements in works of art. A painting, a work of music, or a dance is on some level an expression of an individual artist's perception of, encounter with, or feeling about some aspect of the world. But artistic expressiveness, whatever the genre, can only occur when what is seeking expression is formed or patterned, and when the form and content interpenetrate so as to communicate a unified vision or picture or mood. To think in these terms is to conceptualize dimensions common to all art-making, to identify a place where they may be "strands of similarity."[12]

Somewhat the same can be said about the aesthetic experience, the peculiar experience that occurs when a particular kind of attention is paid to a selected-out portion of some phenomenal field, when a special kind of noticing or listening takes place, to the end of perceiving the internal relations among the elements of a work. Somewhat the same can be said about attending to what is intrinsically pleasant or beautiful or interesting and, finally, achieving the total work of art.

Even as we concern ourselves, however, with what is generally agreed to with regard to art and art experiences, we ought also to pay heed to such critics as Morris Weitz, who insists that "art" be treated as an open concept, since there exists no final definition of "art."[13] Stress is placed on the importance of holding in mind the need to make choices about the proper uses of the term because of the new examples of art that are constantly appearing in the world. Weitz suggests that the various theories of art be understood as recommendations of what to attend to in particular works as we make our choices with respect to them. I find enormously suggestive this concern for choosing, a concern of great importance for the discovery of inter-relationships among the arts. Self-consciousness is needed with regard to the recommendations and the evaluations made; questions must remain open. Otherwise, too much is likely to be taken for granted; we will stop listening to ourselves, stop engaging with works in the concreteness of their particularity.

Aesthetics has often been called a dreary science but it is not dreary if it provides students of the arts with a language and conceptual resources for reflecting upon their own experiences with dance and music and painting, with interrogating what they find. With the questions kept open, the notion of expression can function fruitfully to unify the study of certain art forms. So can the matter of formal embodiment; so can questions of medium and problems of style. Perhaps most importantly, we may then be enabled to consider the multiple decisions made by the artists in whom we are interested, the decisions made as they struggle to present the forms of their feelings. We may be enabled to participate imaginatively in the dynamic processes involved as artists embody in line, space, imagery, gesture, and sound what is subjectively given to them and what is to be communicated to others, at least to those choosing to realize what is thereby transmuted and embodied —in their own inner time.

It is important for music students or students of painting to understand motion in dance, or the dimensions of space, time, and dynamics in which dance exists. It is important to know what it means when a body is the instrument, rather than a palette or a piano. It is important for dancers to understand the element of motion in music, the relation between sounds and colors. This is one reason why I emphasize the uses of imaginative participation in the creation of art works by different artists. If such participation is undertaken by someone with a background in at least one of the other arts, that person can become a rich network of relationships; his or her consciousness can then be a ground for the integrations we seek.

Important, too, is the ability to take a critical stance with respect to the works under study. It is often said that teaching—good teaching— is identical with criticism, especially when it is carried on for the sake of making particular art forms more accessible. To criticize means to elucidate, to describe, sometimes to interpret and explain. It is not necessarily to evaluate or to give a verdict, although it is difficult for any critic to be wholly neutral. Criticism is a type of verbal performance. It involves the application of certain principles, certain ideas concerning the nature of art. It involves discourse about the works of art themselves. It must begin in the critic's (or the teacher's) appreciative and direct confrontation, with his or her own imaginative involvement and intuitions. To sigh, to throw up one's hands, or to laugh in delight in the course of such engagement would not, of course, lead to others' understanding of the work nor would it help anyone else appreciate the play, the painting, the dance, or the symphony. On the basis of the confrontation and involvement, the critic must go on to give "directions for perceiving," as Arnold Isenberg has said. He "does this by means of the idea he imparts to us, which guides us in the discrimination of details, the organization of parts. . . ."[14]

It is as if critics (or teachers) were to take their audiences (or students) on a journey through a work of art, pointing to those aspects of their principles or guiding concepts that make it possible for them to see. They can point to qualities within a work, to color combinations, melodic sequences, metaphors, symbols, the action of a hero, the cinematic space within a film. Pointing, they endeavor to afford those who heed them new perceptions, new disclosures, so that they can more effectually realize the work in question for themselves. And that, after all is the test: whether or not critics (or teachers) can intensify another's appreciation, enrich vision, free him or her to bring a given work into being in his or her inner time.

The importance of certain kinds of criticism must be as clear in other people's experience as it is in mine. Certain critics taught me how to look at *Guernica,* to attend to Rembrandt's use of light, and to note the color facets that give monumentality to Cezanne's work. Some critic taught me to discover the evocations of Africa, Iberia, and Greece in Picasso's *Les Demoiselles D'Avignon,* to encounter a Henry Moore sculpture, to respond to Minimalism, to enter Piero della Francesca's burnished world. The same is true with respect to montage and visual metaphors in film, to camera angles, fade-outs, and discontinuous cinematic space. Criticism enabled disclosures to take place, I am suggesting, and distinctive disclosures, depending on the work of art, but the critical acts involved were not unlike, and I am suggesting as well that attentiveness to criticism may provide another mode of interrelating the things we do.

We need to remind ourselves, of course, that no critic can ever fully translate a symbolic structure or determine the discoveries an individual will make. Crucial for an understanding of the role of criticism is the recognition of our radically diverse, autonomous experiences with works of art. Critics offer lenses, perspectives, visions that enable us to see what their categories have the capacity to reveal. But there always exists something outside the categories, beckoning to us, as one critic puts it, "soliciting our subjugation to its power to change our ways of seeing and living."[15] To engage in critical reflection upon our own art experiences is, then, to heighten self-consciousness—to aid us in clarifying what we mean by "art" and what we take to be the relation among art forms.

The reflecting and disclosing acts of consciousness demanded may also engage us in exploration of the traditions to which works of art belong. If it does, it ought surely to move us to question standard categories and labels. It ought to enable us to trace back significant themes in the history of styles. Beginning with the present and moving back in time to seek out our precursors, we can utilize a notion of style that implies an ordering of expressional forms. These forms may reflect in some manner the changes taking place over time in the felt relationship between consciousness and reality. With a sense of modernism or neo-modernism in mind, representatives of the various arts might move together into a dialogue with the past for the sake of discovering the sources of present break-downs and transmutations. They might disclose for themselves the loss of confidence in the external structures that sustained the 18th century world and created what Blake called "mind-forg'd manacles." They might, by entering the works of Wordsworth, Berlioz, Turner, and Goethe, engage with the upsurge of the expressive, the lyrical, and the strange. Reconstituting the middle years of the last century, they might move into an exploration of the reaction against confession and expression. Confronting the cool and crafted worlds of Symbolistic poets and Impressionist painters, they might rediscover art forms as impersonal equivalents of a reality become problematic, inexpressible in ordinary language. They might recapture some of the latter-day Expressionism, the Surrealist montages and nightmares, the cutting edges of abstract forms, serial music, bars and silences. . . . The point is to break together with being situated in one time, one place, to plunge back in history with a sense of interrogation and the desire to confront an emerging order, an emerging meaning that may somehow bind the arts of humankind.

I do not need to say very much about the equal importance of performance and studio work nor about the ways in which these can provide occasions for integration. Many have talked of the necessity to provide students with an understanding of the interplay of perception and expression. One commentator writes:

> The student needs to know what the past can provide in the way of models of perception, and he will need to experiment with ways to perceive and ways to integrate his own perceptions. To the extent that he is aware of the continuity of his mode of seeing (or hearing, or touching) with that of other men, he will have a sense of rootedness in a tradition which he can accept as his own. But the mode of seeing must be genuinely his. He will be the creator of his own perception, and that means he must know what it means to create an object or event with artistry.[16]

Obivously, there are multiple connections between participation in artistic activity and the ability to enjoy artistry, between such participation and self-discovery. Bennett Riemer talks of the way in which musical performance can contribute to increasing aesthetic sensitivity.[17] Stephen Spender talks of the way in which creative writing can increase sensitivity to the uses and possibilities of language.[18] Harold Rosenberg speaks often of deepening encounters with works of art through studio experiences and contacts with the art world. He believes that the making of paintings and sculptures should always be included in the enterprise of teaching art and that students can be educated in the processes employed by practicing artists—by their attitudes towards their materials and the character of their visual experiences. He continues:

> Art is culture, the culture developed by artists over the milennia of creation. The subject of an art course . . . is the artist and what he does and has done. It is not self-expression, or psychology of creation, or rules of how to match colors and harmonize forms.[19]

So there should be choosing and participation and experience and the search for order in all the arts. And there is the need to push back the walls of time to comprehend developing traditions in their continuities and discontinuities. Finally, each individual must somehow be liberated to transform her or his own reality, to become aware of her or his encounters and of what it means to be present in the world. Music, dance, and painting, if engaged in participatively and thoughtfully, can be distinctive in the confrontations they make possible and the personal possibilities they disclose. Only human beings can experience incompleteness, the gap between what is and what might be. Only human beings can fill the gap by moving out in search of meaning and transcendence, moving out to change their world. The focus must remain on the human being, on his or her achievement, his or her choice.

I want to end with an evocation of Alfred Schutz's notion of inner time, his notion of making music together in outer time in a face-to-face relationship, a community of space. "It is this dimension," he wrote, "which unifies the fluxes of inner time and warrants their synchronization into a vivid present."[20] This is what I see participants in aesthetic education doing, wherever they are: making music together, freeing themselves to future and to be.

References

1. Wallace Stevens, *The Collected Poems* (New York: Alfred A. Knopf, 1964), p. 75.
2. Soren Kierkegaard, " 'The Individual'," in *The Point of View for My Work as an Author,* ed. Benjamin Nelson (New York: Harper & Row, 1962), pp. 110-115.
3. John Dewey, *Art as Experience* (New York: Minton, Balch & Co., 1934), p. 104.

4. Alfred Schutz, "Making Music Together," in *Studies in Social Theory* Collected Papers II, ed. Arvid Brodersen (The Hague: Martinus Nijhoff, 1964), pp. 171-172.
5. Jean-Paul Sartre, *Literature and Existentialism* (New York: The Citadel Press, 1965), pp. 10-11.
6. Maurice Merleau-Ponty, "Cezanne's Doubt," in *Sense and Non-Sense* (Evanston, Ill.: Northwestern University Press, 1964), p. 17.
7. Leonard B. Meyer, "Some Remarks on Value and Greatness in Music," in *Aesthetics Today,* ed. Morris Philipson (New York: The World Publishing Co., 1961), p. 184.
8. Gabriel Marcel, "Bergsonism and Music," in *Reflections on Art,* ed. Susanne K. Langer (Baltimore: The Johns Hopkins Press, 1958), p. 151.
9. Merleau-Ponty, *Phenomenology of Perception* (New York: The Humanities Press, 1967), p. 456.
10. Rene Wellek and Austin Warren, *Theory of Literature* (New York: Harcourt, Brace & World, 1962), pp. 126-128.
11. J.W.N. Sullivan, "Music as Expression," in *Problems in Aesthetics,* ed. Morris Weitz (New York: Macmillan, 1959), p. 412.
12. Ludwig Wittgenstein, *Philosophical Investigations* (New York: Macmillan, 1968), Part I, Section 67.
13. Weitz, "The Role of Theory in Aesthetics," in *Problems in Aesthetics, op. cit.,* pp. 150-151.
14. Arnold Isenberg, "Critical Communication," in *Contemporary Studies in Aesthetics,* ed. Francis J. Coleman (New York: McGraw-Hill, 1963), p. 150.
15. Murray Krieger, "Literary Analysis and Evaluation—and the Ambidextrous Critic," in *Criticism,* ed. L.S. Dembo (Madison: University of Wisconsin Press, 1968), p. 35.
16. Jon Roush, "The Humanities Museum," in *The Arts on Campus,* ed. Margaret Mahoney (Greenwich, Conn.: New York Graphic Society, 1970), p. 37.
17. Bennett Reimer, *A Philosophy of Music Education* (Englewood Cliffs, N.J.: Prentice-Hall, 1970), pp. 126-127.
18. Stephen Spender, "Language and Communication," in *The Humanities in the Schools,* ed. Harold Taylor (New York: Citation Press, 1968), p. 97.
19. Harold Rosenberg, "Where to Begin," in *The Humanities in the Schools, op. cit.,* p. 72.
20. Alfred Schutz, *op. cit.*

PREDICAMENTS
OF WOMEN

15
The Lived World

"THE world," writes Merleau-Ponty, "is not what I think but what I live through."[1] He is describing the ways in which human consciousness opens itself to things, the ways in which—as embodied consciousnesses—we are in the world. He speaks of a perceptual reality that underlies our cognitive structures, of a primordial landscape in which we are present to ourselves.

I want to discuss the lived worlds and perceptual realities of women because I am so sharply aware of the degree to which they are obscured by sex and gender roles. I am convinced that the imposition of these roles makes women falsify their sense of themselves. Muriel Rukeyser says something to this effect when, in one of her poems, she writes of "myself, split open, unable to speak, in exile from myself." And a few lines later, "No more masks! No more mythologies!"[2] In "The Laugh of Medusa" Helene Cixous describes a "unique empire" that has been hidden"[3] and women who "have wandered in circles, confined to the narrow room in which they've been given a deadly brainwashing." I want to point to some of the deformations due to masking and confinement in the hope that they can be repaired. My concern is for the release of individual capacities now suppressed, for the development of free and autonomous personalities. It seems to me that these require an intensified critical awareness of our relation to ourselves and to our culture, a clarified sense of our own realities.

Now it is clear enough that we encounter each other in everyday life by means of roles and patterns of behavior that are habitualized, consciously or unconsciously learned. But what *is* everyday life? It is important to recall that it constitutes an *interpreted* reality—"interpreted by men," say Berger and Luckmann, "and subjectively meaningful to them as a coherent world."[4] As soon as we become habituated in the use of language, as soon as we begin transmuting

213

perceived shapes and presences into symbolic forms, we become participants in that world. This means that we begin interpreting our experiences with the aid of a "stock of knowledge at hand," recipes made available by the culture for making sense of things and other human beings, for defining our situations as we live.

It is interesting that Berger and Luckmann talk of a "reality interpreted by *men*," because the constructs normally used for mapping and interpreting the common sense world are largely those defined by males. It seems evident that, whenever they were developed, the dominant modes of ordering and categorizing experiences of private as well as public life have been functions of largely male perspectives—because, in Western culture, males have been the dominant group, the ones in power. And I include experiences of family life and childbirth as well as those of work, business, politics, and war. Alfred Schutz says that those who are born in any group tend to accept "the ready-made standardized scheme of the cultural pattern handed down . . . by ancestors, teachers, and authorities as an unquestioned and unquestionable guide in all the situations which normally occur within the social world."[5] In other words, the recipes, the interpretations, are treated as wholly trustworthy; they are taken for granted "in the absence of evidence to the contrary." Inevitably, they are internalized by women as well as by men. Once internalized, even such constructs as those having to do with subordination, natural inferiority, and unequally distributed rights are taken for granted. They are objectified, then externalized. They begin to appear as objective characteristics of an objectively existent world.

When Anais Nin writes that, "My maternal self is in conflict with my creative self," when she says that "creativity and femininity" seem incompatible, or that acts of independence are likely to be "punished by desertion,"[6] on some level she is reporting such phenomena as *givens*. On some level, she is unable to recall that they have been constituted, that they are part of an *interpreted* reality, that (as Helene Cixous puts it) "woman has always functioned 'within' the discourse of man. . . ."[7] So it is with the fictional Edna Pontellier in Kate Chopin's *The Awakening*. She is listening to her husband moving about his room, "every sound indicating impatience and irritation."

> Another time she would have gone in at his request. She would, through habit, have yielded to his desire; not with any sense of submission or obedience to his compelling wishes, but unthinkingly, as we walk, move, sit, stand, go through the daily treadmill of the life which has been portioned out to us.[8]

She accedes "unthinkingly." This means she takes for granted, not simply the reality of male domination and conjugal rights but a vision of life as a treadmill, of a fate "portioned out" in a fashion that has nothing to do with choice.

These notions are associated with sex roles, not with the sexuality of the woman concerned, not with the body as an "original source of perspective," the means by which subjectivity enters the world. Because they have to do with roles and not perceived realities, they connect with the everyday or common sense realities in which people live most of their lives. They tend, therefore, to overwhelm or to suppress a variety of alternative interpretations and alternative realities—like those of art, or dream, or play. They do so because the conceived world, the constructed world, is so frequently at odds with the perceived wold; it is difficult, especially for women, to grant to perceived realities the integrity they deserve.

Consider Edna Pontellier again—beginning her life on a Kentucky plantation, grasping her space at first through a bodily situation that involved a sea of grass through which she could run, about which she could feel. As Merleau-Ponty would see it, the smells and colors of that place were "themselves different modalities of (her) co-existence with the world."[9] The distances, the different points in the spaces of the plantation, were "relations between those points and a central perspective," the body of the little girl. In any case, this was where Edna came in touch with the world, where she first grasped it in a here-and-now. And this was where, when ten years old, Edna had a fantasy love affair with a cavalry officer and, when threatened by the stern prayers of her Presbyterian father, ran to take refuge in the grass.

Then the social world takes over; she marries, begins playing the role of wife, taking on what the author describes as a "fictitious self." Her awakening occurs at the seashore, when she turns away from the Creole mother-women and responds to a flirtatious young man. For the first time she begins "to realize her position in the universe as a human being." More significantly, she is seduced by the voice of the sea, "inviting the soul to wander for a spell in abysses of solitude; to lose itself in mazes of inward contemplation." She confuses the stirring of a long-suppressed sexuality with a hidden authenticity, the emergence of a true self; at length, in despair at abandonment, in fear of possible promiscuity, in defiance of the "soul's slavery" of domesticity, she swims out to sea and drowns. Her suicide is not only due to repression and depression, although it can be explained that way. It is due to the falsification occasioned by the role she is forced to play, given the late 19th century moment, her social class, and her husband's demands. It is, in part, a crisis of meaningfulness: she has no way of grounding what she feels; she has no way of confronting her own relationship to the world.

Merleau-Ponty says, "The experience of perception is our presence at the moment when things, truths, values are constituted for us." He writes that, "Perception is a nascent logos; that it teaches us, outside all dogmatism, the true conditions of objectivity itself, that it summons us to the tasks of knowledge and action."[10] It is not simply that perceptual experience is in some sense primordial, that it refers to our original landscapes, and the background of our lived lives. Nor is it simply that perception remains foundational to a developing rationality. Perceptual reality ought always to be considered one of the multiple realities available to us: a recognizable set of experiences, once they are reflected back upon, characterized by a distinctive mode of attention, one too many people have repressed or refused.

I believe that the ability to come in touch with "the moment when things, truths, values are constituted for us" permits us to break some of the hold of the taken-for-granted when it comes to the already constituted categories by which we interpret the world. In the case of Edna Pontellier, an ability to remain grounded in her earliest relations to her surroundings might have given her some awareness of the way she had built up a meaningful world. It might have kept her in touch with her own perspective, her own vantage point, and allowed her to resist the arbitrariness and the distortions of some of the roles she was forced to play. The spiritualization of women like Edna, the infantilization, the mystification that convinced her of inevitability: all these might have been allayed if she had been somehow able to realize that she lived in a constructed reality, that it was possible to choose along with others, possible even to transcend.

My sense of the oppressiveness of gender roles does not move me to think about recovering a "natural," spontaneous, untrammelled self uncorrupted by the world. I cannot conceive Edna Pontellier or Anais Nin or anyone else existing as a human being apart from social relations and social roles. My point has to do with what William James calls the "sense of our own reality, that sense of our own life which we at every moment possess." He talks about the things that have "intimate and continuous connection" with our lives, things whose reality we do not doubt. And he says that the world of those living realities becomes the "hook from which the rest dangles, the absolute support."[11] Without a sense of those realities, we are likely to lose touch with our own projects, to become "invisible" in Ralph

Ellison's sense, to think of ourselves as others define us, not as we create ourselves.

If we can be present to ourselves and look through perspectives rooted in our own reality, we may be in a position to confront arbitrariness and oppression. The alternative may be the narcissism, egotism, touchiness, and the rest that Simone de Beauvoir attributes to powerlessness. Talking about the woman who is shut up in the kitchen or boudoir, de Beauvoir says that, since she is deprived "of all possibility of concrete communication with others," she experiences no solidarity. "She could hardly be expected, then, to transcend herself toward the general welfare. She stays obstinately within the one realm that is familiar to her, where she can control things and in the midst of which she enjoys a precarious sovereignty." Such a woman is seldom able to grasp the masculine universe "which she respects from afar, without daring to venture into it." She develops a magical conception of reality which she projects into the male world; "the course of events seems to her to be inevitable. . . ."[12]

I think of the narrator of Grace Paley's story, "The Used-Boy Raisers," listening to her present husband and her ex-husband (whom she names "Pallid" and "Livid") battling over religion. She is drawn into their quarrel when they remind her that she is Jewish; she tells them that she believes in the Diaspora and is against Israel "on technical grounds," because she objects to the Jews being like every other temporal nationality. She says:

> Jews have one hope only—to remain a remnant in the basement of world affairs—no, I mean something else—a splinter in the toe of civilizations, a victim to aggravate the conscience.
> Livid and Pallid were astonished at my outburst, since I rarely express my opinion on any serious matter but only live out my destiny, which is to be, until my expiration date, laughingly the servant of man.[13]

It may be that she is associating her own plight as a woman with what she sees as the proper destiny of the Jews, but what is striking is the presentation of a woman who stays obstinately in her own realm, who submits to what she thinks of as her destiny. She says marriage "just ties a man down"; she organizes the "greedy day" with its tasks of motherhood and domesticity; she watches her husbands from a distance, moving off "on paths which are not my concern."

There are others, so many others, in and out of literature. The difficulty is (as it was for Edna and for Nora in *The Doll's House*) that their justifications are always in the hands of others. They keep wait-

ing for male approval, male gratitude, male support. Without grounding, without a sense of themselves, they live, at best, in a kind of negation. They are not self-conscious enough, self-reflective enough, sister-
ly enough to undo the work of socialization; their personal development is necessarily frustrated; they are submerged in their roles.

Again, if women are in touch with themselves and in concrete communication with others, they have a ground against which to consider
the mystifications that work on them, the inequities that prevail—even
today in this presumably liberated time. I believe that it is necessary to
look into the darkness, into the terrible blankness that creeps over so
many women's lives, into the wells of victimization and powerlessness.

I am never surprised, for some reason, to discover in many books
written by women that the death of a female heroine creates no stir in
the universe. Consider Edna Pontellier's suicide. There is no scene of
recognition, not even a funeral scene. Think of Lily Bart's suicide in
The House of Mirth. There is a slight, sad stirring on Selden's part; a
small leaf has fallen from a tree. Consider *To the Lighthouse* and the
death of Mrs. Ramsay, who is the glowing, ambivalent center of the
first section of the book. The second, called "Time Passes," deals with
dark nights, an empty house, the winds, and the waves. Suddenly,
parenthetically, there are the following sentences: "Mr. Ramsay
stumbling along a passage stretched his arms out one dark morning;
but, Mrs. Ramsay having died rather suddenly the night before, he
stretched his arms out. They remained empty."[14]

I am not saying that all women's deaths go unnoticed in women's
novels (although I would note that there is undoubtedly more suicide
and madness in women's literature than in men's). I am suggesting
that there is no female version of a Hamlet in women's literature, no
one telling a friend like Horatio to absent herself from felicity a while
"to tell my story." Nor, in women's literature, is there normally an
Ishmael who escapes to tell, to give the tragedy some meaning under
the sky. I suspect that is what Virginia Woolf had in mind when she
concocted her fiction about Shakespeare's sister. Contemplating a
woman of the 16th century with the capacity to render the human
condition in a play, Woolf writes that any such woman "would certainly have gone crazed, shot herself, or ended her days in some lonely
cottage outside the village, half witch, half wizard, feared and mocked
at."[15] Perhaps this is part of our perceived reality too.

But there are other ills, more remediable ills, to be confronted by
the woman grounded enough to see. Listen to Virginia Woolf again,

this time comparing the difficulties faced by a woman writer with those plaguing men.

> The indifference of the world which Keats and Flaubert and other men of genius have found so hard to bear was in her case not indifference but hostility. The world did not say to her as it said to them, Write if you choose; it makes no difference to me. The world said wth a guffaw, Write? What's the good of your writing? Here the psychologists . . . might come to our help, I thought, looking again at the blank spaces on the shelves. For surely it is time that the effect of discouragement on the mind of the artist should be measured, as I have seen a dairy company measure the effect of ordinary milk and Grade A milk upon the body of the rat.[16]

To change the universe of discourse for an instant, listen to Catharine R. Stimpson, talking about National Endowment for the Arts grants to men and women:

> If census data show 66 percent of musicians are male, 88 percent of individual NEA grants are to men. On the other hand, if census data show 63 percent of painters and sculptors are male, they got but 60 percent of the individual grants. Of the three sample years, 1972 was the best for women as a whole, which may show an effect of the women's movement and the new consciousness about sex roles. In 1970, women received just under 15 percent of the individual awards, in 1968 about 18 percent. A preliminary conclusion that might be drawn is that NEA has not only reflected but sustained a masculinized ideology of the working artist. Microcosm may nurture macrocosm.[17]

And then Stimpson goes on to talk about the way male perspectives have dominated the arts and distorted "our visions of sex and gender." This is simply because men and women have dissimilar experiences that affect their perceptions of themselves and of each other; until women are given full access to the arts, their range will be limited, their complexities less than they should be. Again, this is part of what has to be confronted, not as part of a "given" and unchangeable reality, but as a problematic application of gender categories, at odds with our sense of what is real.

Again, I am arguing for an intensified awareness of women's own realities, the shape of their own lived worlds. Not only might this make possible a clear perception of the arbitrariness, the absurdity (as well as the inequity) involved in genderizing such fields as the arts, the sciences, and, yes, school administration. It might also provoke women into confrontations of their authentic corporeal selves. As is well known, women writers—and, particularly, feminist writers—have diversified approaches to the biosocial nature of women. Please note, I am not now speaking of sex or gender roles; I am speaking of sexuality, the distinctiveness of the body that carries subjectivity into the world. As I do so, I want to try to separate what we think about it from the manifold stereotypes, those that associate it with biological destiny, with evil, with the spiritual, the passive, or the irrational. And, certainly, I want to distinguish it from the kind of male view exemplified by Harry Wilborne in William Faulkner's *The Wild Palms*. In that book, Harry muses "on that efficiency of women in the mechanics, the domiciling of cohabitation. Not thrift, not husbandry, something far beyond that, who (the entire race of them) employed with infallible instinct, a completely uncerebrated rapport for the type and nature of male partner and situation. . . ."[18]

Alice Rossi, writing in *Daedalus,* uses a "biosocial perspective" through which to consider some of the new egalitarian ideologies that deny innate sex differences and demand that fathers play equal roles when it comes to child care. Making the point that, "Sex is an invariant ascription from birth to death," she goes on to talk about the cultural determinists among social scientists and activists, who (she says) "confuse equality with identity and diversity with inequality." Diversity, she writes, "is a biological fact, while equality is a political, ethical, and social precept."[19]

It is not necessary to recapitulate Rossi's interesting and complex argument to make the point that she, partly on the grounds of studies in endocrinology and physiology, argues for the central place of women in parenting. She talks about innate predispositions on the part of mothers to relate intensely to their infants, about the influence upon women of hormonal cyclicity, pregnancy, and birth. At no time does she recommend that all women have children, although she does recommend that women who choose to have children avoid giving them over to communal child-rearing centers, where youngsters may become "neglected, joyless creatures." And she does acknowledge the social deprivation of many women and argue for social support systems of many kinds.

I bring up this article not merely for its intrinsic importance; I bring it up because it seems to me to relate to the themes I have been trying to explore. The confusion Rossi talks about—the confusion of diversity with equality—is a function of the general tendency to permit cultural factors to overwhelm the lived world. Once women come in touch not only with the lived world but with their primordial landscapes and with their corporeal involvements, they cannot avoid com-

ing in touch with their sexuality as well. After all, women's distinctiveness as sexual beings affects the ways in which they grasp the world
around; it influences the modalities of their "co-existence" with that
world. Domination by our sex *roles,* I am convinced, is what moves so
many women to deny or belittle or lament their sexual reality. Current
calls for uni-sexism are heard in the domain of social reality; they have
much the same effect as traditional expressions of shame and guilt.
The consequence is, very often, that attention is diverted from significant questions of family policy and child care policy to misplaced calls
for equity. Nothing I have said—and nothing Alice Rossi has said—
is meant to suggest that one way of life is best for all women everywhere; nor has anything been said to suggest that women who choose
to bear children should forever give up ideas of working or composing
or becoming Shakespeare's sisters. Again, it is a matter of grounding,
of rooting choices in perceived realities, and in what women grasp as
their own lived worlds.

There is another modern novel that deals with some of this, albeit
in a mysterious and troubling way: *Surfacing,* by the Canadian writer,
Margaret Atwood. The heroine is Canadian, returning home to the
wilderness where she grew up from a long sojourn in the United States.
In search of her lost father, she is accompanied by three sophisticated,
urban friends, but she is absorbed in the recovery of her own past, her
own landscape, as she is in struggling against all labels, falsifications,
and, finally, all enclosures. An abortion she has had signifies victimization to her; American hunters on the lake signify male violation
and destruction; ordinary language signifies deformation. She dreams
of rejecting passivity by having a baby herself "squatting on old newspapers in a corner alone; or on leaves, dry leaves, a heap of them. . . ."
Alone on her island, she slips out of her clothes, out of human habita-
tion, into inchoateness, a pantheist reality—what she thinks of as her
own space, her ritual plunge. And finally:

> This above all, to refuse to be a victim. Unless I can do that I can do
> nothing. I have to recant, to give up the old belief that I am powerless
> and because of it nothing I can do will ever hurt anyone. A lie which
> was always more disastrous than the truth would have been. The word
> games, the winning and losing games are finished; at the moment there
> are no others but they will have to be invented, withdrawing is no
> longer possible and the alternative is death. I drop the blanket on the
> floor and go into my dismantled room. My spare clothes are here,
> knife slashes in them, but I can still wear them. I dress, clumsily, un-
> familiar with buttons; I reenter my own time.[20]

Her lover appears on the shore, "a mediator, an ambassador, offering me something: captivity in any of its forms, a new freedom?" She knows she must return to words and houses and that they may well fail again. And the only way back she can find is through a freely chosen pregnancy.

This is extreme, of course. The reality explored may be the reality of psychosis; again, salvation lies somewhere in the past, in a retracing of the trail. But the dissonance between the narrator's perceived landscape and the taken-for-granted world of gender roles and power is brutally clear. What happens when ordinary barriers are breached, accepted forms destroyed? If alternative constructs are not devised, madness may be the consequence. Where is the freedom that is not linked to manipulative power? How do we go about remaking the constituted world?

Catharine Stimpson talks about a need for "a compensatory consciousness about sex, gender, and culture," and a recovery of women's contributions to the arts of the past. Carol Gould talks of the importance of demystification and "the elimination of . . . those illusions that bind us to exploitation."[21] Virginia Woolf talks of living "in the presence of reality"—and having a "room of one's own." It is clear that the interest in socialization, in sex-typing, and in role differentiation has led to notable discoveries. We understand more than we ever have about what has frustrated the self-identification of women, what has prevented free choosing in an open world. Many of the inquiries have had the effect of moving certain women to a reexamination of their own presuppositions, their own roles. There has been—and there must be—an increasing effort to transform teaching practice, to revise teaching materials, and to invent new approaches to work and play.

I believe all this must be supplemented by the kind of emancipatory thinking that enables women to confront the ways in which they have constructed their social reality—and to regain touch with their lived worlds. Like Virginia Woolf, I believe in the power of imaginative literature, of novels that allow one to see "more intensely afterwards," that make the world seem "bared of its covering and given an intenser life."[22] A good work of fiction, writes Sartre, is an "exigence and a gift"; also, it is an act of faith.

> And if I am given this world with its injustices, it is not so that I might contemplate them coldly, but that I might animate them with my indignation, that I might disclose them with their nature as injustices, that is, as abuses to be suppressed. Thus, the writer's universe will only reveal itself in all its depth to the examination, the admiration, and the indignation of the reader. . . .[23]

To read Muriel Rukeyser or Grace Paley or Virginia Woolf is to be given a gift, which we can receive if we are attentive, if we are willing to bracket our everydayness, conformity, and fear. Moreover, as Sartre also says, the work of art is an act of confidence in human freedom. Freedom is the power of vision and the power to choose. It involves the capacity to assess situations in such a way that lacks can be defined, openings identified, and possibilities revealed. It is realized only when action is taken to repair the lacks, to move through the openings, to try to pursue real possibilities. One of the strengths of imaginative literature is that it can enable women to assume new standpoints on what they take for granted, to animate certain constructs with their indignation, so that they can see them as sources of the injustice that plagues them, see them, not as givens, but as constituted by human beings and changeable by human beings. The imaginative leap can lead to the leap that is *praxis,* the effort to remake and transcend.

This is another dimension of the effort to define sexual equality in the modern age. The aesthetic and the imaginative can never substitute for social, scientific, or biosocial inquiry, although they may provoke new modes of inquiry because of the manner in which imaginative forms present a reality ordinarily obscured. Without articulation, without expression, the perceived world is in some way nullified; until given significant form, it holds no significance except in the prereflective domain. That is why literature may provide a resource, an inroad into a province of meaning that is associated, not so much with the "reality interpreted by men and subjectively meaningful to them," but with the world of the "nascent logos," the world women live. And considering that world, I choose to end with more lines from Muriel Rukeyser, these from "Kathe Kollwitz":

> *What would happen if one woman told the truth*
> *about her life?*
> *The world would split open.*[24]

References

1. Maurice Merleau-Ponty, *Phenomenology of Perception* (London: Routledge & Kegan Paul, 1967), pp. xvi, xvii.
2. Muriel Rukeyser, "The Poem as Mask," in *by a Woman writt,* ed. Joan Goulianos (Indianapolis: Bobbs-Merrill, 1973), p. 379.
3. Helene Cixous, "The Laugh of Medusa," *Signs,* Summer 1976, Vol. 1, No. 4, p. 876.

4. Peter L. Berger and Thomas Luckmann, *The Social Construction of Reality* (Garden City, N.Y.: Anchor Books, Doubleday and Co., 1967), p. 19.
5. Alfred Schutz, *Studies in Social Theory,* Collected Papers II, ed. Arvid Brodersen (The Hague: Martinus Nijhoff, 1964), p. 22.
6. Anais Nin, *The Diary of Anais Nin,* Vol. III, 1939-44, Jan. 1943, Goulianos, ed., *op. cit.,* p. 303.
7. Helene Cixous, in Goulianos, ed., *op. cit.,* p. 887.
8. Kate Chopin, *The Awakening* (New York: Capricorn Books, 1964), p. 79.
9. Merleau-Ponty, *The Primacy of Perception* (Evanston: Northwestern University Press, 1964), p. 5.
10. Ibid., p. 25.
11. William James, *Principles of Psychology,* Vol. II (New York: Henry Holt, 1950), p. 297.
12. Simone de Beauvoir, *The Second Sex* (New York: Alfred A. Knopf, 1957), pp. 450-451.
13. Grace Paley, "The Used-Boy Raisers," *The Little Disturbances of Man* (New York: Meridian Fiction, 1960), p. 132.
14. Virginia Woolf, *To the Lighthouse* (London: J.M. Dent, Everyman's Library, 1962), p. 149.
15. Woolf, *A Room of One's Own* (New York: Harcourt, Brace, & World, 1957), p. 51.
16. Ibid., p. 54.
17. Catharine R. Stimpson, "Sex, Gender, and American Culture," in *Women and Men: Changing Roles, Relationships, and Perceptions,* ed. Libby A. Cater, Anne Firor Scott, and Wendy Martyna (New York: Praeger Publishers, 1977), pp. 216, 220.
18. William Faulkner, *The Wild Palms* (New York: New American Library, Signet Modern Classics, 1968), p. 53.
19. Alice S. Rossi, "A Biosocial Perspective on Parenting," *Daedalus,* Spring 1977, p. 2.
20. Margaret Atwood, *Surfacing* (New York: Popular Library, 1972) pp. 222-223.
21. Carol C. Gould, "Philosophy of Liberation and the Liberation of Philosophy," in *Women and Philosophy: Toward a Theory of Liberation,* ed. Carol C. Gould and Marx W. Wartofsky (New York: Capricorn Books, 1976), p. 38.
22. Woolf, *op. cit.,* p. 114.
23. Jean-Paul Sartre, *Literature and Existentialism* (New York: Citadel Press, 1965), pp. 62-63.
24. Rukeyser, "Kathe Kollwitz," in Goulianos, ed., *op. cit.,* p. 377.

16

The Impacts of Irrelevance: Women in the History of American Education

"THE notion basic to justice," writes R.S. Peters, "is that distinctions should be made if there are relevant differences and that they should not be made if there are no relevant differences or on the basis of irrelevant differences."[1] The history of women's education in the United States is a history of distinctions made "on the basis of irrelevant differences." That means it is a history of unfairness and inequity. Women were denied equality of consideration over the years; those who denied them that equality felt no obligation to justify what they did. This was because of the way they selected out factors to be considered relevant and because of the way official notions of relevance were imposed and internalized. Righteously and with perfect self-assurance, those in positions of power did what they could to perpetuate the existence of a separate (and subordinate) female sphere.

There is no need to summon up evocations of ancient myths and illusions to explain the exclusion of women from the universe of "all men" presumably "created equal." Natural rights theory, which gave rise to so much of the American belief system, was itself qualified by such remarks as Rousseau's that, "The whole education of women ought to be relative to men."[2] Great apostles of the Enlightenment like Dr. Benjamin Rush called for "a peculiar and suitable education" for "our ladies." The institutions of liberty and equality gave women a

225

special responsibility: they were appointed to instruct "their *sons* in the principles of liberty."[3]

According to the governing construct, women had duties but few rights. It was not only that they were considered mentally inferior and that the "dictates of nature" (as one woman explained) required the home to be each woman's "appropriate and appointed sphere of action."[4] In a country where, for a moment, almost anything seemed possible, where what was thought to be civilized could at any time be abandoned for life on the frontier or in the wilderness, where violence and anarchy seemed always incipient,[5] there was a felt need for a moral anchor—a place where order reigned, along with propriety and control. That, of course, was the responsibility of women: to establish in the home a counterweight to temptation, to maintain moral norms. If females were to be educated, it was (as Catharine Beecher was to say) to fulfill their "peculiar responsibilities."[6] The fact that they were barred from civil and political affairs, the fact that they had no legal identity, the fact that they were, in effect, the chattels of their husbands, all this was compensated for because precedence was given to them "in all the comforts, conveniences, and courtesies of life."

When de Tocqueville visited the United States in 1830-31, he was impressed by the discovery that, here, "The independence of woman is irrecoverably lost in the bonds of matrimony. . . ." He spoke of the many ways in which democracy seemed to modify social inequalities and then made the point that Americans made an exception when it came to equality between the sexes.

> They admit, that as nature has appointed such wide differences between the physical and moral constitution of man and woman, her manifest design was to give a distinct employment to their various faculties; and they hold that improvement does not consist in making beings so dissimilar do pretty nearly the same things, but in getting each of them to fulfill their respective tasks in the best possible manner. The Americans have applied to the sexes the great principle of political economy which governs the manufactures of our age, by carefully dividing the duties of man from those of woman, in order that the great work of society may be the better carried on.[7]

There is some suggestion of economic determinism here, but it must be pointed out that, even before the development of the factory system, the same division was assumed to exist. This was so despite the shared labors characteristic of domestic industry. As on the frontier, women performed many of the chores usually allotted to men; when left alone, they did whatever they needed to do to survive: ran shops, pushed plows, and repaired machinery. Nevertheless, the traditional notion was stubbornly held in mind. Women were considered predominantly spiritual creatures, emotional and delicate; if they were to be educated at all, the purpose was to educate them for dutiful and dependent lives—for subordination and powerlessness.

When, in the 1830s, the reform movement (which included campaigns for abolition, women's rights, war resistance, and prison reform) began to focus on education rather than "conversion," the notion of subordination was made surprisingly explicit. In the first place, the effort to consolidate existing schools and establish an effective school system was fueled by dread of lawlessness. Not only was it necessary to socialize a great diversity of children into a way of life increasingly dominated by industry, it appeared essential as well to Americanize, through schooling, those who had no experience with freedom—and who seemed all too prone to confuse liberty with license.[8] Whether the dominating concern was to create a literate and disciplined working class, to impose a middle-class and Protestant *ethos,* or to erect barriers against corruption and disorder, the expressed commitment was to "social control." This meant, of course, the internalization of respect for the laws of righteousness and for existing social authorities. Anti-social energies and appetites were to be tamped down; "impetuosity" was to be subordinated to "voluntary compliance."[9] The entire effort and the prevailing atmosphere were thought of as redemptive, humane, and benign.

The teachers in those early schools were largely female. Seldom, if ever, provided with more than an elementary school education themselves, they were granted little status, and their wages were abysmally low. But then it was acceptable to hire young women, who would otherwise be totally dependent as daughters or sisters or wards, and pay them less than an ordinary clerk received. Most of them were thought of as spinsters, and, in any case, they were expected to remain unmarried if they hoped to remain in the schools. Few communities could afford better teaching for the younger children, and it is clear enough that women's second-class position allowed school committees, without apology, to tap the pool of the cheapest labor while keeping the lamp of morality alight. After all, who was better equipped to trim that lamp and shelter it from the wind? Henry Barnard, the Connecticut school reformer, was only one of many when he talked of how well prepared such women were—because they were persons "in whose own hearts, love, hope, and patience have first kept school."[10]

Horace Mann, in his Tenth Report as Secretary of the Massachusetts Board of Education, asked his readers to picture the model teacher. Can you imagine a person, he said, whose language is well selected, whose pronunciation and tones of voice are correct and attractive, whose manners are gentle and refined, all whose topics of conversation are elevating and instructive, whose benignity of heart is constantly manifested in acts of civility, courtesy, and kindness, and who spreads a nameless charm over whatever circle may be entered? Such a person should the teacher of every Common School be.[11]

Constant emphasis was placed on gentility and docility, the virtues long associated with the female sphere. What is interesting is the consonance between these virtues, the virtues normally linked to hearth and home, and what was thought desirable in the common school. Women teachers were seldom hired to teach older children nor to deal with more than elementary literacy. Their minds were not considered acute enough to handle mathematics or the natural sciences. Their assigned role, indeed their fate, was to mold other people's children, to bind them to respectability and virtue with cords they could not easily break. They were genteel, intrusive models; they were stern mother surrogates; delegated to impose social control, they often ran their classrooms with iron hands.

Nevertheless, they knew—and the community knew—that they were strictly subordinated to the men who administered the schools. The principals and superintendents were male; they were responsible for the curriculum, for discipline, for the moral regimen the teachers were to carry out, and even for the ways in which the classrooms were arranged. David Tyack quotes a journal article stating that, "Women teachers are often preferred by superintendents because they are more willing to comply with established regulations and less likely to ride headstrong hobbies." And then:

If teachers have advice to give their superior, said the Denver superintendent of schools, "it is to be given as the good daughter talks with the father. . . . The dictation must come from the other end." In 1841, the Boston school committee commended women teachers because they were unambitious, frugal, and filial: "They are less intent on scheming for future honors or emoluments. . . . As a class, they never look forward, as young men almost invariably do, to a period of legal emancipation from parental control."[12]

The primary concern of the common school was to move all children, boys *and* girls, to "voluntary compliance"; it is not hard to imagine the special lessons in compliance taught to girls. The image of the obviously subordinate woman must have been powerful enough, but when this was linked to the materials in, say, the McGuffey

Readers—with their almost exclusive emphasis on "the good boy," "the poor boy," the boy who stood on the burning deck, and the rest[13] —the construct of the second sphere (the inferior sphere) can only have been continuously confirmed.

There were ordinary young women, however, apart from the early feminists, who did break the pattern of submission and conformity— or, at least, who thought they did. They were the mill girls, who left home to work for wages only to find that they were discriminated against in the factories as much as anywhere else. Not only did they have to work from twelve to sixteen hours a day, they were paid far less than men. Frequently they were compelled to live in company dormitories and submit to rigid discipline. This may well be considered to be still another mode of female education: values and skills were intentionally transmitted, not to mention a whole structure of attitudes and beliefs. Lucy Larcom, who first had wanted to "keep school" as her aunt had done, went to work in the Lowell mills in 1835, when she was about thirteen; she wrote that she thought it a good thing for so many strange girls to leave their homes and go to Lowell, because "it taught them to go out of themselves and enter into the lives of others"[14] and because it appeared to be a way of belonging to the world.

The Lowell mills, in fact, became a tourist attraction, largely due to such girls. Charles Dickens and Harriet Martineau both commented on the self-respect, the good clothes, the fine manners of the thousands of young women who worked there for less than three dollars a week on five-year stints. The operatives had libraries and their own newspapers, but they worked seventy hours a week, and payments for their food and lodging were deducted from their wages. Their "education" included regular church attendance, Sunday School classes, and occasional classes in the fundamentals of literacy; they were required to avoid card games as well as "ardent spirits" and to refrain from all modes of dissolute behavior.[15] Their "intelligence" and contentment were widely advertised, but it is obvious that they were being cared for by the factory managers, puritanical father surrogates who could allow little leeway for spontaneity or choice of self. There were male operatives in some mills and male inhabitants of company towns, but there is no evidence of such protective behavior on their behalf, perhaps because working men, though subordinate, belonged to the sphere where protection and care were not required.

Herman Melville, having visited the Lowell mills and seen the workers there, wrote a story about a paper mill based upon his experience. He called it "The Tartarus of Maids"; it deals with blue-white girls sorting rags, serving iron machines, folding paper, moving through the "consumptive pallors of this blank, raggy life. . . ." Near the end, the narrator speaks with the principal proprietor about his machines and his girls:

> "The girls," echoed I, glancing around at their silent forms. "Why is it, sir, that in most factories, female operatives, of whatever age, are indiscriminately called girls, never women?"
>
> "Oh! as to that, why, I suppose, the fact of their being generally unmarried—that's the reason, I should think. But it never struck me before. For our factory here, we will not have married women; they are apt to be off-and-on too much. We want none but steady workers: twelve hours to the day, day after day, through the three hundred and sixty-five days, excepting Sundays, Thanksgiving, and Fast-days. That's our rule. And so, having no married women, what females we have are rightly enough called girls."[16]

The girls are compared at the conclusion with the bachelors the narrator had met near London's Temple Bar, in a "very perfection of quiet absorption of good living, good drinking, good feeling, and good talk,"[17] men who knew nothing of suffering and loneliness. These are the two extremes—a Paradise and a Tartarus—but the distinction between the spheres is highlighted in a kind of lurid glare. Melville was able to make a second, more ambiguous distinction as well: between women and girls—those in the protective circle of domestic life and those infantilized by factory managers, bent (like grateful and virtuous daughters) over work tables and looms.

Infantilization and segregation were too often linked with education in the lives of 19th century women. It is true that the fiction of the happy, well cared for Lowell girls was to a degree destroyed when a Lowell Female Labor Reform Association was organized, in time to be led by Sarah Bagley, who wrote of herself as "a common schooled New England female factory operative. . . ."[18] They engaged in a petition campaign in an unsuccessful effort to move the legislature to enact a ten-hour day. They could not vote, but they tried to exert pressure at election time to defeat unsympathetic legislators. They did not win what they wanted; they were held back by male union members as well as by the factory managers; they continued to be treated as "girls." But the very fact that they moved together for a while suggests that they had not fully internalized the official view of themselves as helpless, docile, and insistently happy. They were schooled, but not well schooled.

Catharine Beecher, daughter of Lyman Beecher and sister of Harriet Beecher Stowe, was perturbed by the spectacle of women going to work in factories, and, because so many eligible men were going west to the frontier, an increasing number of "surplus" females were being forced to earn their own living—more often than not as operatives. After conducting a seminary for young women at Hartford (where *"intellectual* culture" was deliberately subordinated to "the formation of that character which Jesus Christ teaches to be indispensable to the *eternal* well being of our race" and where girls were taught their social duty in the world[19]), Miss Beecher turned, in 1827, to female improvement generally. Struck by the disproportion between the number of people who wanted to hire domestic servants and the number of women who wanted to go into domestic service (because of the larger compensation offered by "our manufactories") and impressed also by the importance of the common schools, she began to elaborate on her Christian notions of women's highest calling:

> When all the mothers, teachers, nurses and domestics are taken from our sex, which the best interests of society demand, and when all these employments are deemed respectable and are filled by well-educated women, there will be no supernumeraries found to put into shops and mills or to draw into the arena of public and political life.[20]

Beecher's contribution to women's education was to suggest that household work demanded intellectual skills and that women of all classes deserved a well-rounded education in such areas as physiology, hygiene, nutrition, and applied mathematics. Women had their "proper work" to do, she was saying, but that work should be viewed as dignified.[21] Nevertheless (and this must be stressed), she continued to assert that "certain relations" had to be maintained "which involve the duties of subordination. ... There must be the relations of husband and wife, parent and child, teacher and pupil, employer and employed, each involving the relative duties of subordination."[22] Her efforts to establish normal schools for teachers, important as they were, were equally permeated with the notion that it was more important "that women be educated to be virtuous, useful, and pious, than that they become learned and accomplished. . . ."[23]

Emma Hart Willard, who herself had received an advanced education, saw the problem of intellectual development quite differently. Largely due to her own fascination with higher mathematics and the frustration she experienced at not being allowed to attend the men's examinations at the University of Middlebury, the Troy Female Semi-

nary she established in 1821 not only included courses in advanced
algebra and geometry but more explicit courses in physiology than had
yet been offered. This did not mean that she neglected religious training nor the "truths" of the Scriptures. Nor did it mean that she
challenged the "service" obligations of women.[24] She did, however,
provide high school opportunities at a time when no high schools were
open to females; as significantly, she began—at least by indirection—
to erode the conventional belief that there were differences in mental
capacity between men and women.

She did not, and undoubtedly could not, go as far as the Scotch
feminist, Frances Wright, who arrived in the United States in 1819 and
launched her campaign for educational emancipation and social justice.
An associate of the utopian thinker Robert Owen, she worked at New
Harmony, edited a newspaper, and lectured to audiences of work-
ingmen throughout the East and Middle West. Not only did she demand equal education for women, she launched a critique of religious
dogmas and, like other Owenites, called for the establishment of free
boarding schools to promote the eradication of class differences and
class control.[25] Probably of most importance was her continual demand that people begin thinking for themselves. Like Henry David
Thoreau, she called on men and women to examine the *grounds* of
their beliefs, to open their eyes and inquire; unlike Thoreau and his
transcendentalist contemporaries, she spoke directly to those who
were subordinated in society, to those—women and workers both—
she thought to be oppressed.

And, indeed, the oppression was multi-faceted. The maintenance
of the two spheres made it immeasurably difficult for women to overcome the feeling that they were the creatures of outside authorities.
Harriet Martineau, after one of her visits, spoke directly to the problem when she described the ways in which American women were even
deprived of the right to determine what precisely their duties were:

> If there be any human power and business and privilege which is
> absolutely universal, it is the discovery and adoption of the principle
> and laws of duty. As every individual, whether man or woman, has a
> reason and a conscience, this is a work which each is thereby author-
> ized to do for himself or herself. But it is not only virtually prohibited
> to beings who, like the American woman, have scarcely any objects in
> life proposed to them; but the whole apparatus of opinion is brought
> to bear offensively upon individuals among women who exercise free-
> dom of mind in deciding upon what duty is, and the methods by which
> it is to be pursued.[26]

Emma Willard, Elizabeth Peabody, Margaret Fuller, and the others who were courageous enough to identify themselves and their commitments belonged, it must be recalled, to a privileged class. In most cases, they were admired or indulged or sustained by their fathers or by interested male friends. It was *possible* for them to demand, as Margaret Fuller did, total fulfillment,[27] to reject renunciation, and to enter and enjoy "the Paradise of thought."[28] Numerous others, middle-class and working-class women alike, retained the image of themselves as destined to subordination and dependence; the schools, with few exceptions, reinforced what they had internalized from their earliest days.

Even Mary Lyon, who tried so hard to provide the female students at Mt. Holyoke Seminary with the same academic education men were receiving, wrote to her mother, "O how immensely important is this work of preparing the daughters of the land to be good mothers!"[29] Convinced as she was of the importance of domestic knowledge, she herself worked desperately hard outside the domestic sphere. It took her about four years to raise the necessary money from the surrounding community. Frequently she was forced to rely on male representatives and spokesmen, so that people would not think women were originating such far-reaching plans. When the seminary opened in 1837, Miss Lyon inaugurated a curriculum as rigorous and academic as the one at Harvard. The students were carefully selected; they were expected to attend for three years, during which they took such courses as grammar, rhetoric, human physiology, algebra, natural philosophy, intellectual philosophy, astronomy, chemistry, ecclesiastical history, logic, and natural theology. They also performed domestic duties, of course, but, as Eleanor Flexner has written, Mary Lyon helped to demonstrate "that women's minds were constituted, in bulk and cell structure and endowment, the same as those of their masculine counterparts. . . ."[30] What was required, as always, was opportunity to act on such capacities—opportunity at least more likely for the daughters of businessmen and ministers than for the children of the poor.

The atmosphere was restrictive at Mt. Holyoke in spite of some of the liberating ideas. Emily Dickinson attended the seminary briefly in 1847 and found it too confining. Some time later she wrote a poem about respectability, which may in some sense incorporate part of her response:

> *What soft, cherubic creatures*
> *These gentlewomen are!*

One would as soon assault a plush
  Or violate a star.

Such dimity convictions,
  A horror so refined
Of freckled human nature,
  Of Deity ashamed,—

It's such a common glory,
  A fisherman's degree!
Redemption, brittle lady,
  Be so ashamed of thee.[31]

Like many poems, this one means variously; among the possibilities it opens to the reader is an ironic view of the second sphere. The "gentlewomen," exposed to knowledge, equipped with what they believe to be "convictions," are the same conventional creatures Harriet Martineau described: people who did not have the "freedom of mind" required for deciding themselves what their duty was—for identifying a meaningful "redemption," one that was their own. Surely more was needed than an education in grammar and natural philosophy. It was possible for women to have minds equal to those of "their masculine counterparts" and, at once, to perpetuate a delicate, "dimity" conception of themselves. Only a few succeeded in emancipating themselves; only a few, in the mid-19th century, transcended the "fisherman's degree."

It seemed to some that Oberlin College, founded in 1833 to serve both men and women and both whites and blacks, would overcome the traditional separation. It was a school founded in the spirit of abolitionism and reform, but, in fact, it reinforced the idea that educated women were to be helpmates, responsible for the mental health and moral balance of men doing evangelical work upon the frontier. Again, the old distinction was made: the attitude of the college was that, "women's highest calling was to be the mothers of the race, and that they should stay within that special sphere in order that future generations should not suffer from the want of devoted and undistracted mother care."[32] Women were segregated from men at the college, and they were required to do domestic work, including the laundry of their male fellow-students.

Lucy Stone and other feminists-to-be attended Oberlin in the early 1840s, but only on occasion did they break into such male fields as theology. Lucy Stone had already been a district school teacher and was older than many of the other students. She was active in peace and anti-slavery work on campus, and, when ready to graduate, she was selected to write a commencement oration. When she discovered that the oration would have to be read for her by a male student, she refused to accept the honor at all and went on, of course, to become a public speaker for the anti-slavery cause and for women's rights.

Lucy Stone was an exception—another exception. Most of the women at Oberlin acquiesced: they would live their lives as inferior and sustaining beings; they would accommodate to the "special sphere." But, as the years went on and the country became more industrialized, more diverse, and more complex, increasing numbers of women became restive in the bonds of gentility and segregation. After the Civil War, more and more colleges opened for women, as high schools became available to girls.

There were Vassar, Smith, and (notably) Bryn Mawr. M. Carey Thomas, herself educated at Cornell, Johns Hopkins, and the University of Leipzig, was Dean and then President of Bryn Mawr. Like other women's colleges, Bryn Mawr created an island of intellectual commitment in a wilderness of acquisitiveness and exploitation, but M. Carey Thomas articulated, more boldly than many others, the necessity for loosening family ties and emancipating young women from traditional roles. The "Bryn Mawr type" was to effect a new equality in human relationships; Miss Thomas saw no reason why women should not enter all the technical and professional fields. "There is no reason to believe," she said, "that typhoid or scarlet fever or phthisis can be successfully treated by a woman physician in one way and by a man physician in another way. There is indeed every reason to believe that unless treated in the best way, the patient may die, the sex of the doctor affecting the result less even than the sex of the patient."[33]

Invigorating though these ideas surely were, successful though many Bryn Mawr graduates turned out to be, the separation between the spheres was not overcome. For educated, middle-class women, it was simply recast. For M. Carey Thomas (and she was in many ways exemplary) intellectual prowess and domesticity were irreconcilable; marriage and childbearing both were anathema to her, and she communicated some of this to her studnets. Ordinary sexuality seemed to her to be irrelevant; for the intellectual woman, friendships could and probably should take the place of the dependency required of the wife. Indeed, the majority of women college graduates in the late 19th century never married; the professional roles that most of them chose were nurturing roles, traditionally feminine roles: social worker, librarian, nurse, and teacher most of all. Because they chose in that fashion, it seems clear that their own internalized conflicts were seldom resolved. Few were so aggressively committed to the "intellectual renunciation" M. Carey Thomas prescribed. Most were afflicted by the ways in which social reality was interpreted by the people around, by the "official" definitions of women's powers and women's proper spheres. And, indeed, the schools—through the models they presented and in the absence of any effort at critique—could not but perpetuate what was taken for granted.

Novelists exposed it: women writers like Kate Chopin,[34] Mary Austin,[35] Mary Wilkins Freeman,[36] and Edith Wharton,[37] and certain male writers like Frank Norris,[38] Theodore Dreiser,[39] and Henry James.[40] In 1892, Henry James noted the "growing divorce between the American woman . . . and the male American immersed in the ferocity of business, with no time for any but the most sordid interests. . . . The divorce is rapidly becoming a gulf—an abyss of inequality, the like of which has never before been seen under the sun."[41]

But on all sides the separation of the sexes was encouraged by censors, pastors, and even by frightened women's groups who feared the loss of support. In a speech at a Baltimore meeting of the American Academy of Medicine in 1895, a Professor Ward Hutchinson said:

> The woman who works outside of the home or school pays a fearful penalty, either physical, mental, or moral, or often all three. She commits a biologic crime against herself and against the community, and woman labor ought to be forbidden for the same reason that child labor is. Any nation that works its women is damned, and belongs at heart to the Huron-Iroquois confederacy.[42]

And Dr. Hutchinson was only one of many. Henry Adams talked that way; scientific and educational writers emphasized the dangers implicit in making women learned; G. Stanley Hall at Johns Hopkins celebrated what he called the "madonna conception"[43] and called for monthly programs centered around the "Sabbath" of menstruation.

Faced with such a campaign of mystification, Jane Addams was undoubtedly not alone in being almost paralyzed early in her life by the conflicting claims of femininity and the desire to make a difference in the world.[44] She resolved the conflict when she discovered the existence of a British reform movement called "Christian Renaissance" and the possibility of becoming a kind of womanly saint through social reform. The establishment of Hull House turned out to be the solution. Her religious approach to education as the saving of souls and her involvement with early progressive thought led her to talk of "social control"[45] when she addressed the problem of inducting immigrant children into the society of the early 20th century and even when she discussed the importance of pluralism or the recognition of cultural diversity. She resembled Lillian Wald, founder of the Henry Street Settlement, in considering teaching and social work to be her "natural" provinces; there is no question but that such women, displacing aspects of their femininity, played more sophisticated (and more knowledgeable) versions of the roles enacted by the "elevating and instructive" young women who first taught in the common schools.

For all the separateness of the spheres, however, and for all the tendency of women professionals to accede to the need for social control, some remarkable female educators appeared on the scene in the early part of the 20th century—the century known to some as the "century of the child."[46] There was Ella Flagg Young, who worked with John Dewey in the Laboratory School he established at the University of Chicago and who later became the first woman superintendent of schools in Chicago. Not only did she work against the daily supervision that degraded so many teachers, she argued strongly for more women superintendents, because she said (not surprisingly), "It is woman's natural field and she is no longer satisfied to do the greatest part of the work and yet be denied the leadership."[47]

There was Julia Richman, the first Jewish woman superintendent in New York City, who helped lay the foundations for testing by proposing that children be divided in terms of their ability into "the brightest material," "medium material," and the "poorest material."[48] In many respects, she was similar to Horace Mann in her righteous passion to improve, to Americanize, to tamp down incorrigibility, and to remedy through schooling the deprivation she found among the immigrants and the very poor.

And there were the great progressive innovators and educators: Margaret Naumburg, who founded what was to become the Walden School in 1915; Caroline Pratt, who opened the Play School (later, the City and Country School) in 1914; Marietta Johnson, who established an Organic School in Fairhope, Alabama, in 1907; Lucy Sprague Mitchell, who founded the Bureau of Educational Experiments (later, the Bank Street College of Education) in 1916, and others. With some exceptions, these women belonged to the stream of progressivism that carried with it interests in art, play, and therapeutic self-expression—what has been called the "romantic" dimension of progressive thought.

This was not, in their cases, because they were not well-educated or intellectual. All had had rich experiences in learning in the United States and abroad, and a number were well grounded in aesthetics and psychology. It has partly to do with the inherent appeal of the new freedom then associated with progressive ideas. Educators, particularly in the twenties, selected out different aspects of the approach: some responded to the scientific component; others, to the implications for measurement; others, to the "life-adjustment" overtones; still others, to the concern for social control. The tendency of women educators to act on the possibilities of personal freedom in what *they* understood to be progressivism (and to reconceive the "child" each one was supposed to be) is an indication of their own awareness of constraints.

It was not nearly so simple for women to attain leadership positions in the public school systems, as it was not nearly so likely for women public school teachers to achieve autonomy. Diane Ravitch writes of the poorly trained women teachers in the early part of the century in New York:

> School officials preferred having female teachers, because they could save money by paying women less than men. Women were glad to have teaching jobs, because it was one of the few respectable occupations open to them. And women were blatantly discriminated against by the school system. They were paid less than half of what men received for the same job.[49]

Until 1904, in fact, there was a bylaw in New York City that required the immediate dismissal of a female teacher who married. As late as 1932, the sociologist Willard Waller was commenting on the low social standing of the teacher, the paltry rewards, "the assimilation of the teacher to the female character ideal." In fact, he said, "It has been said that no woman and no Negro is ever fully admitted to the white man's world."[50] He wrote, as others had before him, of the teacher as child and of the negative status of the teacher being partly due to the extension of the child's perceptions of that teacher into his or her adult life.

Looking back, we may find it startling that so few women considered themselves or openly defined themselves as oppressed. Now and then in history there has been an expression of identification with the black person, slave or free, sometimes following the lead of Frederick Douglass, who made his sympathy with the women's rights movement so eloquently clear.

The Grimké sisters, Sarah and Angelina, are glowing examples. Not only did they, as slaveholders' daughters, perceive the full horror of slavery, they left the South on that account. Active in the antislavery movement, they were often barred—because they were women —from public platforms. Sarah Grimké wrote an essay on "The

Equality of the Sexes," which makes clear the relation between the subordination of women and the plight of the slaves. She talked about women's "deficient education," the way in which they were treated as "pretty toys or mere instruments of pleasure," and the differential pay scales for men and women. "A man who is engaged in teaching, can always, I believe, command a higher price for tuition than a woman— even when he teaches the same branches, and is not in any respect superior to the woman."[51] The same things was true, she wrote, in tailoring, laundry work, and other fields where males and females worked side by side. And then she wrote:

> There is another class of women in this country, to whom I cannot refer, without feelings of the deepest shame and sorrow. I allude to our female slaves. Our southern cities are whelmed beneath a tide of pollution; the virtue of female slaves is wholly at the mercy of irresponsible tyrants. . . . Nor does the colored woman suffer alone: the moral purity of the white woman is deeply contaminated. In the daily habit of seeing the virtue of her enslaved sister sacrificed without hesitancy or remorse, she looks upon the crimes of seduction and illicit intercourse without horror, and although not personally involved in the guilt, she loses that value for innocence in her own, as well as the other sex, which is one of the strongest safeguards to virtue.[52]

At the end of the passage, she asks, "Can any American woman look at these scenes of shocking licentiousness and cruelty, and fold her hands in apathy, and say, 'I have nothing to do with slavery'? *She cannot and be guiltless."* Clearly, Sarah Grimké saw the connection between one mode of subordination and another. More significantly, however, she appeared able to identify the connection between *personal* liberation and commitment to human liberation. And she made this clear in the context of a reasoned critique of what she ironically called woman's "appropriate sphere."

There were women, after the Civil War, who did not necessarily express themselves on the interrelationships among various modes of oppression, but who did voluntarily go South to teach the freed slaves. They went immediately after the fighting ended, when the campaign to maintain white supremacy was becoming vicious and violent. The school teachers who came from the North were treated as subversive, particularly when they tried to establish integrated or "mixed" schools. One teacher is quoted as saying, with reference to the freed slaves, "Oh what a privilege to be among them when their morning dawns, to see them personally coming forth from the land of Egypt and the house of bondage."[53] Henry Perkinson writes of the "schoolmarms" who even tried to teach Latin and Greek to their students and, most particularly, that blacks were the economic and social equals of whites. Teachers were flogged or tarred and feathered; frequently, their schools were burned. Thus far, we know relatively little[54] about the Yankee school teachers' feelings about themselves as women; it is reasonable to believe that, however religious and traditional their motivation, on some level they could identify with those who had been in chains.

Some years later, at the start of the new century, Margaret Haley, an organizer for the Teachers' Federation in Chicago, was asking teachers to begin perceiving themselves as a white-collar proletariat.[55] An anonymous college-trained worker said, in answer to a survey in the 1890s, "The same work exactly, which I am engaged in, is done by men in the New York Department at double the pay. I find where women are employed and men are at the head, favoritism plays a very decided part on the matter of salaries. One reason for the inequality in women's wages, as compared with those paid men, is that women are patient in their willingness to earn something, be it ever so little. They *earn* it. They are not situated in life to apply the nerve required to demand what should be theirs justly. . . ."[56] Managers and administrators in the school systems resisted self-assertion on the part of women workers and women teachers. The leaders in the school systems tried to utilize whatever socialization techniques they had available to keep their women employees docile, to make sure that they would never "apply the nerve required. . . ."

On the surface, things have changed for women in education. There are no dual wage scales; there are few controls where, at least, traditional marriage is concerned. Women can, to some degree, attain leadership positions in organizations and unions. There are still relatively few female school administrators and college presidents, affirmative action legislation notwithstanding.[57] Work has only just begun to repair sexist practices in classrooms, to rewrite sexist literature, and to alter attitudes towards work and future expectations. Nevertheless, the existence of the "separate sphere" seems to me unquestionable, even today. There is little evidence of women identifying their subordination with the subordination of other groups in society. There is little explicit recognition of the need for critical consciousness —what Paulo Freire calls "conscientization"[58]—to overcome internalized oppression and perhaps to bring about (even within an inequitable system) a kind of equity.

There must be critique. There must be an ongoing demystification, as there must be an enlarging conversation among those who have the courage to identify themselves as subordinate, as oppressed. The connection between the kind of subordination imposed on women and the kind of subordination imposed on schoolchildren must finally be exposed. Illusions have to be eliminated, writes Carol Gould, the "illusions which bind us all to exploitation." Only when we can develop the kind of critique that liberates us from such illusions will there be a possibility of freeing women "to discover and to *choose* what they want to become."[59]

That is indeed the next step for women in education, the step never taken in time past. The problem is to discover whether it *can* be taken apart from the kind of *praxis* that might transform both men's and women's common world.

References

1. R.S. Peters, *Ethics and Education* (Glenview, Ill.: Scott, Foresman, 1967), p. 51.
2. William Boyd, ed., *The Emile of Jean-Jacques Rousseau* (New York: Teachers College Press, 1960), pp. 134-135.
3. Benjamin Rush, *Thoughts on Female Education* (Philadelphia, 1787), p. 6.
4. Mrs. A.J. Graves, *Woman in America: Being an Examination into the Moral and Intellectual Condition of American Female Society* (New York: Harper and Brothers, 1841), p. 143.
5. Lawrence A. Cremin, ed., *The Republic and the School: Horace Mann on the Education of Free Men* (New York: Teachers College Press, 1957), p. 57, p. 90.
6. Catharine Beecher, "On the Peculiar Responsibility of American Women," in *Roots of Bitterness, Documents of the Social History of American Women*, ed. Nancy F. Cott (New York: E.P. Dutton, 1972), p. 171.
7. Alexis de Tocqueville, *Democracy in America*, Vol. II (New York: Colonial Press, 1889), pp. 223-224.
8. Horace Mann, in Cremin, *op. cit.*, p. 58.
9. Ibid., p. 57.
10. Henry Barnard, "Gradation of Public Schools, with Special Reference to Cities and Large Villages, *American Journal of Education*, Vol. 2, December 1856, p. 461.
11. Mann, "The Massachusetts System of Common Schools; Being an Enlarged and Revised Edition of the Tenth Annual Report of the First Secretary of the Massachusetts Board of Education" (Boston, 1849), p. 86.
12. David B. Tyack, *The One Best System* (Cambridge: Harvard University Press, 1974), p. 60.

13. See William Holmes McGuffey, *Newly Revised Eclectic Second Reader* (New York and Cincinnati, 1848).
14. "Lucy Larcom's Factory Experience," in Cott, ed., *op. cit.,* p. 128.
15. Alice Felt Tyler, *Freedom's Ferment* (New York: Harper Torchbooks, 1962), p. 212.
16. Herman Melville, "The Paradise of Bachelors and The Tartarus of Maids," *Selected Writings of Herman Melville* (New York: Modern Library, 1952), p. 210.
17. Ibid., p. 211.
18. Quoted in Eleanor Flexner, *Centuries of Struggle: The Woman's Rights Movement in the United States* (Cambridge: The Belknap Press of the Harvard University Press, 1975), p. 58.
19. Beecher, "The Education of Female Teachers," in *The Educated Woman in America,* ed. Barbara M. Cross (New York: Teachers College Press, 1965), pp. 68-69.
20. Beecher, in Flexner, *op. cit.,* pp. 30-31.
21. Beecher, "Ministry of Women," in Cross, ed., *op. cit.,* pp. 94-95.
22. "On the Peculiar Responsibility of American Women," in Cott, ed., *op. cit.,* p. 172.
23. Cross, ed., *op. cit.,* p. 70.
24. See Merle Curti, *The Social Ideas of American Educators* (Totowa, N.J.: Littlefield, Adams and Co., 1959), p. 181.
25. Tyler, *op. cit.,* pp. 206-211.
26. Harriet Martineau, *Society in America* (1837), Vol. I (New York: AMS Press, Inc., 1966), pp. 229-230.
27. Margaret Fuller, "Schoolteaching," in Cross, ed., *op. cit.,* pp. 109-111.
28. Cross, Introduction, *op. cit.,* pp. 19-30.
29. Curti, *op. cit.,* p. 185.
30. Flexner, *op. cit.,* p. 36.
31. Emily Dickinson, "What soft, cherubic creatures . . .," *Selected Poems and Letters of Emily Dickinson,* ed. Robert N. Linscott (Garden City: Doubleday, Anchor Books, 1959), p. 125.
32. Robert S. Fletcher, *History of Oberlin College to the Civil War* (Oberlin: Oberlin College Press, 1943), p. 373.
33. M. Carey Thomas, "Education for Women and for Men," in Cross, ed., *op. cit.,* p. 147.
34. Kate Chopin, *The Awakening* (New York: Capricorn, 1964).
35. Mary Austin, *Earth Horizon* (Boston, 1932).
36. Mary Wilkins Freeman, *Madelon* (New York, 1896).
37. Edith Wharton, *The House of Mirth* (New York, 1905).
38. Frank Norris, *The Pit* (New York: Doubleday, 1928).
39. Theodore Dreiser, *Sister Carrie* (New York: Modern Library, 1947).
40. Henry James, *A Portrait of a Lady* (New York: Washington Square Press, 1966).
41. James, *The Notebooks,* ed. F.O. Matthiessen and Kenneth B. Murdock (New York: Oxford University Press, 1947), p. 129.
42. Quoted in Larzer Ziff, *The American 1890s: Life and Times of a Lost Generation* (New York: Viking Press, 1966), p. 280.

43. G. Stanley Hall, *Adolescence,* Vol. II (New York, 1904), p. 627.
44. See Allen F. Davis, *The Life and Legend of Jane Addams* (New York: Oxford University Press, 1963).
45. See Clarence Karier, Paul Violas, and Joel Spring, *Roots of Crisis: American Education in the Twentieth Century* (Chicago: Rand, McNally, 1973).
46. Cremin, *The Transformation of the School* (New York: Alfred A. Knopf, 1961), p. 105.
47. John T. McManis, *Ella Flagg Young and a Half-Century of the Chicago Public Schools* (Chicago: A.C. McClurg, 1916), p. 144.
48. Tyack, *op. cit.,* p. 202.
49. Diane Ravitch, *The Great School Wars: New York City, 1805-1973* (New York: Basic Books, 1974), p. 103.
50. Willard Waller, *Sociology of Teaching* (New York: John Wiley, 1932), p. 50.
51. Sarah Grimké, "Letters on the Equality of the Sexes," in Cott, ed., *op. cit.,* p. 183.
52. Ibid., p. 185.
53. Henry J. Perkinson, *The Imperfect Panacea: American Faith in Education, 1865-1965* (New York: Random House, 1968) p. 18.
54. See John Hope Franklin, *Reconstruction: After the Civil War* (Chicago: University of Chicago Press, 1961).
55. Margaret Haley, "Why Teachers Should Organize," *NEA Addresses and Proceedings,* 43rd Annual Meeting, St. Louis, 1904, p. 150.
56. "Testimony on Compensation for Educated Women at Work," in Cott, ed., *op. cit.,* pp. 336-337.
57. See Suzanne E. Estler, "Women as Leaders in Public Education," in *Signs: Journal of Women in Culture and Society,* Vol. 1, No. 2, Winter 1975, pp. 363-386.
58. Paulo Freire, *Pedagogy of the Oppressed* (New York: Herder and Herder, 1967).
59. Carol Gould, "Philosophy of Liberation and the Liberation of Philosophy," in *Women and Philosophy,* ed. Carol C. Gould and Marx W. Wartofsky (New York: Putnam, 1976) p. 38.

17

Sexism in the Schools

MY concern is with autonomy and the capacity to choose. My concern is with work as a mode of acting on the world. Sexism, to me, is emblematic of constraints and closures. It is one of the ways of drowning out the summons to an open future; it cancels personal possibility. The sexist much resembles the anti-Semite Jean-Paul Sartre has described:

> He chooses the irremediable out of fear of being free; he chooses medi-ocrity out of a fear of being alone, and out of pride he makes of this irremediable mediocrity a rigid aristocracy. To this end he finds the existence of the Jew absolutely necessary. Otherwise, to whom would he be superior? Indeed, it is vis-a-vis the Jew and the Jew alone that the anti-Semite realizes he has rights.[1]

All we need to do is substitute "female" for "Jew," and the picture comes clear. It is a picture of fixity, of dull tenacity. Nothing could be more at odds with what we think of as the educative, especially if we associate the educative with open-ended growth, with the reflective action and full communication that permit people to be free.

Sexism can be called miseducative in the Deweyan sense; it is an attitude, a posture that shuts persons off from "occasions, stimuli, and opportunities for continuing growth in new directions."[2] Young female persons are not the only ones affected by frustrations like this; young male persons are affected too, as are male and female adults who are (consciously or unconsciously) sexist in point of view. They may be the kind of people who appear to profit from the limits imposed on those they think of as "others," and who suspect that they have rights only vis-a-vis those "others," but this does not diminish the damage that is done.

Virginia Woolf once wrote:

244

All this pitting of sex against sex, of quality against quality; all this claiming of superiority and imputing of inferiority, belong to the private-school stage of human existence where there are "sides," and it is necessary for one side to beat another side, and of the utmost importance to walk up to a platform and receive from the hands of the Headmaster himself a highly ornamental pot. As people mature they cease to believe in sides or in Headmasters or in highly ornamental pots. . . . No, delightful as the pastime of measuring may be, it is the most futile of all occupations, and to submit to the decrees of the measurers the most servile of attitudes.[3]

Her linking of taking sides to measuring demonstrates her own sensitivity to the absurdity (as well as the internal logic) of certain of our social constructs. When Woolf moved to talk of alternative modes of being alive, she did not use logic to criticize the dominant mode. She said to her listeners and her readers:

So long as you write that you wish to write, that is all that matters; and whether it matters for ages or only for hours, nobody can say. But to sacrifice a hair of the head of your vision, a shade of its color, in deference to some Headmaster with a silver pot in his hand or to some professor with a measuringrod up his sleeve, is the most abject treachery, and the sacrifice of wealth and chastity which used to be said to be the greatest of human disasters, a mere flea-bite in comparison.[4]

She obviously could not think of freedom or authentic visions without thinking of self-initiated action, the kind of action (be it writing or any other kind of working) that would allow those visions to be expressed.

When John Dewey wrote about freedom in educational contexts, he had much of the same thing in mind.[5] He knew that the possibility of freedom is deeply grounded in individuality. He knew also that, "Freedom or individuality . . . is not an original possession or gift. It is something to be achieved, to be wrought out."[6] Much of his life work had to do with identifying the conditions required for permitting that achievement to take place. As he saw it, the actualization of freedom was all one with the release of individual capacities; so he devoted most of his philosophical energies to defining the kinds of environments that would promote the development of intelligence and the "power of vision and reflection."

And, indeed, freedom has everything to do with the capacity to identify openings in situations, possible courses of action. It signifies individual choosing in the light of the spontaneous preferences that compose each person's individuality. The measuring Virginia Woolf described, the comparing, the ornamental pots: these can only thwart choosing and cripple spontaneity. They close off opportunities for self-creation. They enclose individuals in "sides" or molds; they leave only a restricted place in which to move.

More, of course, is required for the elimination of sexism in schools than the elimination of pots and measuring rods. It is never enough to enact a negative freedom, freedom *from* interference and constraint. Educators are challenged to think about what it might signify to actualize freedom for every person—to move individuals (both male and female) to define their spontaneous preferences, to act intelligently on their visions. What kinds of conditions can be created? What sorts of interactions do we want to see?

We can answer conventionally, of course. We can talk about individualization, "whole" children, and the rest. We can obscure the distinctions so frequently made, covering over the thwarting that comes from sexist tenacity. This, actually, would be a traditional response, because educational spokesmen, including proponents of the open classroom, have not drawn attention to the "claiming of superiority and imputing of inferiority" where the sexes are concerned. Dewey did often write of boys and girls being indiscriminately involved in cooking, weaving, and carpentry; but, when he did so, he was governed by a view of the educative value of such activities, not by a desire to overcome the stereotypes of his time. The progressives who followed after did not feel embarrassed by the tool tables and the doll tables in their classrooms. If they thought about sex discrimination at all, they were likely to think that the miniature communities they were ostensibly creating would counteract what was unjust outside the schools. Contemporary open classroom teachers have not tended to divide children into "sides," but very few have as yet confronted the effects of sexism on textbooks, curriculum, and even the language spoken day to day.

On occasion, there is evidence of some unexamined sexism. Lillian Weber has been quoted as saying (in a classroom where a boy proudly wrote, "I made an astronaut") that the boys were reading and writing as well as the girls because the boys had "male things to do, in sharp contrast to the femininity of the usual elementary school classroom"[7] Another proponent of the open classroom described a Central Harlem school where children seemed happier than usual. "You could see it in the bodies of the girls dancing to soul records," she wrote. "You could read it in the eyes of the boys who were building airplanes and scooters at the worktable."[8] Both are, in some sense, responding to the old charge that the American classroom has been consistently "feminized" over time because of the dominant presence of women elementary teachers and (it is sometimes said) because of the emphasis on "feminine" virtues like docility, modesty, patience, and self-constraint. Granting the need to problematize the so-called "hidden curriculum" in the schools, we do not need to acquiesce in the traditional categories. Clearly, a more critical approach is needed; most educators have tended to avoid the problems presented by sexism over the years. (Dewey, for instance, participated in the Suffrage movement but seems to have never talked explicitly about the need to combat pedagogically the injustices associated with the inability to vote.)

Members of the women's movement, not America's educators, were the first to call attention to the impact of sexism on the schools. The reasons educators were unable to *see* are probably to be found in a range of unexamined assumptions shared with the community at large. Among these is the assumption that there are separate spheres for men and women: another that there are insuperable biological differences, not to speak of differences in temperament and physique. The crucial point is that critical thinking has not been done with respect to such assumptions. There are many educators, even today, who are not convinced that attention should be paid.

Little authentic change is likely to take place in classroom situations if the educators involved are not wide-awake to such matters— and present to themselves. I do not believe that good teaching proceeds according to sets of rules externally imposed, anymore than I believe in predefined techniques, repertoires, or competencies. Similarly, I find it hard to accept the idea that previously unacknowledged sexist practices—or any of the practices that cripple and demean—can be fundamentally altered by changing the rules or even the laws. Of course it is essential to legislate for equity in hiring to establish the kinds of regulations that limit unjust discrimination. Of course we have to insist that girls be given opportunities to look through microscopes, use chisels, learn computer languages, and play punchball with the boys. Obviously we have to do something about the textbooks that create and perpetuate stereotypical behavior. But first and foremost is the need to attend to and perhaps reconceive our fundamental project —which is teaching.

Teaching involves deliberate and purposeful action carried on by a live human being who can reflect upon what he or she is doing, who is not an automaton, but self-conscious and self-aware. Teaching involves such a person in interactions with (or dialogue with) a variety of other live human beings. These others are, by means of the dialogue, to be enabled to learn how to learn. Or, to put it somewhat differently, they are to be enabled consciously to enter into the learning process, to choose to become members of a particular learning community.

To speak of teaching in this fasion is to disclose the risks intrinsic to the activity, the inevitable uncertainties. Once a teacher acknowledges that learning takes place only when a learner takes responsibility for his or her own learning, once a teacher acknowledges the role of the student's "resolute will," that teacher cannot but confront with new ideas the factors that close off opportunities. He or she, after all, is positing and, indeed, encouraging the autonomy of each of the students in the class. Autonomy signifies a sense of personal agency; it carries with it a conviction of moral responsibility. To create the kinds of social conditions that provoke and sustain autonomy demands the most critical consciousness of the forces that seduce people into acquiescence and mindlessness. It requires a profound self-understanding on the part of the teacher, who has to live in a kind of tension simply to function as a free agent, to make choices appropriate to the often unpredictable situations that arise.

Existentialists have talked a great deal about the ways in which "othering" affects people—about the tensions experienced when individuals are distanced and seen as "types," or as objects. On one level, when teachers treat their students as "others," when they label them or define them by means of sex or I.Q., those students are likely to rebel internally. But the rebellion is likely to be ineffectual and, in fact, turn into what is called *rassentiment* unless conditions are such that they can express their own preferences and, in some degree, act upon them. This applies most poignantly to females, because of the culture's long tradition of fixing them in molds. We need only look to novels about women to see how often the flame of rebellion has been doused. Sometimes, as in Kate Chopin's *The Awakening,* it dies out because of the woman's own sense of powerlessness when it comes to defining options. Sometimes, as in Edith Wharton's *The House of Mirth,* it dies because of the pressure of conventions, of "manners," all that is required of a needy woman in search of approval and support. Not accidentally, novels dealing with the lives of women in the United States ordinarily end in suicide, submergence, or defeat. This is because the female characters are unable to find openings for work and authentic action and cannot actualize themselves.

Again, my concern is with teaching and the provision of opportunities for all young people, not merely to identify themselves as persons, but to act upon their visions of possibility. I am suggesting that only a teacher who is present to herself or to himself, who has achieved some personal autonomy, can take the risks required to move others to choose themselves. There is support for this in the available research on, for example, motivation and aspiration, meaning "goal-setting and effortful striving,"[9] and on the relation between aspiration and what is called "expectancy."

It is evident that, although the achievement motivation (or the propensity to strive for success) exists both in men and women, young girls orient differently to achievement situations, even in elementary school. They do better on tasks defined as "feminine," just as boys do better on "masculine" tasks. This is one reason why girls appear to be more intelligent than boys in elementary and junior high school. It takes some time before males see studying as a masculine activity or discern the connection between studying and later success. It also takes a while before females receive the message that work is not their true destination and that there is something fundamentally unfeminine about striving too hard and achieving too much. The very idea that high achievement might lessen opportunities for marriage still accounts in many places for the fear of success. Obviously, sexism and its ideology reduce expectancy in many ways. The important point in this context, however, is that the kind of teaching that does indeed close off openings in experience (as it must if aspiration and "expectancy" are reduced) cannot conceivably be effectual teaching. It may be a kind of training, even a species of indoctrination, but it is difficult to conceive it as the kind of activity that arouses others to their own choosing, their own significant questioning and work.

We are likely to forget the profound consequences for teachers when there is, as there has been in the United States, a habit of treating women as a "second sex."[10] It is not merely a question of surface patterns of behavior; the social reality in which most of us were born was and is constructed by means of distinctions and discriminations no longer believed to be just. There has been a bland taken-for-grantedness about such notions as males do the important work of the world and females who seek jobs for the sake of fulfillment are in some sense unfeminine. People who believe these things seldom remark that this is the way they have learned to interpret experience. They seldom acknowledge that they share a certain conventional way of seeing things. Again, like Sartre's anti-Semite, they are convinced they are making judgments about what is objectively true.

American literature is replete with passages that highlight the ways in which American women have been treated and conceived. The inferiority, the duties, the destiny of women have been repeatedly spelled out by men and, far too frequently, internalized by women themselves. Critical consciousness of a rare sort is necessary if teachers of young people are not to perpetuate such views. They are interpretations, not reports of demonstrable facts, but few educators have been inclined to think very much about the ways in which they have constructed their realities. Educators, like most other people, have been reared in such a way as to repress their background consciousness, their awareness of their own perspectives on the intersubjective world. They have been taught to accept and accede to traditional descriptions of cultural phenomena, including those descriptions that make women appear to be the dependent ones, the incomplete ones, the beings incapable of autonomy. And if educators themselves are women, they are likely to distance themselves from that reality as effectively as from their own childhoods. To do otherwise is to see too much that is problematic; it is (at least for some) to threaten the ground on which they think they ought to stand.

My argument is that a denial of the problematic is a denial of cognitive possibility. If students are to be taught in such a way that they become conscious of what they are doing and conscious of significant participation in some learning community, their teachers need to retain an awareness of how their own meaning-structures were built up over time. To be aware of this is to be aware of the crucial questions to which such structuring responds. If barriers are raised against questioning, if only certain problems are defined as worth attending to, critical thinking becomes unlikely. The student is reduced to ferreting out what the teacher has decided in advance is the "right" answer. No attention can be paid to open-ended inquiry or to the norms of truthtelling, because the game (as it were) has been fixed. This, of course, is an extreme example of what follows from closing off opportunities, but it is not far from what Virginia Woolf had in mind when she wrote of silver pots and measuring rods. And it is not an unusual consequence of the categorizing and limiting associated with schoolroom sexism.

Again, it is profoundly important for teachers themselves to subject their own assumptions to searching criticism, using whatever tools they have at their disposal (precisely the tools their students need, if they are to learn) and avoiding the one-dimensional vision that freezes, fixes, and constrains. There are innumerable works in history and the social sciences today that sweep away the mists; there are plays, films, and always increasing numbers of novels and poems. Consider but two. The first was written in 1700 by Anne Finch, Countess of Winchilsea:

> *Did I, my lines intend for publick view,*
> *How many censures wou'd their faults persue. . .*
> *True judges might condemn their want of witt,*
> *And all might say, they're by a Woman writt.*
> *Alas, a woman that attempts the pen,*
> *Such an intruder on the rights of men,*
> *Such presumptious Creature, is esteem'd,*
> *The fault can by no vertue be redeemed.*[11]

The second was written recently by Dilys Laing:

> *Staunch Anne! I know your trouble. The same tether*
> *galls us. To be a woman and a writer is double*
> *mischief, for the world will slight her*
> *who slights the 'servile house', and who would rather*
> *make odes than beds. Lost lady! Gentle fighter!*
> *Separate in time, we mutiny together.*[12]

The vistas can widen and multiply as we look as well through historical perspectives and the perspectives of the social and natural sciences. Taking into account more than a single reality, we ourselves become freer to make sense and, yes, to choose.

This is as important for men as it is for women, for boys as it is for girls. Freedom increases as possibilities of action, of being, expand. My concern about sexism and its constraints is not mainly due to the fact that boys are treated differently from girls. Boys will continue to be expected to run and be winners, to be strong and masterful and the rest. Girls (no matter how bright and hopeful) will still be expected to hold back, to avoid too much risk-taking, to be passive and nice to look at—constantly to please. My interest, however, has to do primarily with a desire to set each person, male or female, free to choose among a range of alternatives—to choose in terms of his or her spontaneous preferences and not solely in terms of some "given," whether embodied in mold or style or "side."

Of course distinctions will be made. But when they are made, we ought always to be asked to justify our decisions to treat people differently. There is a general moral principle that says distinctions should not be made if there are no relevant differences. One philosopher has written that, "The notion basic to justice is that distinctions should be made if there are relevant differences and that they should not be made if there are no relevant differences or on the basis of irrelevant differences."[13] The point is that the distinctions made, especially when expressed through differences in treatment, have to be justified. Too few people consider what is involved in such justification. Too few, perhaps especially where treatment of the two sexes is concerned, feel themselves bound to give reasons when they discourage girls from going to shop or playyard or when they discourage boys from choosing painting over gymnastics. Not only ought teachers attend to the principles that govern their decisions, not only ought they to feel bound to give good reasons; they ought to draw attention, far more than they normally do, to the processes involved in justification. This is focal to moral education, among other things; it would seem essential to a just school. There needs to be sensitivity to principles like fairness and, indeed, like justice, which surely is the prime value in any polity.

If we are to create the kinds of social conditions that allow for the expression of spontaneous preferences and for the actualization of individual freedom, we all have to become peculiarly sensitive—in ways we have never been before. There is a sense in which our attitudes towards work become the touchstone of what we do, since it is by means of work that freedom comes into being in individual lives. Alfred Schutz, who drew attention to the multiple realities that compose human lives, made the point that the world of working is the "paramount reality." The world of working is the world of physical things; "it is the realm of my locomotions and bodily operations; it offers resistances which require effort to overcome; it places tasks before me, permits me to carry through my plans, and enables me to succeed or to fail in my attempt to attain my purposes. By my working acts I gear into the outer world, I change it; and these changes, although provoked by my working, can be experienced and tested both by myself and others, as occurrences within the world independently of the working acts in which they originated."[14] He wrote of how we share the world with others and how the world of working is the reality in which such sharing becomes most meaningful. This description of the significance of working for self-identification may well make us painfully aware of the ambivalence often displayed with respect to work where students are concerned, the work they do in school and the work they are permitted to anticipate. Also, it may remind us of the kinds of things women have been traditionally expected to do, activities many teachers still have in mind when they look at the female students in their classrooms.

Simone de Beauvoir has written that a basic inequality in marriage still lies is the fact that the husband finds concrete self-realization in work and action, whereas liberty often has only a negative aspect for the wife. "In certain privileged cases," she said, "the wife may succeed in becoming her husband's true companion, discussing his projects, giving him counsel, collaborating in his works. But she is lulled in illusion if she expects in this way to accomplish work she can call her own, for he remains alone the free and responsible agent."[15] Even though, in this period, more and more married women are beginning to work, the presumption that girls will grow up to be mainly helpmates still underlies many of the things they are told and taught.

To create the conditions necessary for self-expression in the classroom, educators must provide openings for a sense of agency where work is concerned, as they present the possibility of varied callings for both males and females. We need to allow for aspirations of unprecedented kinds. Males, after all, can be nurses and caseworkers; females can become forestry workers and engineers. Nevertheless, the ancient emphasis continues underground: decent women have a domestic destiny; the separate spheres can never be one. There remains a familiar guilt in too many women's experience. Work, even today, appears to be unfeminine; gearing into the world *sounds* unfeminine. Controlling and changing the world remain the province of men; men themselves still experience shame if they prefer less active, quieter roles.

When there is ambivalence towards and confusion about work in the classroom, openings cannot but be closed. Of course it is true that many kinds of work in this society are considered meaningless and depersonalizing. It is also true that many good arguments can be raised against encouraging women to "liberate" themselves by moving into corporate bureaucracies. All of this is too frequently a mask, since the crucial issue has to do with the right of women to choose for themselves. Robert Coles, writing in *Daedalus*[16] has reported on a number of interviews with working people, who are quite aware of the meaninglessness of some of the jobs they perform. Coles found, nevertheless, that self-respect still seems to be linked to having work and that men and women both gauge their successes as persons by referring to the work they do. This is not a disguised argument for career education in the school; it is simply a suggestion that respect for persons in some sense involves respect for them in their "paramount reality," whether they are male or female. Freedom, again, has to be expressed in some kind of action. What teachers can do is to provide the conditions that will permit preferences to emerge.

Obviously, the inhumanities in this society raise many barriers. There are countless difficulties in the way of creating the open spaces for freedom we have in mind. Nevertheless, we must do more than pursue equality of treatment within the traditional forms. Women's novels, in the recent period, have supported the view that too many of the structures devised in our society are simply insufficient. Clearly, more critical reflection is required if what is limiting is to be properly exposed and what is humane transformed. This is in many respects the same as working for openings; in some sense, it is the same as good teaching, because it is part of the struggle against closure and fixity. It is what is required for a new conception of power, a new idea of space.

A woman speaks; in a way, she speaks for all: "This above all, to refuse to be a victim. Unless I can do that I can do nothing."[17] De Beauvoir has talked about the impossibility of fashioning a female human being who would be the precise copy of a male. But, she said, if we imagine a society in which the equality of the sexes is concretely realized, such equality would find new expression in each individual. And this suggests still another reason for our attempting to create social situations in which such equality is realized (by each individual) through action and productive work.

There are new goals before educators willing to renew their sense of calling, willing to commit themselves to setting persons free to be. There are new personal and interpersonal goals, centering on the expansion of meaning and the release of human power. To achieve such goals, we have to break with either/ors. We need to discover new fusions of what have been thought of as male and female characteristics. Perhaps a new revolution can then take shape, an educational revolution generated by the rejection of sexism. In the course of such a revolution, we may all rediscover ourselves.

References

1. Jean-Paul Sartre, *Anti-Semite and Jew* (New York: Schocken Books, 1948), pp. 27-28.
2. John Dewey, *Experience and Education* (New York: Collier Books, 1963), p. 36.
3. Virginia Woolf, *A Room of One's Own* (New York: Harcourt, Brace & World, 1957), p. 110.
4. Ibid.
5. Dewey, *Democracy and Education* (New York: Macmillan Company, 1916), pp. 352-356.

6. Dewey, "Individuality and Freedom," in *Intelligence in the Modern World: John Dewey's Philosophy,* ed. Joseph Ratner (New York: Modern Library, 1939), p. 627.

7. Charles Silberman, *Crisis in the Classroom* (New York: Random House, 1970), p. 305.

8. Ibid., p. 304.

9. Judith Long Laws, "Work Aspiration of Women: False Leads and New Starts," *Signs,* Spring 1976, Vol. 1, No. 3, Part 2, p. 45.

10. See Simone de Beauvoir, *The Second Sex* (New York: Alfred A. Knopf, 1937).

11. Anne Finch, Countess of Winchilsea, "The Introduction," in *by a Woman writt,* ed. Joan Goulianos (New York: Bobbs-Merrill Company, 1973), p. 71.

12. Dilys Laing, "Sonnet to a Sister in Error," in Goulianos, ed., *op. cit.,* p. 329.

13. R.S. Peters, *Ethics and Education* (Glenview: Scott, Foresman, 1967), p. 53.

14. Alfred Schutz, *The Problem of Social Reality,* Collected Papers I, ed. Maurice Natanson (The Hague: Martinus Nijhoff, 1967), p. 227.

15. de Beauvoir, *op. cit.,* p. 474.

16. Robert Coles, "Work and Self-Respect," *Daedalus,* Fall 1976, pp. 29-38.

17. Margaret Atwood, *Surfacing* (New York: Popular Library, 1972), p. 222.